MORE THAN JUST A GAME

MORE THAN JUST A GAME

FOOTBALL v APARTHEID

Chuck Korr and Marvin Close

Collins

*To the men of Robben Island
and the free South Africa
they helped to create.*

First published in 2008 by Collins

an imprint of

HarperCollins Publishers

77–85 Fulham Palace Road

London W6 8JB

www.collins.co.uk

12 11 10 09 08

10 9 8 7 6 5 4 3 2 1

A catalogue record for this book is available from the British Library.

HB ISBN-13: 978-0-00-727879-4

TPB ISBN-13: 978-000-728411-5

Designed and typeset by Richard Marston and Jeremy Tilston

Printed and bound in Great Britain by Clays Ltd, St Ives

Contents

Preface by Sepp Blatter

This book strives to preserve and convey the amazing history of the Makana Football Association, founded on Robben Island. Following FIFA rules, principles and statutes, the association used football to create a space of dignity, respect, and democracy on this infamous island, symbol of apartheid.

More Than Just a Game is about those who played football on Robben Island and who have since become South Africa's leaders: Jeff Radebe, Jacob Zuma, Mark Shinners, Anthony Suze, Marcus Solomon, Tokyo Sexwale, and Dikgang Moseneke, the first chairman of the Makana FA who was democratically elected in 1969. Above all, it is the story of the thousands of relatively unknown prisoners whose lives were enriched by football and whose sacrifices made possible the eventual creation of a free South Africa.

Expelled from FIFA in 1976, South Africa was finally readmitted in 1992, thanks to the efforts of my predecessor, Dr João Havelange. It was an emotional day on Saturday 15 May 2004, when I had the privilege to open the envelope and announce South Africa as organizers of the FIFA World Cup 2010, the first one ever to take place on the African continent.

This book celebrates football, the universal game, and the passion of millions of fans. But it is more than just a game, since it unites us in a world which is becoming increasingly divided.

Football is indebted to the footballers of Robben Island.

For the game! For the world!

Joseph S. Blatter

Introduction

It was an unlikely sight: football legends Pelé, Samuela Eto'o, Ruud Gullitt, George Weah, and many other of the world's top players gathered behind razor-wire prison fences and sentry towers on a tiny, windswept island 12 kilometres off the coast of Cape Town. They lined up on a bumpy, rutted pitch and took it in turns to shoot eighty-nine footballs into a set of rusting goal posts, one for each of Nelson Mandela's years on his birthday.

They were there, along with FIFA officials, South African World Cup 2010 organizers, and prominent South African politicians to honour Mandela at the place with which he is most identified – Robben Island Prison: the high security jail that for three decades housed Mandela and thousands of other political prisoners.

But there was another reason that FIFA had chosen to stage this unorthodox birthday celebration on the ex-prison's football pitch. Once the mighty band of football greats had finished striking the balls into the goal, five former prisoners, Anthony Suze, Sedick Isaacs, Lizo Sitoto, Mark Shinners, and Sipho Tshabalala, stepped out onto the grass and took centre stage. These men knew the pitch well, for they had laid, rolled, and irrigated it many years previously, and they had made the goal posts and nets with their own hands, from debris washed up on the shingle beach around Robben Island.

The five were unknown outside South Africa and scarcely known to anyone in their own country. They had survived long-term imprisonment on Robben Island by never losing faith that one day their fight would lead to a free South Africa, and football had played a major role in their battle. Though much has been written about how prisoners organized themselves politically on the island, the outside world knows little about how vitally important the game of football was to helping keep the men sane and focussed despite their cruel surroundings. Against all the odds, this dedicated bunch of prisoners spent four long years trying to persuade the prison authorities that they should be allowed to play organized football. Even more incredibly, they then kept the league, which they named the Makana Football Association, running for over twenty years, in accordance with strict FIFA rules, playing in weekly league fixtures, cup competitions, and friendly matches. This simple, universally popular sport became an impassioned symbol of resistance against apartheid.

FIFA's top officials then strode out onto the pitch to formally welcome the men and to conduct a remarkable ceremony. For the first time in its history, football's ruling body conferred membership on an organization, rather than a country or an individual. The recipient was the Makana Football Association. This public event was a measure of just how far the nation had come since the end of apartheid in 1990 and the subsequent declaration of a multi-racial South Africa. In a message read out at the Robben Island ceremony from FIFA President Sepp Blatter, he observed that what happened on Robben Island decades earlier showed just how football could give hope and make a difference in people's lives.

Out on the pitch, a FIFA spokesman recounted that in 1971 when Tshabalala was released from Robben Island, he had written to his comrades telling them how proud he was they had mastered football, and that he hoped that someday they would meet 'the giants of the game'. This dream had come true, for there they were, surrounded by some of the world's best footballers. The ceremony brought together players in a dramatic reunion across generations and circumstance.

Before arriving on Robben Island, Nelson Mandela was hardly a keen football fan, but as he became increasingly interested in what the game meant to the men in the prison, it began to teach him important lessons about the unifying nature of sport. He became acutely aware, through smuggled information, just how much sports-obsessed Afrikaners were wounded by a succession of sports boycotts that effectively isolated South Africa from the rest of the world.

Throughout the 1960s and early 1970s, the country was globally banned from taking part in all team sports, plus many tournaments for individual sportsmen and women. It opened Mandela's eyes to how important sport was to people across the world – and how important it was to their politics and sense of right and wrong. When South Africa staged the Rugby World Cup in 1995, Mandela famously posed for the world's cameras, wearing the shirt of the team's white captain Francois Piennar. It was a highly symbolic act and demonstrated once again how the then president used sports as a way to forge national unity across racial lines.

This helps explain the significance of South Africa's future hosting of the 2010 FIFA World Cup and why it is time to tell the extraordinary story of the Makana Football League. What follows is the incredible account of how this determined group of prisoners and freedom fighters used what Pelé called 'the beautiful game' to bring a sense of dignity to one of the ugliest hellholes on Earth. How against all odds, they turned football into an active force in their struggle for freedom.

The cover of this book shows the only known photograph in existence of the prisoners playing organized football on the island.

This image was taken by a member of the South African security services in the 1960s, and subsequently passed on to the international press as part of a carefully orchestrated propaganda exercise to reassure the world just how well prisoners were being treated on Robben Island at the time.

Notice that the faces of the players have all been blacked out and obscured. The apartheid authorities steadfastly refused to view the prisoners as human beings or individuals. They were faceless terrorists, without names, known only by their prison numbers. We hope that this book puts the faces back onto these players.

1

The Apartheid State

'The goal is that eventually there will be no black South Africans.'
Cornelius Mulder, Republic of South Africa Cabinet Minister

Cape Town, 1964. Sedick Isaacs stood on a downtown street corner reading a newspaper and trying to look nonchalant. The unassuming, bespectacled young high-school teacher contemplated the enormity of what he was about to do. He gazed at the front page in his hands, which informed him that Nelson Mandela had been taken into custody. He was not a sports fan, but if he had flicked to the back page, he would have read that football's world governing body, FIFA, had banned the all-white apartheid South African team from playing international soccer. But Sedick wasn't really taking in much of what he read. He glanced up and down the street, decided that the coast was clear, and disappeared into a chemist's shop.

Minutes later, he stepped back out on to the street carrying a large parcel wrapped in brown paper. His heart skipped a beat when he spotted an armoured police van draw to a halt on the other side of the road. Sedick pressed himself into the shadows of a doorway and watched carefully as police officers jumped out on to the pavement and proceeded to ask a couple of black pedestrians for their passbooks.

The apartheid government had brought in the Pass Laws in the Fifties and, since then, black men and women had been restricted as to the areas in which they were allowed to live, work, and move around. Passbooks, known as *dompas*, had to be carried at all times, effectively turning black men and women into foreign guestworkers in their own country. The passbook contained all their personal details, their photograph, and fingerprints, and had to be shown on request to any white civil servant, police officer, or government official. Not surprisingly, the *dompas* were much hated.

Sedick was of Asian descent and therefore not strictly required to carry a passbook, but he knew that, having a non-white face and being in such a white area of the city, he was bound to attract attention. If the policemen spotted him, they might want to body-search him and, more worryingly, demand to look inside the parcel he was carrying.

What he had just purchased from the chemist's was perfectly legal – a number of different household products and chemicals that anyone could buy over the counter – but, once mixed together, they formed the basis of an explosive. A trained chemist, Sedick had bought the ingredients in order to manufacture bombs.

A softly spoken intellectual, Sedick had grown up in the Bo Kaap district of the city, where he attended Trafalgar High, one of the best non-white schools in South Africa. It was there that his teachers had taught him about the way in which democracy was practised in other parts of the world and how various revolutions had been necessary to bring about justice and change. These lessons made a lasting impression upon Sedick, who had grown up in a South Africa torn apart by the inequalities of apartheid.

When he was at university studying chemistry, he had become involved in various political discussion groups. However, the thought of demonstrations and armed struggle was alien to Sedick and his friends. It was only when a friend of his father introduced him to people living in the black township of Langa that he became acquainted with brutal oppression at first hand. His father's friend was a tailor and would send his salesmen out into the black townships to tout for business. As a teenager, Sedick would accompany them into the corrugated huts and breezeblock sheds that were home to the black people of Langa.

There, he met young, politicized radicals who were talking about taking direct action to overthrow the apartheid regime. At first, their angry commitment shocked him rigid but, the more he came to know the impoverished day-to-day lives they were forced to live under apartheid, the more he came to understand.

He became a member of the Muslim Youth Movement and met other people who wanted to take protest politics that little bit further. Some members of his group had got hold of small arms while others spoke about the possibility of sabotaging government-run buildings and installations. Sedick's contribution had been to use his skills as a chemist to test gold, and then to help smuggle it to help raise funds for the group but, recently, he'd been learning how to make explosives – and teaching other members of the movement to do the same.

Now, pulling back into the shadows, trying to keep out of sight of the police, he pondered the irony of possible capture. If the police called him over, he could be arrested without having set off a single bomb. His own personal battle against apartheid would be nipped in the bud. This time, however, he was lucky. The passbooks were clearly in order, the black workers were waved on, and the police van disappeared down the road. Sedick drew a silent sigh of relief and began cautiously to make his way home with his explosive ingredients.

Introduced by the racist National Party in a whites-only election in 1948 when Sedick was just a child, apartheid forced a system of total racial segregation on South Africa in order to ensure white domination over all aspects of the country.

During the Second World War, hundreds of new factories and workshops had opened in urban areas across the nation, making everything from munitions and military equipment to uniforms, army boots, and tents. To drive this rapid economic growth, industry had needed labour and, attracted by the promise of better wages and jobs, thousands of poor black and Asian workers migrated to the towns and cities. Cumulatively, this caused massive overcrowding. The authorities couldn't cope. Housing was hopelessly inadequate, and shanty towns and squatter camps began to spring up in places like Johannesburg, Pretoria, and Port Elizabeth – and in Sedick's home city of Cape Town.

By the end of the war, for the first time in South Africa's history, there were more blacks than whites living in the cities. Many whites, particularly those aligned to the Afrikaaner Right, saw this as a dangerous development and feared that blacks would come to dominate these urban areas. They came up with apartheid – in Afrikaans, 'separateness'– to counter what they described as 'black danger'.

In practice, what it meant for black people and non-whites such as Sedick was a life choked and constricted by the injustices of discrimination. The belief underlying the system was that all white people were superior to blacks and coloureds, and their 'uniqueness' needed to be protected with all the power of the state. There had been a lot of racial discrimination and separation between the races in South Africa before 1948 but, from that year onwards, it was legally sanctioned.

As Sedick grew into childhood, the regime officially classified every individual in the country by race – white, Asian, coloured, and black. Members of the same family who did not share exactly the same skin colouring or even had a different hair texture could be classified as racially different. Individual government officials could and did enforce the rules selectively and arbitrarily. Many families were split up as a consequence, children being taken into care. Such measures were justified by the claim that they were necessary in order to maintain the system and to avoid the inevitable catastrophe that would be caused by racial mixing.

The government passed laws making interracial sex illegal and prohibiting mixed marriages. Police went to extraordinary lengths to impose these laws, even raiding houses and breaking into bedrooms to photograph couples as evidence.

New signs and hoardings went up all over South Africa: 'Whites Only'. To separate the races further, racially divided schools, universities, and hospitals were created. All public amenities, from swimming pools and beaches to public toilets and parks, were split into white and non-white areas. Restaurants, cinemas, hotels, and cafés were segregated. Whites rode on white-only buses, waited at 'white' bus stops. Naturally, it was the whites who got the very best of everything, especially when it came to economic benefits such as jobs and land. More than 80 per cent of the land, including any that was rich in valuable minerals, was reserved for 12 per cent of the population.

The apartheid government then introduced laws that would effectively make black people foreigners in their own country. These laws created *bantustans* (homelands) – impoverished rural territories akin to reserves for Native Americans in the US and Aboriginal peoples in Australia. They covered less than a tenth of South Africa's land mass. The plan was to herd the entire black population into them, effectively partitioning the whole country into white and non-white districts and thereby alleviating apartheid fears of black domination in the towns and cities. Administratively, the homelands were to be run by puppet chiefs hand-picked by the government. They had little power and had to defer to their white masters on all aspects of local governance.

More than three million people were forcibly evicted from their homes and banished to areas too small and lacking in resources to support the numbers living in them. Vibrant, thriving multiracial districts such as Sophiatown in Johannesburg and District Six, near Cape Town, were demolished and destroyed. Sophiatown was one of the oldest black areas in Johannesburg, with a population of over fifty thousand. Famous throughout black South Africa and beyond for its jazz music, its thriving art and culture, it was cleared virtually overnight. During the hours of darkness, gun-toting soldiers and police arrived in scores of flat-bed trucks to remove its population by force, taking them against their will to rough, undeveloped land 15 miles from the city centre. The government dubbed the area Meadowlands; black Africans called it Soweto, a corruption of Southwest Township.

Once the forced evacuation of Sophiatown was complete, its homes were bulldozed and all evidence of its previous occupants airbrushed from history. A new town was built for blue-collar whites. The government planners named the new suburb Triumf – 'triumph' in Afrikaans.

This pattern of enforced repatriation was to repeat itself across South Africa as Sedick grew into his teens. It soon came to include Asians, coloureds, and Chinese. Over three hundred thousand people were forcibly exiled from the towns and cities and banished to the poorer rural areas of South Africa.

However, without the largely manual, semi-manual, and domestic labour provided by blacks, Asians, and coloureds, the white districts would have ceased to operate. They were so reliant on non-white labour that the government had to find a means to allow other races to continue working in the towns and cities but at the same time strictly control their movement – hence, the introduction of the Pass Laws for blacks. The government did, however, keep a cold, vigilant eye on other non-whites – particularly men such as Sedick, already known to be a member of an organization critical of apartheid. As Sedick had come to understand, the tentacles of South Africa's secret police stretched out into every area of life in the country. Desperately poor blacks and non-whites were paid and blackmailed into informing on their more militant friends and neighbours. Security agents infiltrated most, if not all, of the organizations committed to opposing apartheid and exerted an increasingly iron grip on dissent.

To a degree, Sedick sensed that it would be only a matter of time before he was arrested for his activities. For the moment, however, he was still in the game. He walked nervously back home from the chemist's shop, desperate not to attract attention to himself as an Asian face in a white area of the city. He passed further police patrols but, that day, luck was on his side. He reached his home without being stopped, and began his experiments.

One evening some days later, Sedick drove out with three comrades to test his newly made explosives in the Strandfontein beach area of Cape Town. A long expanse of white sand that ran for many miles along the west coast at its furthest point away from the city, it was remote and secluded. Out here, Sedick and his colleagues hoped to be far from the attention of the security forces. They set off a couple of devices in the sand and then, on the drive back home, stopped outside a power sub-station, pondering whether to blow it up with their last remaining bomb. However, Sedick's luck had run out: the police were waiting for them.

It soon became clear that the security police had been watching Sedick for weeks. He guessed that the reason had little to do with his nascent bomb-making activities. Sedick had become friendly with a local white girl, something that both violated the 'immorality laws' and offended the deeply held prejudices of most white South African policemen.

Along with his three comrades, he was taken at gunpoint to Woodstock police station. They were questioned overnight and the following day transferred to Cape Town's notorious Caledon Square police HQ.

There was not enough room for him in the block used for prisoners detained for security reasons so he was placed in a cell with a man charged with common-law criminal acts. Staring at the peeling, grey-painted walls and trying hard not to despair about what the future might hold, Sedick started to chat with the man, asking what he was in for. The answer turned out to be multiple counts of murder, rape, and attempted murder. The man then returned the question and, when Sedick said he had been charged with political offences, the prisoner, several inches taller and a hundred pounds heavier than Isaacs, let out a long, slow whistle. 'Wow, that's dangerous stuff, man!' he said. Sedick was soon to discover precisely how dangerous.

Many of Sedick's interrogators were hard-line right-wingers who positively despised black and coloured political agitators and reserved their most savage and sadistic interrogation techniques for them. In their eyes, Sedick was a terrorist, incapable of understanding that he was challenging a system that had been created by the racially superior whites to build a better, happier, more prosperous South Africa. The only thing holding the country back was men like this Sedick Isaacs trying to take the law into their own hands. He threatened the security of the state and therefore had to be punished.

Flouting every international agreement on human rights and the treatment of prisoners, a team of interrogators worked in shifts from eight o'clock in the morning until midnight, taking it in turns to work Sedick over, both mentally and physically. First, he was threatened with torture. Members of the security police described in graphic detail and with great relish what they intended to do to him if he refused to co-operate. They wanted information – about Sedick's comrades, about the plans his group had for future sabotage, where and when it would happen.

When Sedick didn't give them the information they wanted he was subjected to long bouts of sleep deprivation, to soften him up for future beatings and punishment. Used as a weapon by torturers the world over, depriving a prisoner of their sleep leads to disorientation, reduces a body's tolerance to physical pain, and makes them highly suggestible to cutting a deal or volunteering information.

Then his interrogators made good their earlier, graphic promises and set about Sedick with fists, rifle butts, and feet, following up the beatings by attaching electrodes to various parts of Sedick's body. The torture lasted for days. Sedick learned really to 'expect hell' if the guards stepped unsteadily into an interrogation session smelling of alcohol. Fortified by 'Dutch courage', the torturers would launch brutal physical attacks on the prisoners, any last inhibitions spirited away by drink.

His interrogators continually informed Sedick that his comrades had told them everything, there was no reason for him to hold back, but to Sedick that made no sense. Why would his torturers continue to beat him and give him electric shocks in order to extract information if they already knew everything?

For many prisoners, as with Sedick, the torture would continue throughout the hours of darkness. Inmates in another section of the police HQ cells were woken one night and subjected to an insidious form of psychological torture. A prison guard crept sinisterly up and down the corridors whispering through the grilles in each of the doors that one of the men was going to be killed that night.

Prisoners were also set against each other. Common-law inmates were paid with extra rations and privileges to attack, beat, and sexually assault political prisoners. The torturers thoroughly explored every single possibility to destabilize, disorient, and put the fear of God into the reviled politicos.

Torture, however, in Sedick's case, served only to harden his resolve, to make him determined to survive the ordeal of detention and continue the fight against apartheid, whether in prison or on the outside. Inevitably, it would be the former. South Africa's security services had arrested Sedick as part of a much wider 'anti-terrorist' project with the object of rounding up as many active anti-apartheid resistance fighters as possible, either to make them disappear or to lock them away. The government increased the security forces' budget and gave them almost unlimited powers to track down anti-apartheid activists – not just in South Africa but abroad, too.

While Sedick awaited trial, a group of men who, in the future, he would count among his closest friends in prison, was also being targeted by the South African security services.

Lizo Sitoto was a bear of a man. He was unusual among the majority of black South Africans in that he revelled in playing a sport that many regarded as 'the white man's game' – rugby. In the Eastern Cape, however, black sportsmen had long played top-quality rugby and saw the game as their own. Indeed, they took pride in claiming that, if they had been given a fair chance to compete, many blacks would be representing South Africa internationally as members of the Springboks. For Lizo and his soon-to-be fellow prisoners, Marcus Solomon and Steve Tshwete, as for many blacks, culture in the Eastern Cape revolved around the twin pillars of church and club rugby.

Big, strong, and physically powerful, Lizo volunteered to join the African National Congress's armed military wing, Umkhonto we

Sizwe (MK), 'The Spear of the Nation'. The MK never presented a great threat to the stability of white South Africa, but the government exaggerated its importance for reasons of propaganda and exploited its existence as a means of justifying further repressive policies. The MK was sufficiently well organized and funded to run military training camps over the borders in neighbouring countries such as Zambia and Botswana. Lizo was sent to Northern Rhodesia to undergo training.

The African National Congress (ANC) had originally been formed as a multi-racial national organization, its aim the end of all racial discrimination, and universal suffrage irrespective of colour, race, or creed. It based its beliefs on Gandhi's principles of peaceful protest. This, however, was to change in response to a series of shocking events in 1960 which convinced the leadership of both the ANC and the new movement formed from it, the Pan African Congress (PAC), of the need to take up armed struggle.

In 1960 Lizo was eighteen years old and already politically mature. Growing up in the Eastern Cape, he had been heavily influenced by his mother, who was a member of the black Women's League political movement. As with many thousands of non-whites across South Africa, the events of 1960 shocked him into pursuing armed, direct action as a response to the evils of apartheid.

It began in a place called Sharpeville, a suburb of Johannesburg. At around ten o'clock on the morning of 21 March 1960, a crowd of over five thousand black people gathered outside the local police station to take part in a peaceful demonstration which formed part of a five-day-long non-violent campaign calling for an end to the Pass Laws. Protesters were asked by the organizers to leave their passbooks at home and then formally and peaceably present themselves at police stations across the country for arrest.

The demonstrators anticipated that they would be imprisoned, that prison and police cells would be filled to overflowing, and that the resultant shortage of labour would deal a major blow to the South African economy. They also assumed that, since the government was trying to convince its allies in the West that it was reasonable and had been elected as a result of a free vote, it would not resort to wholesale violence, at least not in such a public arena. Tragically, the opposition had misread the government's position. They had no idea just how far government officials would be willing to go.

As the crowd began to swell in number throughout the morning, the military sent in low-flying jets to intimidate the demonstrators into dispersing. The crowd stood its ground. Police then set up a line of Saracen armoured cars between the station and the protesters, who, according to reports at the time, sat down in front of the police and sang hymns.

At 1.15 p.m., just over three hours into the hitherto peaceful demonstration, local police commander D. H. Pienaar claimed that a rock had been thrown at his car. His men trained their guns on the unarmed crowd and shot indiscriminately at men, women, and children, even as they turned and ran. Eyewitnesses said those in the crowd fled like rabbits and fell like stones. Sixty-nine people were killed, 180 injured. Scores of people were ferried in the backs of cars and lorries to the Bagawanath Hospital near Johannesburg, suffering from gunshot wounds. Many of the wounded were later put under arrest in their hospital beds, bundled into police vans to be taken away for questioning.

The massacre led to a storm of international protest, including an official condemnation from the United Nations, who called upon South Africa to abandon apartheid and racial discrimination. The apartheid government resolutely turned its back on the world's protests and cracked down even harder on its non-white population.

The response from the ANC and PAC was to target government buildings for sabotage. Explosives were made, arms purchased, and volunteers trained in combat. Thousands of young men such as Lizo Sitoto were driven to make a conscious decision to go into active opposition against the regime. These new recruits to what became known as 'the struggle' came from every region of the country, had very different ethnic, racial, and cultural backgrounds – and often disagreed on both political goals and the tactics to achieve them. What they did have in common was their renewed determination to smash apartheid and their willingness to accept the risks involved in trying to change their society.

Shortly after the Sharpeville massacre, Lizo found himself in the back of a car with a group of young ANC comrades, being driven through Northern Rhodesia to join a secret MK military training camp – but the men were soon to discover that the existence of the camp and their journey to it was a fairly open secret. White Rhodesian policemen had been tipped off by South African security agents that Lizo and his compatriots were arriving upon their soil to be trained in terrorism. The young men were arrested and sent back into South Africa – into the less than welcoming arms of the security police, who subjected Lizo to the same regime of interrogation that Sedick had suffered.

One of the charges levelled against Lizo was that he had left South

Africa without permission. Ironically, though at the time being transported back to the country in the custody of security agents, he was also charged with returning to South Africa without proper permission.

Marcus Solomon never even made it over the border. A few years older than Sedick Isaacs, he had also attended Trafalgar High. Like Sedick, the studious and intellectual Solomon was planning to become a teacher. The secret police, however, knew all about his extracurricular activities. Throughout 1964, white Cape Town newspapers had run scare stories about a particularly dangerous bunch of subversives, the Yu Chi Chan Club (the name came from a book on guerrilla warfare written by Chairman Mao), also known as the National Liberation Front.

In truth, the club's numbers were small and its members more interested in discussing theories of resistance and how to build a socialist society than in training for armed struggle. However, given the fervent, almost paranoid anti-communism of the government and their fears of a militant communist China, it was easy for the press to portray the Yu Chi Chan Club as a genuine threat to a 'free' Christian capitalist South Africa. Security operatives put its members under constant surveillance.

Solomon and one of his comrades in the club were leaving the country to help raise support for their cause. They had established a connection with some members of the ANC, who had set up their departure, and were now in a car with Winnie Mandela and her driver, being taken to a rendezvous that would be the next step on their journey. They were stopped by security forces, who demanded that Marcus and his friend go with them. Mrs Mandela and her driver were allowed to go on their way.

By 1963, much of the leadership of the ANC and PAC were in detention or in exile but, as more men became actively involved in trying to bring down apartheid, so the security forces redoubled their efforts to sweep up the very youngest members of the ANC and PAC, to make sure they would not supply new forces for the struggle. The government mass-produced laws that allowed it to detain and imprison opponents for any number of new 'offences', which went well beyond the legally enshrined crimes of treason and sabotage. Due process no longer mattered to a government claiming to protect society from a communist revolution – even if the suspects were little more than children.

Across South Africa, in a Pretoria township, a young student called Tony Suze was playing football in his school playground. By his own admission, Tony was football mad. Abundantly skilled and very athletic, his schoolmates knew never to go into a game against him half-heartedly. He played hard and always to win, even if it was just a kickabout during break.

Tony was good enough to harbour hopes of making it into the top ranks of black South African football but, like Lizo the rugby player, he knew that, under apartheid, he would never stand a chance of playing for his country, or in a racially mixed team. South Africans played football as they lived – apart. White teams and leagues were given the best playing facilities and by far the most funding. Black and coloured teams had to battle hard just to win the right to gain land for their own football pitches.

Tony's township school was tidy, if not pretty. The staff tried hard to make the students' lives there as enriching as possible, but the truth was that Tony's school, like all the other black township educational establishments across South Africa, was starved of cash and even the most basic resources, such as books and writing materials. In 1964, the apartheid government spent one-sixth of the amount it spent on each white child on a black child's education. The state saw no sense in educating blacks: it would only give them knowledge and skills for employment they would never obtain, and might give them designs above their station.

Cruel first-hand experiences of injustices such as this inspired Tony to become an active youth member of the PAC – an organization which the apartheid government had banned in 1960, along with the ANC, as part of its clampdown on opposition.

That day, as Tony and his mates pretended to be Bobby Charlton, Pelé, and Di Stefano on their school pitch, an unmarked car cruised slowly to a stop outside the school fence. Two men in suits eased themselves out of the front seats and shaded their eyes from the hot sun. Tony spotted them walking towards the school gates and knew that the inevitable was about to happen.

Some days earlier, Tony had been off school, unwell. In the late afternoon, a classmate had come to his house, not to see how he was feeling but to warn him that the secret police had come into the school and had been asking about him. Maybe he should stay off for a few days. With typical defiance, Tony told his friend, 'If they want me, they can have me.'

He went back to school, full of youthful bravado – and more than a little naïve. To his way of thinking, what did a couple of years behind bars matter when you were only a teenager, at the start of your life? When the security police came to take him away, Tony handed the football over to a friend, laughed, and followed them defiantly to the car.

Once the security services had extracted what information they could from the political prisoners, Sedick, Tony, Marcus, and Lizo were transferred to prisons around the country to await trial. For almost all of them, their trials were a formality. However good their lawyers were, however weak the government's case, conviction was virtually guaranteed. After all, in the logic of apartheid, the men wouldn't have been charged if they hadn't been opponents of the state. Security officials did not make mistakes. The only important questions were: what would the prison sentence be and where would it be served?

From Caledon Square police HQ, Sedick was transferred to Pollsmoor Prison to await trial. Later to become home to Nelson Mandela after his transfer from Robben Island, this massive correctional facility was built to house as many as six thousand common-law prisoners. Its grey maze of corridors and barrel-shaped cells stood incongruously in the plush white Cape Town suburb of Tokai – not that Sedick could see any of its manicured lawns and swimming pools from his cell deep within the prison's bowels.

There, Sedick took his mind off the pain and loneliness of detention by applying his curiosity and scientific knowledge to figuring out ways to dismantle the bars and escape. In conjunction with a fellow prisoner, Eddie Daniels, they bribed a guard to get a hacksaw and set up transportation for when they broke out of the cell.

To work on the bars undiscovered, they had to rely on the

co-operation or at least silence of fellow activists. Dullah Omar frequently risked his personal safety and his career to act as attorney for many political prisoners, including Sedick. On one of his visits to Sedick, it became clear that the men in neighbouring cells were singing in order to mask the noise of the hacksaws at work on the bars. Dullah Omar was shocked and, when he recovered his composure, warned Sedick that the guards positively relished the opportunity to shoot escaping prisoners.

At no time did he ever suggest he would no longer act as Sedick's attorney, even though he knew he could be accused of conspiracy if the escape plan were discovered. Dullah Omar continued to champion the politically oppressed and in 1994 was chosen by President Mandela to be the Minister of Justice in the first democratically elected government in South African history.

After weeks of work, Sedick and Eddie Daniels managed to loosen the grille but, a few days before the intended escape, a group of warders came through the cells banging on the bars to test them, and the loose grille was discovered. Allegedly, the search was the result of a common-law prisoner informing the warders that a hacksaw blade had been sold to a fellow common-law prisoner, and that the same prisoner had been seen talking to the political prisoners. However, the warders were as keen to avoid embarrassment as the prisoners were to avoid punishment. They concocted a story that the bars were faulty as a way of diverting blame from themselves and on to the contractors, who must have installed sub-standard equipment. The story may have precluded any direct reprisals on the would-be escapees but, from now on, as far as the guards were concerned, Sedick was a marked man.

When the trial of Sedick and his three co-defendants came up it was heard by two 'assessors' rather than a jury. The basis of the case against them was simply that, since explosives had been found in the car in which they were travelling, they were all guilty of conspiracy. Sedick decided not to take the stand, but his brother was called to testify and was asked to identify handwriting found on documents in the car. He pretended not to be certain whether it was Sedick's writing, but the judge ruled that, if his own brother could not definitively deny that it was Sedick's handwriting, then this failure must be construed as positive identification. As Sedick would discover on many occasions over the next couple of decades, surreally skewed logic was lodged at the heart of the apartheid sense of justice.

Sedick was sentenced to twelve years, and given a long lecture about letting down staff and students, past and present, at Trafalgar High School. He had to smile at the irony – it was staff at Trafalgar who had helped to stir his political awareness in the first place.

When Tony Suze's case came to trial in Pretoria, he was astonished to be handed down a fifteen-year sentence for treason, sabotage, and crimes against the state rather than the couple of years he had been expecting. Despite his age, the courts had decided to make an example of him. Back in Cape Town, Marcus Solomon was given ten years for sedition and conspiracy, and Lizo Sitoto was given the longest sentence of all: a whole raft of charges levied against him resulted in a sentence of sixteen and a half years.

These four men – Sedick, Lizo, Tony, and Marcus – from different backgrounds and of different political affiliations, were soon to discover that they would serve their sentences in a place that was to be the site for a new security-service experiment. Concerned that the militants would turn other, common-law prisoners and make them sympathetic to the terrorist cause, the government had decided to behead the resistance movement and isolate its senior leaders, active members, and – potentially the most dangerous to the regime – its foot soldiers. They would all be sent to a place where they could no longer pose a threat: Robben Island.

A windswept lump of rock 7 miles off the coast of Cape Town, Robben Island was known as South Africa's Alcatraz (the infamous island prison off San Francisco), and had for hundreds of years been the place where successive regimes banished the unwanted. The island was battered by harsh Atlantic currents, and the seabed nearby was littered with shipwrecks. Over the centuries, many sailors had lost their lives in the turbulent, shark-infested waters.

The Dutch used the island as a makeshift prison for army deserters and criminals until 1795, when the British seized the tip of Africa. For the next century, Robben Island was a hell hole. Lepers, the mentally ill, and prostitutes suffering from syphilis were all forcibly extradited to the island to live in squalor.

The British set a precedent for the island by using it as a prison for political opponents. It was here that the great African general Makana was incarcerated. His tribe, the Xhosa, went to war with the British after the colonial power stole their cattle, and Makana was captured and banished to Robben Island. He died attempting to escape. Almost a hundred and fifty years later, in 1964, another prominent member of the Xhosa tribe was imprisoned on Robben Island – Nelson Mandela.

The island was cleared of its inhabitants in the Thirties, all dispersed to prisons and hospitals on the South African mainland. The military took possession of the island, burned down the ramshackle old buildings, and began to turn it into a fortified sea defence, complete with gun emplacements and underground workings. In the early Sixties Cape Town's first line of wartime defence was to become South Africa's first line of attack on the men who opposed its apartheid regime. The security forces requisitioned the island from the military and erected 20-foot-high razor wire fences to mark out the perimeters of a new high-security prison, a vast institution that would house well over two thousand men. Those men would in a couple of years include Sedick, Tony, Lizo, and Marcus.

2

The Price of Resistance

'*We would be better off fighting the system than trying to live in it.*'
Dikgang Moseneke, Prisoner 491/63

It was the middle of December. As the white people of Cape Town packed out the city-centre department stores and shops buying presents and decorations, a group of black, coloured, and Asian Pollsmoor Prison inmates were about to receive the most unwelcome of Christmas surprises.

The prisoners were herded out of their cells, shackled together at the ankles and wrists, and pushed into the back of a truck. Under heavy guard, the lorry drove off from Tokai and into the centre of Cape Town, past the twinkling Christmas trees and decorated shop windows and down along the concrete harbour front to an isolated wharf. It was early evening and there was a chill in the air.

Sedick Isaacs was in an extra set of shackles. He was regarded by the prison guards as a major security risk, thanks to his unsuccessful escape attempt. He and his fellow prisoners were kicked off the back of the truck, made to line up, and then jogged across the dock to a waiting boat. Bound with a chain, the prisoners struggled hard to stay on their feet, steel cuffs biting into wrists and ankles as they staggered, like drunks, towards the boat.

The hold was opened up and the prisoners were ordered to jump off the jetty and inside. Because of the shackles, everyone fell together in a painful heap. It was becoming clear to Sedick that every stage of the journey had been carefully planned to maximize the humiliation of the prisoners.

Crouched in the hold, he looked up and saw a mass of leering faces. One guard gleefully told him that he would never see his family again, another that it would be so long before he managed to get off the island, when he did cars would no longer drive on the roads but across the sky. Then everything went dark, as the doors of the hold closed and the engine was fired up.

Though it took less than an hour, the crossing from Cape Town to Robben Island breached a stretch of water notorious for its unpredictable storms and turbulent crosscurrents. Many of Sedick's fellow travellers had never been in a boat before and, as the craft heaved its way through the choppy waters, they were badly seasick. The smell of the diesel fumes made it even worse. Still manacled together, the prisoners arrived on the island soaked in one another's vomit, shaken by the uncertainty of their future.

They had all heard stories and rumours about Robben Island, but none of them had any concrete knowledge of what really awaited them. They had every reason to expect the worst, and more. Back on the mainland, the guards had warned the prisoners of 'carry-ons' (a euphemism for beatings) with rubber batons and pickaxe handles, and that they would have to work long shifts in a quarry, sweating out their guts in summer and freezing in the winter.

As the boat made its way into Murray's Bay Harbour on the south of the island, the prisoners were herded up top. Two dog-legged concrete jetties stretched out from the harbour, drawing the boat into the island like the pincers of a claw. A phalanx of olive-green-uniformed guards was already waiting on the wharf. Judging by the long batons and truncheons they were brandishing, Sedick figured they were unlikely to be the most cordial of welcoming committees.

Gazing beyond, Sedick caught his first sight of the place that was to be his home for the next thirteen years. Many prisoners would share his initial impression, experience the same gut-churning sense of grim foreboding. Flat and barren, the island was crisscrossed with rough tracks and roads bordered with low, scrubby vegetation. It looked roughly oval in shape and was smaller than Sedick had expected. It was just over half a mile wide.

On the western side, a lighthouse blinked out into the Atlantic Ocean, warning vessels of the island's treacherous offshore reefs. Tucked down a road to the south of the lighthouse was an Anglican church, what looked as if it might be the warders' barracks, and a small village of houses Sedick would later learn was home to the married guards and their families. The east appeared to be the 'business end' of the island. A few hundred yards down a gravel track sat the old prison buildings, ringed by a 20-foot-high double-corridor fence topped with razor wire. At each corner of the compound, brooding watch towers stood sentinel.

Further down the jetty, an army truck waited for the boat to disgorge its convict passengers. Still hobbled together, the men scrambled and struggled off the boat and on to the bare concrete. A row of armed guards jeered and spat, delighting in seeing the prisoners fall over one another, relishing the fact that many had vomited on each other. As the wind swept in off the sea, the Afrikaaner warders shouted the chilling words: *'Dit is die Eiland. Hier gaan julle vrek!'* ('This is the island. Here you will die!'), then ran at the men without warning, beating them around the head and shoulders with their truncheons and batons, chasing them on to the back of the truck. It was a brutal and unjustified attack, but totally premeditated. It was the regime's declaration of intent: for prisoners, life on 'Devil's Island' would be savage and unremittingly punishing. They were there to be broken and demoralized – for as long as they survived.

Its human cargo now on board, the truck lurched off down the gravel road towards the prison compound. Drawing closer, the new inmates could see that the cell blocks in which they were to live had been crudely converted from ramshackle old military buildings. They were basic in the extreme.

On arrival, the prisoners were thrown off the back of the lorry as if they were nothing more than sacks of millet and made to queue for their first meal on the island – a porridge of thin maize served up from big metal drums. All of the men had been held in mainland prisons before sentencing and, although rations there had hardly been *haute cuisine*, they had at least been nourishing and sufficient in quantity.

At Sedick's first meal, some of the new arrivals were still so sick from the boat ride they were unable to keep their food down and, although they were beyond hungry, they left most of their porridge. It would, however, be the first and last time they would refuse food on the island. The maize gruel tasted dreadful and smelled brackish and sour, but the prisoners soon learned that, for them at least, food on the island would be in short supply. A few months earlier, when Tony Suze arrived on the island, the food had been out, uncovered, in the open for a long time. It was cold and speckled with bird droppings. As he spooned the slop hungrily into his mouth, he remembers, seagulls flapped around his head, screeching. It sounded to him as though the birds were laughing at the new prisoners, mocking them, vowing to return, to scavenge and sabotage each and every meal the men ate.

Each man was identified by his prison number. In the case of Isaacs that was 883/64, signifying he was the 883rd prisoner to be sentenced in 1964. After the meal, the men were forced to strip and change into their prison uniforms. The uniform for coloured and Asian prisoners consisted of a top, long trousers, socks, and shoes. These men were also afforded slightly better conditions across the board. Blacks were issued with shorts, to remind them that, in white supremacist eyes, they were nothing more than boys and, on their feet, they were allowed to wear only rubber sandals roughly fashioned from old car tyres, no socks. Racial distinctions would permeate every area of life on the island.

All the men were ordered to carry four items in their shirt pocket at all times – their identification card, tooth brush, spoon, and towel. The spoon was used for all food, no knives or forks would be needed. The towel was so small that it fitted easily into the pocket.

In fact, when Sedick was kitted out, he fared little better. He was given shoes, but they were hardly a pair: one was a size seven, the other a nine. A fellow new arrival became itchy after having worn his shirt for a few minutes. Looking inside, he discovered it was alive with lice.

Each of the men was then assigned a cell block. Black prisoners were ordered to remove their car-tyre sandals before entering their allotted block and throw them into a pile outside in the yard. All the men's hearts sank when they were marched inside. Old military dormitories that would once have been home to a maximum of twenty men now housed as many as sixty prisoners, sleeping cheek by jowl on meagre sisal mats. Most of the buildings were poorly maintained, and damp and draughty, and all the inmates had to keep them warm at night were a couple of almost transparently thin blankets. There were no pillows.

Once inside, Sedick swiftly realized that Robben Island Prison was home not only to political prisoners such as himself, but also to some of the most notorious murderers, gang leaders, and violent criminals in South Africa. It was deliberate policy to house the 'terrorists' with common-law felons who were bound to give them a tough ride. The political prisoners would be fighting enemies on two fronts.

The principle of divide and rule lay at the heart of everything. Along with virtually all the 'politicals', Sedick had been classified as a D-category prisoner. A-category inmates enjoyed the most privileges – newspapers, even radios; B and C progressively fewer; D prisoners were allowed virtually none. Prisoners in this lowest category were not eligible for parole. No matter what his behaviour, Sedick would serve at least every day, every hour, of his twelve-year sentence. His formal complaints and efforts to publicize the abuses in the prison led to a charge of attempting to 'undermine the good order and reputation' of the prison service. A year was added to his sentence. When asked today if he was guilty of such offences, Isaacs just nods and says 'Of course, I was.'

To further promote disharmony, the prison authorities tried wherever possible to mix African National Congress members with inmates who held allegiance to other organizations, such as PAC and the South West Africa People's Organization (SWAPO). They assumed that holding adherents of these different factions in close proximity to one another would bring out the worst in the men and that their differences would cause disunity and fractiousness in the prison population.

The men who ran the prisons were, however, accustomed to dealing with traditional criminals, and this led them to make a number of mistakes in their policies towards political prisoners. Their assumption that nothing could ever unify the men on Robben Island was one of their worst errors of judgement. The prison brought together committed political opponents of apartheid from across the country. Men who might otherwise never have met had the opportunity to discuss and debate issues and to build on one another's experiences. They quickly found common cause in their opposition to both apartheid and the efforts of the prison to break them, and that became the first step towards finding other things that would unite and bring them together.

At eight o'clock, the prisoners were ordered to sleep, but it was freezing cold and the sparse matting that served as a mattress was unyielding and desperately uncomfortable. Lights in the cell blocks were left burning throughout the hours of darkness, and warders patrolled the corridors, often removing their shoes and tiptoeing in stocking feet so inmates wouldn't hear their approach. Talking was banned and anyone found so much as whispering would be in for a beating.

Most of the prisoners found that the nights were the worst. Left in silence, alone with their thoughts, their minds would drift back across the unsettled waters to the mainland, to home, to their family, their wife and children. Of course they missed their loved ones and had understandable concerns about their financial and domestic well-being – whole families were left without a breadwinner, struggling to put food on the table and clothe their children – but there was also the constant and very real fear that family members were themselves in danger: of being put under surveillance by the security forces, persecuted because their father, brother, uncle, cousin, or nephew was incarcerated on Robben Island. After over a decade and a half of apartheid, by 1964, South Africa was virtually a police state. Torture and murder in police and military cells was abetted by freelance, vigilante justice carried out by members of the security forces. The families of Robben Island prisoners were particular targets.

All the inmates could do was hope – hope that comrades and friends would still be at liberty, and helping their families to survive. The prisoners had to believe this, but doubt crept in at night, 'the enemy within', as Nelson Mandela called it. The prisoners had all come to know what the apartheid regime was capable of, had suffered its interrogation and torture. What if a loved one were being subjected to the same treatment? Visits were restricted and letters heavily censored. With no knowledge or information about what might be happening back at home, countless nights were spent fretting. Was it morally right to commit singlemindedly to a political cause, whatever the personal sacrifice, whatever the cost to one's family?

From day one, life for the prisoners on the island fell into a monotonous pattern. Awoken at 5.30 a.m. by the harsh clang of an iron bell, they were allowed to wash and shave in cold brakish sea water before being whipped, naked, out of their compound and subjected to the humiliation and indignity of a full body-cavity search.

For the black prisoners, each morning would start with a mad scrum, a frantic search through the pile of car-tyre sandals for a pair that might remotely fit. On Tony Suze's first morning, he realized that the order of the day was simply quickly to grab whatever sandals you could. Perhaps they wouldn't be a pair – one too small, another far too big, maybe two left feet; probably they would not be the right size – and prisoners would regularly spend the rest of each day trying to swap for something that did fit. The next morning, the 'challenge' would start all over again.

The guards justified throwing the sandals into a pile in the yard by claiming that common-law prisoners had been hiding blades and sharp objects in their footwear for night-time fights and score settling. The truth, though, lay more in the petty, infuriating lengths the authorities would go to in order to humiliate, frustrate, and punish the political prisoners. A lot of days would be spent barefoot, which, given the work that Tony and his fellow politicals were forced to do, was a painful proposition. Common-law inmates were given the less strenuous jobs, working in the kitchens, the offices, or the library. The toughest work was reserved for the political prisoners: toiling eight hours every day in the quarry.

Having been harried to finish their miserable breakfast of porridge, the prisoners were marched in columns, double-quick time, down a rough gravel road enclosed on either side by high walls of barbed wire. The track led to the east coast of the island, to Rangatira Bay. When they reached the bay, the men were corralled in a barbed-wire pen so that the warders could divide them up into work details. In the pen, prisoners were harassed, beaten randomly, and set upon by Alsatian guard dogs which snapped and chewed at their arms and legs. This was their introduction to the stone quarry, the place former prisoners refer to as 'where everything happened, where life was really lived'.

The quarry itself was a bleak spot, cold and inhospitable. Both Sedick and Tony recalled their first sight of it. The Atlantic's gunpowder-grey waves roiled and swelled and then crashed into the quarry, sending walls of spray flying across the grim natural bowl of rock, filling it with seawater. The men's initial task would be to pump out this water and build dykes across the shingle beach to stop the quarry being re-flooded. For their first few weeks and months on the island, they worked in bone-chillingly cold water, hewing out and then carrying heavy boulders to the beach.

Once the quarry was cleared and sealed off from the ocean, the men were set another task: building cell blocks for themselves and the new prisoners who were being brought on to the island. The old military buildings were full to bursting point, and inmates who arrived after Tony were warehoused in iron sheds, *zinktronk* (zinc jail), which were freezing in winter, baking hot during the summer months. Despite their lack of concern at the poor living conditions, the prison regime had decided, with a sadistic ingenuity that would come to seem typical, not to go to the expense of employing government contractors but to force political prisoners to build their own jail – the only convicts made to do so in modern times.

The work was backbreaking. Wielding hammers weighing over 13 pounds, the men were driven hard by the warders, day in and day out.

It was particularly tough for prisoners such as Sedick and Marcus Solomon, who were not used to such hard physical labour. On Marcus's first day working in the drained quarry he had to push an iron wheelbarrow, loading and unloading rocks. By mid-morning his hands were a mass of blisters which soon began to chafe, burst, and bleed.

No medical aid was provided and prisoners were expected to carry on working at full tilt irrespective of injury or fatigue. Those who fell behind were beaten and put on short rations. It did not seem to occur to the prison regime that denying prisoners full rations would further diminish their ability to work.

Tony Suze spent his first few days on the island on a work detail cutting stones inside the quarry. He used his vantage point to try to find his school friend Benny Ntoele. The two had played football together for years, and Tony knew that Benny had been shipped out to Robben Island a month before him. He was one of Tony's oldest friends, and finding him would be a real morale-booster – or so he thought.

A work party passed Tony's group, and another prisoner said that Benny was part of it. Tony did not see him and the next day he asked someone to point him out. Tony peered long and hard towards where the man was indicating but couldn't recognize his friend. His work-mate pointed again, singling out a small, crook-backed figure. Tony couldn't believe what he was seeing. Back in Pretoria, Benny had been a chubby little guy. This man was a skeleton, drawn and aged. The two exchanged waved greetings before a guard stepped in to make Tony return to his stone cutting. The sight of Benny scared the life out of Tony. As he worked, tears trickled down his cheeks. He thought to himself, if they can do that to someone in just one month, did any of them have a hope of getting off Robben Island alive?

The sheer physical burden of working in the quarry was punctuated by acts of violence perpetrated by the warders. It did not take the prisoners long to understand the depth of their sadism. The warders patrolled the work groups in the quarry relentlessly, enforcing a strict no-talking rule with rifle butts to the head and beatings with batons and truncheons. One warder, an Afrikaaner Nazi, proudly sported a swastika tattoo on one arm and was nicknamed 'Suitcase' Van Rensburg by the prisoners because of the case he carried around with him.

Many of the older guards shared Van Rensburg's far-right views. During the Second World War a pro-Nazi movement called the Ossewabrandwag was formed in South Africa. By the end of the conflict it boasted 300,000 members. The party even had its own version of the Brownshirts, the Stormjaers. Many ex-members of the Ossewabrandwag went on to work in the military, the police, and the prison services.

Tony was taken aback by the venom of some of the senior guards. Warder Delport was known as the 'terror of the quarry'. He despised the black prisoners and regarded them as vermin, a danger to the white race. Delport was determined to make their time on Robben Island a living hell. Strong and muscular, he was free with his baton and encouraged his junior guards to be the same. Prisoners in Delport's area of the quarry quickly became used to regular beatings and assaults. Being young and naturally defiant, Tony often found himself a target.

Before he arrived, there had been a number of coloured warders on the island guarding the common-law criminals. Once the political

prisoners began to arrive, however, the coloured guards were transferred back to mainland prisons and replaced with an all-white staff.
The authorities feared that the coloured guards might empathize
with the political prisoners or at least see them as persons, rather
than as objects or numbers. Many of the new junior warders were
young, poor, illiterate Afrikaaner whites who were malleable, totally
unquestioning supporters of apartheid. The senior guards taught
them to view the political prisoners as nothing more than terrorists
and communists committed to driving the white man out of Africa.
The propaganda they were fed by their government stressed 'black
danger' to both South Africa and white civilization.

Over time, the prisoners would work patiently on the attitudes of
the warders, but their initial, fundamental lesson was learned swiftly.
Although the Minister of Justice had overall control of the judicial
system, the Department of Prisons in Pretoria set policy, and the
commanding officer on Robben Island was the head of their institution, none of these mattered to the prisoners anywhere near as much
as the warders in charge of individual sections and work groups.
These were the men whose actions directly affected the daily lives of
each and every prisoner; these were the men who could sabotage or
ignore any policy established by Pretoria or the senior officers.

In the beginning battle lines between warders and prisoners were
strictly drawn and the entrenched prejudices of the warders seemed
intractable. Warders were positively discouraged by their officers
from having 'unnecessary communication' with prisoners and forbidden to discuss politics or talk about any of their family members.
The guards were not to grow close to the prisoners but rather to
impose a regime of institutional violence and random persecution

across the entire quarry. No warders embraced this more enthusiastically than the Kleyhans twins, Pieter and Ewart.

One blazing hot day in the quarry senior ANC member Johnson
Mlambo questioned an order given by a guard. As he was carried away
from his workplace, kicking and screaming, the Kleyhans ordered
other prisoners to dig a deep hole in the grey, dusty soil. Mlambo was
then buried up to his neck in the ground and left to swelter in the hot
sun. A couple of hours later, Ewart Kleyhans swaggered back over to
Mlambo with a group of other guards and sneeringly asked if he
wanted water. Yes? Well, Kleyhans would go one better – he would
give Mlambo 'whisky'. And, with that, Kleyhans unbuttoned the flies
of his trousers and urinated into the prisoner's face.

Another inmate to fall foul of the Kleyhanses was one of the first
political prisoners on Robben Island, Andrew Masondo. He complained about conditions in the quarry. Ewart dragged him away and,
in a vicious rage, beat Masondo until he bled through his eyes, his
mouth, and his ears. The prisoner spent a month in the sick bay and
became short-sighted as a consequence of the attack.

Masondo was lucky to make it into the sick bay. Ill or injured
prisoners were often abused and hit, accused of being 'lazy blacks'.
When men complained of feeling sick, guards would swing a baton at
their heads. If he ducked, the prisoner was 'obviously' well. The other
method applied to determine if a prisoner was ill or merely shamm-
ing was to order him to take a dose of castor oil. If he refused, there
would be no medical examination or treatment. The authorities
provided the prisoners little in the way of medical help or support,
and the sick were mostly nursed back to health by fellow prisoners
who happened to have had training in first aid.

36

In addition to beatings and threats from the guards, the men were deliberately robbed of their dignity at every possible turn. Tony soon discovered that if he wanted to relieve himself or fetch a drink of water, he had to hand over his work card and literally negotiate permission. Often, the request was refused for no reason other than malice.

The warders missed no opportunity to trick and belittle the prisoners. Early on, Marcus and his work group were gathered together and made to stand to attention in the quarry. Any man who had a driving licence was asked to put his hand up. Hoping they might get an easier, less strenuous job driving a lorry or a tractor, a number of men enthusiastically raised their arm aloft. A grinning guard pulled them out of the pack and led them to a nearby shed. It was full of wheelbarrows with rusted and bent iron wheels. 'You can drive? Good. Then you can drive these.'

The barrows had a big heavy wheel on the front, were notoriously difficult to push and keep balanced, especially when they were full of rocks, and regularly toppled over. Whenever this happened, the prisoner responsible would immediately be beaten and the warders would scoff triumphantly, 'You want to govern the country? You can't even govern a wheelbarrow,' or 'What's the problem? Is this wheelbarrow tired?'

At midday, the prisoners were allowed a short break for lunch, which was eaten in the quarry. Once again served up from metal drums, it was usually a slop made from maize. Sometimes, but rarely, it might contain a little meat gristle and fat, or fish scrapings. Food was allocated according to race. Blacks received 340 grams of meal each day; Asians and coloureds, 400. Officially, coloured and Asian prisoners were allowed 170 grams of fish or meat four times a week; blacks 140. In practice, though, prisoners were seldom given their 'official' ration. Run by the common-law inmates, the prison's kitchens bubbled over with corruption. The cooks kept the best food aside for themselves and their gang associates or used it to bribe the guards in order to gain favours.

After the brief break for lunch, it was back to an afternoon of hard labour. The pace of work became more and more frenzied as the day progressed. Each group had a strict quota it had to satisfy and, whatever the job, each prisoner was given a daily target. If he failed to reach it, his work card was taken away from him and the prisoner placed on a 'spare diet' as punishment. Meagre though normal rations were, the men soon learned to fear being put on the spare diet – two days with nothing but rice water, which contained little in the way of energy, sustenance, or calories. Working in the quarry with only that in your belly was ravaging.

In his first few days on the island, Sedick found life in the quarry almost impossible. Slight in build and distinctly unathletic, he struggled desperately to meet his daily quota of broken stones. However, help was at hand, and it revealed to Sedick a growing sense of unity and selfless solidarity among the prisoners on the island. He would turn around from hewing out a rock from the quarry face to discover that the amount of stones in his pile had suddenly multiplied. The stronger, fitter men were keeping a running daily check on those who were older, weaker, or just plain ill. Wherever humanly possible, they hit their own targets and then surreptitiously helped other comrades to attain theirs.

After a day in the quarry, the exhausted men were jogged back down the barbed-wire corridor to their cell blocks, once again in double-quick time, harassed by dogs and swinging batons, harried to move faster, always faster. The routine of humiliation, however, was far from over. Back in their compound, prisoners were made to perform the most degrading of acts: the 'tausa dance'. Naked, they were ordered to leap up into the air and click their tongues so that the guards could make sure there was nothing hidden in their mouths, then they had to twist around, clap their hands, and land with their backsides exposed so that the warders could check they weren't smuggling anything back from the quarry between their buttocks. The political prisoners steadfastly refused to perform the tausa – and paid the consequences with further beatings and abuse. They received the same punishment for their defiance in not addressing the guards as *baas* or 'master' – terms of utter submission.

As the vast majority of the political prisoners were locked up for the night in their cramped cell blocks, a few hundred yards across the prison, Nelson Mandela, ANC leader Walter Sisulu, and a score of other imprisoned black and coloured party leaders were led back to the isolation block, having spent their day labouring in a smaller, lime quarry in the middle of the island.

The isolation section was a quadrangle of buildings separate from the rest of the prison, made up of three double rows of cells, each with a corridor running down the middle. On the fourth side of the quadrangle there stood an imposing wall just over 20 foot high, on top of which armed guards with Alsatian dogs patrolled twenty-four hours a day.

Inside the isolation block, the political leaders lived in tiny, single, seven-foot-square cells, the walls and floors of which were riddled with damp. These men were permanently segregated from the main jail, and the prison regime worked hard to ensure that they had no contact with their party lieutenants and foot soldiers. The policy proved to be unsuccessful.

Common-law prisoners who served in the isolation block as trustees could be bribed to pass messages, news, and information between the various leaders and their men. Sedick was particularly impressed with a method that had been developed by the prisoners on the island to produce 'invisible notes'. To all intents and purposes, these appeared to be blank scraps of paper but, when exposed to heat, the note revealed orders, directives, and advice, which had been written with milk. Other prisoners perfected a system of quasi-semaphore or wrote in the sand in order to pass messages between the two areas of the prison.

The overwhelming message that came back to the main prison from the political leadership was that Robben Island must be turned into a 'university of struggle'. The political education of the prisoners was positively encouraged, as were discussion and debating groups that would plan for a new, apartheid-free South Africa of the future.

This message reinforced the existing desire of the other prisoners to start studying, and this soon became a vital and important way of boosting morale and helping the political prisoners to create their own sense of community. Studying was not a solitary exercise; the men would teach and learn from one another. Those who threw themselves into studying provided an example for comrades who might otherwise have allowed prison to turn them into passive human beings. It served to create a sense of self-respect in the most dire of circumstances – but it also allowed the prisoners to believe that they were wresting back some degree of control over their lives in the prison.

Skilled teachers such as Sedick and Marcus directed all their energies into organizing study sessions with the other prisoners, and in so doing instantly gained a real sense of purpose. Some of their comrades were unable to read and write, so a concerted effort was made to wipe out illiteracy in the prison. Soon, in the evenings, the cell blocks were abuzz with a whole range of educational activities. The prisoners organized a variety of seminars, many of them dealing with political and economic matters. However, throughout the early years of the prison, the discussions and seminars were segregated strictly along political lines.

The men also took advantage of the prison regulations concerning educational opportunities for inmates, which enshrined the right to take approved correspondence courses at both the matric (secondary school) and university level. Essentially, this 'right' had been instituted as a piece of window dressing, which the apartheid regime could point to as an example of its 'fairness', because, in truth, only an isolated few had ever asked to exploit the opportunity. Suddenly, though, the Robben Island prison authorities were swamped with requests to take correspondence courses. Scores of prisoners signed up, half expecting the chief warder to turn them down – but they were all granted. This was an early indication to the men that strength could be found in numbers. If they were to change any of the conditions in the prison, they would have to do it together.

Yet studying and correspondence courses were not the only pastimes in the prison. Most of the prisoners were young and learned to find their fun where they could. Their ingenuity knew no bounds. They made dice from stolen pieces of soap, playing cards from scraps of paper, and chess pieces from lumps of driftwood salvaged from the shingle beach next to the quarry. Men from the Eastern Cape such as Marcus showed their fellow inmates how to play draughts, while inmates from the Transvaal introduced the game of ludo.

The prisoners did not expect the authorities to tolerate any of this. The regime did not want prisoners to enjoy a single moment on Robben Island; they were to have their spirits broken at every possible turn. Any attempt the inmates made to alleviate the tedium of the prison routine was cruelly stamped on. Regular searches were carried out and cells shaken down. The guards took sadistic joy in breaking up players' games, and anything that the prisoners had created out of debris or for their own pleasure was immediately destroyed.

A cellmate of Tony's had spent countless hours carving a pattern on to a prison-issue spoon. During a search, one guard shook the man's bedding and the spoon fell on to the concrete floor. The warder picked it up, rolled it around and around in his hand and, clearly admiring the delicate and intricate carving, smiled, snapped it into little pieces, and then cast the pieces to the floor. Other prisoners suffered the same fate when they were discovered to have found ways to manufacture personal items from driftwood and pieces of slate.

There was only one game it proved virtually impossible to stop. It was simple to set up and easy to hide from the warders. Football-mad Tony Suze had only been on the island a short time when he and fellow fans of the game got the idea to bundle up and bind together a couple of the men's shirts to create a makeshift football. If the guards came to search the cells, it could be quickly pulled apart.

Soon, the long, dull evenings were enlivened by enthusiastic cell games. Bedding was pushed to the sides and short five- and eight-a-side mini matches took place, one prisoner acting as look-out.

As time went on and more and more football players of a high standard came on to the island, the more passionate these matches became but still, in 1964, it was all completely ad hoc. In those early days, when Sedick, Tony, Lizo, and Marcus were on the island, it seemed utterly inconceivable that the regime would allow the prisoners to play organized sport – but it would not be too long before the men who had been brought together from across South Africa to serve their sentences on Robben Island would dare to dream.

3

The Struggle for Prisoners' Rights

'Sport was a human right. We prisoners had the right to spiritual and physical development.' Isaac Mthimunye, Prisoner 898/63

For decades, football had been by far the most popular national game in non-white South Africa. Throughout the Twenties and Thirties an extensive web of black and coloured leagues had sprung up around the country and, as more blacks moved into the urban areas during the Thirties and Forties, a number of now-legendary clubs were born – the Orlando Pirates, the Mokone Swallows, and the Bucks among them. The players, though largely unpaid, became superstars and role models in their own neighbourhoods, achieving on the pitch and bringing joy and self-respect to their communities off it.

By the Fifties, unlike white South African football supporters, black fans could also bask in the reflected glory of having their own world-famous football star – the legendary Steve 'Kalamazoo' Mokone. Though he had to leave the totally segregated South African leagues to make his name, and wait months for his international passport to be granted, Steve Mokone was an inspiration, even to black South Africans who had little interest in sport.

Mokone was already a national star playing for the Bucks club when scouts from England's Coventry City Football Club persuaded him to play in Britain in 1955. Though he thrived on the pitch, he became disillusioned by the racism of English fans. Non-white faces were rare in British sport at that time, and the abuse heaped upon Mokone during matches by both players and fans was relentless.

After three years he moved to Holland to play for the premier-league Dutch side Heracles and, as their star striker, raised the club's game, leading them to finish near the top of the Dutch Eredivisie (premier division) for two high-scoring, breathtaking seasons. He was so loved by the Dutch fans that a street in Amsterdam was named after him.

In 1961 Mokone made his most important move – to Torino, in Italy, where he became the first black footballer in the world to earn the then phenomenal salary of £10,000 a year. In his first game for the Turin club, Mokone immediately proved his value by scoring all five goals in his team's 5–2 victory over Verona. Before long, the Italian sporting press had dubbed him 'the Maserati of soccer players'.

Back home, black South Africans kept a close eye on his international success, and in their own amateur football league were themselves enjoying something of a golden age. In the early Fifties, matches in Durban, Johannesburg, Cape Town, and Pretoria were attracting crowds of ten thousand; by the end of the decade, top black teams like Bush Bucks, the Wanderers, Zulu Royals, and City Blacks were regularly drawing attendances double that.

In 1956 the coloured Western Province team played a rare one-off friendly against the white Western Province side. The all-white team was the best in its league, having just won South Africa's Currie

Cup – a competition black and coloured teams were banned from entering. Captained by future cricket international Basil d'Oliveira, the coloured team trounced its white rivals 5–1. After eight years of apartheid, this win represented more than just victory on the field, and the rejoicing was epic.

Throughout the decade to follow, top English sides such as Manchester United, Wolverhampton Wanderers, and Tottenham Hotspur toured the country regularly. Their players might have been white, but at least they weren't white South African, and the non-white sections of the South African stands echoed with roars of encouragement urging the English teams to put one over on apartheid's players – and the black and coloured spectators weren't disappointed. Occasionally, however, they had to pay the price of their support: it wasn't unheard of for a non-white head in the crowd to be batoned and beaten by the security forces who policed the matches.

As it is throughout the world, football was central to the lives of many young South African men. Wherever there was an open space, inevitably, before long, there was a kickabout, so it wasn't surprising that among the almost two thousand political prisoners who joined Tony, Marcus, Sedick, and Lizo on the island in the course of 1964 and 1965, there were many dozens of talented young players itching for a game.

Dimake Malepe was one of them. At just sixteen, he was one of the youngest prisoners on the island and also one of the best footballers. Before arriving at Robben Island, he played full-time in Cape Town and was soon nicknamed 'Pro' by his prison comrades. Others who were to make their mark early on were cousins and fellow trialists

Mark Shinners and Dikgang Moseneke, who arrived on the island together, goalkeeper Sipho Tshabalala, and tough defender 'Big Mo' Masemola.

Indress Naidoo, too, although not himself a football player, would take on an important role in the prisoners' crusade for the right to play. Imprisoned for sabotage, Indress had endured heavy torture while in detention but had never cracked. The authorities had a particular interest in him because most of the members of his family were active members of the ANC and well known to the security police.

The casual cell kickabouts that started in 1963 provided a vital diversion from the brutality of the prison and brought some much needed fun into the prisoners' lives. The men may have been committed freedom fighters but they derived the same sense of achievement and release from football as any young man in any circumstances anywhere – and, again as with young men anywhere, the games became increasingly competitive. Tony Suze and Mark Shinners began to coach the other prisoners in ball skills but, despite this, there was a sense of frustration: in the end, they weren't playing proper football. The more the men kicked their makeshift balls around the cells, the more they hungered for the real thing.

Of course, the men realized that this was against prison rules. Their desire to play real football on a proper outside pitch stood in stark contrast to the reality – the authorities' almost total control over the prisoners' lives. Initially, political prisoners on Robben Island weren't allowed to talk to one another, let alone congregate in groups. Pencils were banned, and even board games such as chess, ludo, and draughts; team sports played outside were out of the question. If they were ever going to change things, to take football out of the cells and into the open air and play in proper teams, the men would, somehow, have to change the rules and gain official permission from the prison authorities.

When the cell-block players first talked openly about wanting to play organized football, some of their fellow prisoners laughed. They could not believe that the prison regime would ever even consider granting them permission. However, the footballers had been doing their homework and had formulated a way of using the prison system's own rules to help them make their case.

According to these rules, prisoners confined in a cell for more than seventy-two hours had to be allowed out in the fresh air for exercise. Up until now, the prisoners' exercise had taken the form of walking aimlessly round and round the compound – but why shouldn't they be allowed to use this time to play football?

The first obstacle the prisoners had to overcome in this improbable protest campaign was to work out how to even ask this question. It wasn't as if they could just pop along to the chief warder's office, knock on the door, and waltz in with their demands. Again, prison regulations played into their hands. They would make their request during Saturday-morning *klagtes* and *versoeke*, a session which allowed the prisoners to raise any 'complaints' and 'requests' they might have.

These sessions were held in each of the cell blocks and gave the prisoners an audience with the chief warder, Captain Theron. The right to complain was enshrined within South Africa's prison regulations and had to be seen to be enforced regularly at penitentiaries throughout the country. The apartheid regime prided itself on following rules and regulations to the letter, and was keen to give the impression internationally that it was fair and respected due legal process. However, there was no official obligation actually to act upon any of the prisoners' complaints.

So, every Saturday morning, an empty charade was played out on Robben Island. The prisoners would file forward and register their objections – about the poor quality of the food, the clothing, and the working conditions. They would complain about the treatment meted out by the guards and the lack of any privileges. And each week, the chief warder would stare uninterestedly into the middle distance, shrug his shoulders, and dismiss the inmates and their complaints. Nothing changed, but the regulations had been observed.

Now, from late December 1964, inmates began to take it in turns to make the same request every week: 'We would request to be allowed to play football.' Early attempts were met with sneering derision by Captain Theron, who could hardly believe the audacity of the prisoners, and the prisoners' campaign soon became the talk of the warders' barracks. The staff were infuriated by the prisoners' demand: in their eyes, it was totally unreasonable. These terrorists weren't on the island to play sport and enjoy themselves, they were there to be punished, through hard labour and intimidation. Something would have to be done. There would have to be reprisals.

A few weeks into the campaign, Tony took his first turn at that Saturday's complaints and requests session. He phrased the prisoners' request in the same words – 'We would request to be allowed to play football' – and, without looking up, the chief warder demanded that a guard take Tony's 'ticket', i.e., he was to be given no food during the following weekend. In the months to come, this was the form the authorities' reprisals would take.

Despite the punishments meted out week on week, the prisoners continued to show resolve and unity. The men in each cell agreed among themselves who would make the request the coming Saturday, in the full knowledge that whoever it was would be put on a spare diet for two days. Perhaps not surprisingly, the keenest footballers on the island, such as Mark Shinners, Big Mo Masemola, and Pro Malepe, were among the first to step forward and sacrifice their food tickets. The prisoners tried to make sure that older men and those who were ill did not make complaints, but everyone was keen to participate. The men had used this selective approach successfully in the hunger strikes that had led to improvements in diet and clothing.

The prisoners' persistence confused and baffled the prison regime's hierarchy: why would men living an already harsh life wilfully set themselves up for further discomfort and punishment – and all over a stupid game?

The war of attrition dragged on through 1965, each side determined not to back down. It took a lot of strength for the prisoners to carry on but, as time went by, the campaign to secure the right to play football became a cause in itself, something for the men to rally around. It also brought additional, perhaps longer term and broader benefits: the will to play, and the mens' efforts to win the right to do so, transcended political divides. Political divisions between parties permeated the men's lives on the island, extending into all their activities but, now, supporters of PAC and the ANC began to mix to discuss their crusade, and men from both parties volunteered to step up at Saturday-morning complaints. And the longer they battled in common cause against their shared enemy, the intransigent prison authorities, the more the prisoners began to realize exactly how far-reaching the benefits of playing organized football might be.

Of course there was the sheer physical enjoyment of the sport, the thrill of pulling together as a team, the adrenalin of competition, and the motivation of pitting your own abilities against others', but on Robben Island there was even more to be gained. The men's fight to play league football was all about proving to themselves and to the prison regime that they were capable of organizing themselves, of acting with discipline, and of working in harmony together. It was about self-respect and developing a sense of community, despite everything.

There were also the psychological aspects to consider. Back on the mainland, Sedick Isaacs had read a number of books about the effects of long-term imprisonment, the mental vacuity and listlessness to which inmates could succumb. To survive and maintain some kind of emotional wellbeing, it was vital for the prisoners to keep physically and mentally active. They had to resist the efforts of the prison staff to grind them down. The introduction of studying had given many prisoners a purpose. Football would give them a passion.

Sedick could already see just how much of a boost the protest had given the men. The cell-block footballers held meeting after meeting to discuss how they would organize the matches, were permission granted. The meetings were always animated and often heated, and the prisoners became willing, and positively keen, to hold meetings to discuss other matters. If they won their campaign, football would also keep the men healthy and fit, in shape to resume their struggle against apartheid on their release, to effect the revolution Sedick firmly believed would eventually take place in South Africa.

The Saturday-morning requests and the officers' reprisals continued into 1966. The chief warder remained as stubborn as the men were patient, the irresistible force against the immovable object. Things, though, were about to change.

The first clue came in the unlikely form of chunks of meat in the prisoners' porridge and a delivery of clothing for a good number of the inmates. A few days later, a delegation from the International Red Cross (IRC) arrived on the island. The prisoners had found an important and unexpected ally.

The irony of the visit was not lost on some of the men. The official remit of the Red Cross is to visit sites of detention to monitor conditions for refugees and/or political prisoners and prisoners of war. It is not their task to do this for common-law prisoners. However, in the vocabulary of apartheid, there was no such thing as a 'political prisoner' in South Africa. The greater majority of the Category-D prisoners on Robben Island were officially termed 'enemies of the state' and regarded as nothing other than terrorists. With no inmates recognized as political prisoners and none granted the status of prisoners of war, why would the regime sanction a visit by the IRC?

As with its albeit shallow adherence to the complaints procedure, it was all to do with appearances, and with South Africa's desire to be accepted as a fair player, and an ally, in a conglomerate of western democratic states.

International opinion of South Africa had become overwhelmingly negative, and the government was becoming increasingly concerned. In the wake of a number of sporting bans a couple of years previously that had drawn worldwide attention to the true excesses of apartheid, it was having to learn fast how to deal with outsiders intent on applying political pressure on the country.

In 1961 FIFA had imposed a ban on South Africa's whites-only national team playing competitive or friendly games against other countries. However, its then president, the Englishman Sir Stanley Rous, a die-hard colonialist, had campaigned long and hard against what he described as political interference. He was content to ignore the fact that the South African government's racial policies were a political decision that ensured that only whites could participate in international football at the highest level.

In 1963, the world ban was withdrawn based largely on Sir Stanley's assessment that 'South Africa's coloured footballers are happy with the relations that have been established.' He came to this conclusion after a short visit to South Africa in which he met men who were approved by the government and South African football officials. His opinion certainly would have come as a big surprise to the men on Robben Island.

White South Africa was playing international football again – but not for long. The following year, the annual FIFA conference was attended by a much larger contingent of delegates from Africa, Asia, and the Eastern Bloc than previously, most of whom roundly condemned any policy of segregation based on colour or race. The ban was put in place once more, in 1964. For the prisoners, this was morale-boosting news. South Africa would not be invited to rejoin the international football community for almost thirty years. In 1974, Sir Stanley lost his presidency to the Brazilian João Havelange, who used Rous's actions concerning South Africa as a major focus in his campaign to unseat the long-serving Englishman.

New prisoners flooding on to the island brought more sports-related good news: the International Olympic Committee had followed FIFA's example. It had demanded that South Africa formally and publicly renounce all racial discrimination in sport. The government refused to comply and was therefore not invited to participate in the 1964 Olympic Games in Tokyo. South Africa became the first country to be kicked out of the IOC, the first country to be banned from taking part in the Games. Also in 1964, it was learned that several tennis players at Wimbledon who had been drawn to play against white South African players had pulled out of the tournament.

On the mainland the security services had never been more completely in control of dissent and opposition, but the government was becoming more and more concerned at these sporting organizations' attempts to isolate the nation. It had no intention of changing course over apartheid but was worried about the potential effects of international boycotts on its economic partners around the world – governments and large companies who wanted to invest in South Africa. Begrudgingly, the South African government began to see the sense in allowing the International Red Cross on to Robben Island.

During that first visit, the prison authorities did everything within their power to pull the wool over the delegation's eyes. As well as making a show of the improved food and new clothing, warders were encouraged to be courteous to the prisoners. The prison was to appear to offer all inmates a range of activities and recreation opportunities. To this end, Nelson Mandela and the other senior political leaders in the isolation cells were supplied with sewing kits and material. Category-D prisoners in the communal section were let out of the cell blocks for an exercise session, and Red Cross officials were allowed to conduct a few short, unsupervised interviews with a number of inmates. Their complaints and accusations about life on the island seemed curiously at odds with the sanitized version presented to the delegation by the prison authorities.

Although this first visit from the Red Cross did lead directly to the provision of better clothing for the inmates, the delegation was generally conservative in its judgements and restrained in its criticism of the Robben Island regime. Over time, this would change, thanks in no small part to one fiercely independent critic of the effects of apartheid on South African life, Helen Suzman MP.

Helen Suzman MP was a white politician who fought tirelessly for liberty and equality for all South Africans. She was one of that rare breed in the Sixties, a female politician. She was isolated in other ways because of her party affiliation. In 1961, eight years after having entered Parliament, she was the only remaining member of parliament of the Progressive Party. She would continue to be a lone member until six colleagues joined her in 1974. She justifiably had no faith in the official opposition party, which had become virtually indistinguishable from the ruling National Party on important issues affecting the majority of South Africans. Suzman was not afraid to stand as a lone independent and shine a light on the darker recesses of the regime. Her status as an MP gave her the right to visit prisons and, much to the staff's irritation, she arranged visits to Robben Island, starting in 1967, to see for herself the conditions and talk to the inmates.

When Suzman arrived on the island, she was the first woman many of the men had seen for well over three years. She spoke with Nelson Mandela in the isolation block and dozens of prisoners in the general section. One of the men told her that there was a guard with a swastika tattoo on his arm, and Suzman complained to South Africa's Director of Prisons. He dismissed her concerns initially but soon took notice when she threatened to call a press conference, inviting representatives of the world's newspapers. A few short weeks later, to the jubilation of the inmates, 'Suitcase' Van Rensburg was quietly transferred to a less high-profile prison on the mainland.

Suzman continued to make conditions on Robben Island known to the public, putting pressure on international agencies such as the Red Cross to do more than scratch below the surface and to investigate the prisoners' complaints more fully.

Successive visits from the IRC became increasingly critical of the prisoners' life on the island. The prison regime grew to dread the agency's arrival and, in a game of cat and mouse that was to be ongoing, they did everything they could to hoodwink its representatives. Their efforts were not to meet with lasting success. The barren island off the tip of the Cape, South Africa's most heavily guarded, most controlled patch of land, was to become the government's most public Achilles' heel.

Sensing their opportunity, the would-be soccer players regularly made the same appeal to members of the Red Cross as they did at Saturday-morning complaints. In turn, the Red Cross asked the chief warder why their request could not be granted.

Coming under increasing pressure to make concessions, the prison administrators presented a variety of excuses. Allowing the prisoners to play football would be a major security issue. The prison didn't have the manpower to guard and supervise large numbers of men in the open (other, of course, than for their work in the quarry). Matches would have to be played at the weekends, when fewer staff were on duty. In any case, there was no pitch. The prisoners didn't have kit, football boots – or even a ball. Furthermore, football would be bad for the prisoners' health: they were too weak to take part in regular matches.

The men were heartened by the pressure being put on the authorities from outside but were also aware that the Red Cross came only on periodic visits. The prisoners' most potent weapon remained their resolve and, in the end, their single-mindedness paid off.

In early December 1967, after three years of unremitting requests, the prisoners were informed that the chief warder had granted them permission to play football for thirty minutes every Saturday. They had won.

The chief warder told his officers that it was almost certain that the prisoners would tire of playing football, that they were too feeble to play a vigorous sport. It wouldn't last two weeks. In his white supremacist eyes, not only were the prisoners too physically weak, they were also far too undisciplined to organize regular matches and teams. If they didn't lose interest in the whole project, the regime could use the threat of withdrawing the privilege as yet one more means of controlling the prisoners. If football meant that much to them, being deprived of it would hit them hard. In addition, it was good propaganda. What better way to appease opinion in the West, and the Red Cross, than to make such a magnanimous gesture towards their prisoners? What better way to show how unafraid the regime was of its enemies than to let them play games? The regime was on a winning ticket.

In the cell blocks, the men were ecstatic, but intense debates immediately began to take place about whether or not the prisoners should actually take up the authorities' offer. Marcus Solomon, for one, wanted to exploit the opportunity they had been given, to make political capital out of it, and use it to try and improve the prison diet. In order to play football, the men would need more calories and energy – but should they wait until they were granted better food before playing, or should they play and then launch their campaign for a better diet?

To the men, it was obvious that their campaign to win the right to play outside matches was about much more than just the game of football itself. Having joined together to pursue the campaign and won this concession from the prison regime, they had recaptured a sense of self-determination, and they now realized that they could capitalize further on the situation, exploit their new right as a bargaining chip. Food was the first issue, and their initial debate was decided: they would take up their privilege and play, and campaign for better food later.

On a windy Saturday morning in December 1967 warders strode into Cell Block Four and chose two teams of prisoners at random from those who had volunteered to play. One side chose the name Rangers, the other Bucks, and they ran proudly on to the playing area that had been cleared next to the cell blocks. It had less grass than the township pitches the men had played on as free men and was treacherously bumpy. The prisoners had no kit or football boots, so they played in their prison uniforms and most were barefoot. One thing, however, had been taken care of: there was a small crowd of spectators gathered around the makeshift pitch. The guards had allowed a handful of other inmates out to watch the match.

From the opening whistle, it was obvious that the poor physical condition of most of the men was affecting the quality of the football being played, as was the length of time they had been prevented from playing a proper game. Three or four years of not having played with a real ball, or on a pitch that was not made of cement and enclosed by the walls of a shared prison cell, had taken its toll. The game was riddled with poor passes and badly timed tackles, and the men's lack of match fitness and stamina were obvious. None of this mattered to the players or the gaggle of fans. For them, it was the most exciting event that had ever taken place on Robben Island.

The final result of this thirty-minute match is not recorded, but everyone who took part walked off a winner. They were the pioneers, and they returned to their cell blocks with cheers and applause ringing in their ears. Football on the island had begun.

Matches took place every Saturday – of course, the men's enthusiasm and dedication endured, confounding the chief warder's confident prediction that it wouldn't last two weeks. The standard of play continued to be poor, but no one was poking fun at the players' lack of stamina or skill – it seemed nothing short of a miracle that they were out there kicking a football at all – and morale among the inmates couldn't have been higher. Spectators waved homemade banners and sang football chants, demonstrating not only their allegiance to their team but their own growing sense of identity and comradeship.

Though Sedick Isaacs had no real interest in the actual sport of football, he was as excited by what was happening out on the pitch as any of the sports-mad spectators. Rather than the quality of play or the results, he was interested in what being involved in the sport actually meant to the men, the difference it was making to their lives. Not only did they derive enjoyment from playing and watching the game, organizing the physical set-up of the matches tested their ingenuity. Goals were constructed from planks of wood and fishing nets washed up on the shores of the island. An inmate who had worked as a cobbler cut and moulded stud shapes into the soles of the car-tyre sandals. Physically, the men were pushing themselves, and making game plans and establishing a league system honed the prisoners' organizational and negotiating skills.

The footballers knew they were rusty and not properly match fit. Despite the punishing labour they had to endure daily in the quarry, to improve, they had to train. The more talented took on the responsibility of lifting the standard of play by organizing clandestine coaching sessions in the cells. The one man everyone wanted to train them was Pro Malepe.

Already a handy player, Mark Shinners soon learned what a skilled coach Malepe was, and felt privileged to share a cell with him. Pro led gym exercises in the cell-block bathroom – not in the cell itself, because the players wanted to respect the space of others not involved in the games. To toughen the men up, Pro would start them off with thirty to forty minutes' worth of running on the spot, squats, splits, toe touches, and press-ups. Then the players would work on specific footballing skills – dribbling, passing, shooting, and tackling – all within the restricted area of the cell blocks.

Even though they'd done a hard day's labour in the quarry, no concessions were made. Pro would not put up with an unfit player. He would focus his attention on the men who were showing signs of fatigue and be really hard on them – 'Jump higher! Run faster!' He wanted to make a point: those who were struggling could always give more. Gradually, the men's fitness – and the level of competition – grew.

Indress Naidoo acted as a referee in some of the early half-hour matches. Like Sedick, he saw what a huge morale booster playing football was for the men. He too resolved that, now the prisoners had won the right to play the game, they had to force home their advantage by giving it a more formal structure. It was time to seize the moment.

The players negotiated with the warders to let them stay out longer and longer to play and, as they gained more time on the pitch, they began to form bigger and more courageous plans. First, the men tried to take more control over their game by insisting that the teams were no longer randomly chosen according to cells by the warders. They wanted to select their own teams – and, more ambitiously, to form clubs and establish a competitive football league on the island. What was more, they intended to run their football association strictly according to FIFA rules. Plans were already in hand for the most knowledgeable footballers to give referees and match officials rigorous training.

The prisoners lived their lives in such proximity to each other, rules and structure were vital. Passions and tensions could run very high and were exacerbated by enforced intimacy and confinement. Without strict guidelines, everyday life in the cells could be volatile. For the political prisoners, forming a football league was a chance to organize themselves, to practise the skills they would one day need when they had won the right to run their own country – and, if they were going to do it, they were going to do it right. Four days after the inaugural match between Rangers and Bucks, representatives from various cell blocks met surreptitiously in the quarry to draw up their manifesto.

It was an auspicious day. The ground rules were set but, even more importantly, men from different political factions were working together. Before the concerted campaign to win the right to play football, members of the major political groups on the island had been pretty much segregated from each other. They had different work gangs in the quarry, held separate seminars, greeted one another with different phrases and hand signals, and rarely co-operated. This cross-factional meeting was an indication of how far they had already come.

The men established their guidelines. Each club was to elect its own president, secretary, and officials. Committees were formed to oversee the running of each club and of the association itself. Within these structures, some of South Africa's future leaders would learn how to organize, negotiate with, and inspire the men around them.

These early meetings were not, of course, without their problems. They often became heated and hostile, with suspicions on either side that one political grouping or the other was attempting to wrest control of the association. Each of the seven clubs that were created – Rangers, Bucks, Hotspurs, Dynamos, Ditshitshidi, Black Eagles, and Gunners – were formed along party lines.

This changed quickly when an eighth club, Manong FC, captained by Tony Suze, was admitted to the association before the first season began. It was the first club to select players irrespective of party allegiance and did so in an open manner. On page five of its seven-page handwritten constitution it stated:

> 1. Membership of Manong Football Club shall be open to all persons. Indiscrimination is therefore herein enshrined.
> 2. This indiscrimination embodies ordinary membership and membership to any part of the club.

In most non-Robben Island contexts, 'indiscrimination' refers to race, gender, religion, or nationality but, in the cells, it had a different meaning. The members of Manong FC would not be chosen along political lines: ANC and PAC members would play together in the same team.

The founders of the club, among them Tony, were adamant that they had taken this step in order to break down the barriers between political factions and ensure the successful launch of the football league. When one of the other prisoners pointed out to Suze that the clause gave the club free rein to recruit players purely on the basis of their skill, he just smiled: 'Yes, we did benefit by doing something that we thought was the right thing to do.' The club was living by its motto: 'A *lapile*' – 'the vulture is hungry.'

The men held meeting after meeting in the quarry and the cell blocks to discuss the aims of the football association. At one gathering, a motion put forward by Tony was adopted unanimously: the association would be called the Matyeni Football Association. 'Matyeni' meant stones, a nod to one of the central features of their lives – the quarry.

Indress Naidoo nominated Dikgang Moseneke to be chairman. Dikgang was a PAC member (as were the majority of prisoners) and one of the youngest prisoners sentenced to the island. Indress showed shrewd political skill in making this nomination. Given the tight political organization on the island, Naidoo would not have taken this step before the ANC had a caucus to develop a policy about the new FA. Despite Moseneke's youth, the men had great respect for him, believing that he was someone who could bring about harmony between occasionally antagonistic factions. Indress was elected secretary, a position he would serve in with great care and diligence.

The aim of the Matyeni FA was to involve as many of the political prisoners as possible, not just as players but as referees and linesmen, club secretaries and officials, first-aid units, coaches, trainers, and groundsmen. Its official philosophy was that football on Robben Island should be all-inclusive, offering sport, exercise, entertainment, or some other kind of enjoyment and involvement to all. To promote this ideal practically, the creators of the football league decided that each club should field three teams.

The A teams would contain the cream of the island's footballers, skilled players such as Tony Suze, Mark Shinners, Pro Malepe, and Benny Ntoele – all young men who, if they had been free, could have been pressing for places in some of black South Africa's league teams. The B teams would consist of useful, fairly handy players, and the C teams of footballers of varying abilities, from beginners to older men, who enjoyed a kickabout. This was sport for all.

4

The Need to Organize Football

'I taught Tony Suze mathematics and he taught me how to kick a ball.'
Sedick Isaacs, Prisoner 883/64

It was a Saturday morning early in February 1968. Tony Suze, Freddie Simon, and the rest of the footballers in the cell block were limbering up, stretching, and getting in some last-minute training before taking to the pitch for the game they'd been looking forward to all week.

However, as the training session went on, the men's anticipation took on a different form and they began to exchange troubled looks. Though the men were banned from wearing watches, the rigid routine of their average day meant that they had developed an internal sense of time that was astonishingly accurate. The footballers were released from their cells at 10 a.m. for the first game of the day, but it was now becoming clear that it was past that time. One inmate stepped up to the bars of his cell and called out to the guard, asking when they were going to be allowed out to play. The guard answered dismissively, 'No football today.' The men were incensed but, having become skilled at negotiating with the warders, tried to stay calm and gently persuaded the officer to explain why. Casually, he informed them that a couple of warders were off sick. There weren't enough staff to guard the footballers while they played.

This wasn't the first time it had happened. The regime had realized from the outset how much football meant to the prisoners and that it could be used as a weapon against them; the men, too, had been aware from the very beginning of their campaign to be allowed to play football that victory could prove to be a double-edged sword. There had always been the danger that the authorities would exploit the opportunity it had granted the prisoners, withdrawing the right at will and thus transforming it into a punishment, and it was the prisoners' bad luck that they gained permission to play just at the time major changes were about to occur on the island.

In early 1967 a new administration had taken over the running of the prison. It was a tough regime, out to get revenge on the prisoners for revealing so much to the International Red Cross about living conditions on Robben Island. The authorities and the guards were also enraged by ex-prisoners who had served shorter two- and three-year sentences then left the island and gone out of their way to publicize the human-rights violations that regularly occurred there.

One former prisoner who had been released was the black poet Dennis Brutus. He had served an eighteen-month sentence for crimes against the state. On his release he gave testimony to the UN Special Committee on Apartheid about the reality of life on Robben Island. It garnered a lot of attention around the world and drew widespread condemnation of apartheid. The South African regime was attracting more and more negative publicity. This was brought home to the warders on the island when their own Commissioner of

Prisons attended an international conference in Stockholm. The purpose of the summit was to discuss standard minimum regulations for prisoners around the world. On arrival, he was met by angry demonstrations and then humiliatingly quizzed by journalists who seemed to know more about conditions on Robben Island than he did.

Football was one way in which the authorities could both take their revenge on the inmates for this negative exposure and reassert their control. It would, however, be hard for them to justify a wholesale withdrawal of the right to play to the Red Cross so, instead, they set out to disrupt and destabilize the prisoners' weekly programme of matches.

Week after week, the footballers would have their hopes of playing dashed by 'staff shortages'. When matches did take place, severe limits were placed on the number of spectators allowed to attend. Warders would deliberately wander out on to the pitch and interrupt play, sometimes pretending to take part in the games, mischievously taking pot shots at goal. If a prisoner had annoyed or crossed one of the guards during the week, the warder would make sure that his cell block wasn't allowed to play that Saturday. Known 'troublemakers' had imaginary charges laid against them, too – the penalty: no football.

Guards opened cells late on purpose, allowing the prisoners only to have a few precious minutes out on the football pitch and, instead of allowing the prisoners to send out their club teams, the prison officials disrupted the league programme of matches by picking their own random teams of players from among the men in the cells. Everything the prisoners had organized, the authorities were now trying to sabotage. The prisoners' response was bravely defiant and totally mystified the guards.

One Saturday morning in April 1968 the warders opened up the cell blocks and informed the prisoners that it was time to play football. The men moved not a muscle. One of the inmates calmly told the guards: 'No football today.'

The footballers had held a series of meetings in the cell blocks and the quarry and had decided that, if the prison regime was going to use their right to play football as a stick to beat them with, then the prisoners would try to turn the tables and cease playing the game until the administration stopped sabotaging their efforts and allowed them to have control over their sport.

Up until June no matches were played in the prison, apart from some friendlies on 31 May, Republic Day. The following year, July 1968 to June 1969, just a handful took place. Some prisoners may have regarded the action as counter-productive, in that they were denying themselves the very game they so loved to play, but nothing could have been further from the truth. The men had every intention of resuming organized football, but it had to be on their terms.

There was no question that the action did hurt the men – the footballers missed playing and the fans had lost an important, morale-boosting focus to their otherwise tedious weekends, but they regarded the self-imposed privation in the same way that they viewed the increasing number of hunger strikes on the island. The prison diet was dreadful and the only way to improve it was to go without and thereby put pressure on the authorities. Though, from the prison authorities' point of view, the men were there to be broken and demoralized, prisoners dying of hunger were not a good advertisement for the South African regime in the outside world or to the International Red Cross.

One astonishing incident on the island made the prisoners realize just how far-reaching the effects of their protests could be. After one hunger strike to protest against the perennially poor quantity and quality of their food, the men, weak and miserable, were unexpectedly buoyed up by some astonishing news: following the prisoners' example, the junior warders had begun to boycott the guards' cafeteria, demanding better food.

Apartheid revered hierarchy, even among whites. Senior and married guards were routinely given the best of everything in the island's staff canteen. The younger warders were offered a far inferior menu, and they were tired of it. Their protest won the day. The inmates had taught the young warders a lesson in solidarity.

The prisoners, too, saw a slow improvement in their diet throughout the late Sixties, thanks to their actions, highlighted by selective hunger strikes. They had also proved to themselves, in their battle to get permission to play football in the first place, that if they stood together and presented a united front, the authorities were more likely to come to a compromise; so they stood their ground, hoping that their refusal to play football would again put pressure on the authorities – and attract the attention of the delegates of the next International Red Cross visits to the island.

With the appointment of another new and less draconian senior prison team in June 1969, the prisoners saw their chance to act. Living on Robben Island, they'd long ago learned to stay attuned to the rising of an opportunity, however faint its murmur.

The South African government had responded in its customary cat-and-mouse way to pressure from abroad about conditions on Robben Island and put in place what appeared to the outside world to be a more liberal prison regime. It was a purely pragmatic move. If international concerns could be appeased by the odd concession here, the odd compromise there, then it didn't hurt to make a minor volte-face.

Ever more politically astute, the prisoners judged the situation correctly. This was the moment they had been waiting for: a chance to fight for the right to relaunch serious football and gain more control over their day-to-day lives. The incoming prison authorities regarded support of organized football on the island as an acceptable 'minor' concession to make, to help hoodwink the wider world into believing that Robben Island was not the 'Devil's Island' it was made out to be in the foreign press.

Having re-won the right to play, a committee of prisoners charged with organizing the teams and matches voted unanimously to change the name of the league from Matyeni to the Makana Football Association. The word *matyeni* (stones) reminded the players too much of hard labour in the quarry. The committee chose something that combined the history of the island with pride in their own heritage. 'Makana' would have meant little to the white guards on Robben Island, but the prisoners knew that it was the name of the Xhosa warrior-prophet who had been banished there by the British military in 1819 for fighting against colonialist powers. He died the following year when the boat carrying him and thirty men attempting to escape the island capsized. To the men on the island, his inspiration was legend, his name a fitting one for their new football association.

To begin playing proper league matches in earnest, the new MFA first had to organize itself, to elect officials to run the association. It was no surprise that the talented young Dikgang Moseneke was once again chosen to head up the reformed association or that the ever influential Indress Naidoo would remain his right-hand man.

Together with the likes of Tony Suze and other prominent football personalities, they sat down to write, rewrite, and redraft a formal constitution for the MFA. It took months of debate and sometimes heated discussion to hammer it out, and members of both the ANC and PAC were prominently involved. It was finally unveiled in June 1969.

The constitution filled many pages and articulated the new FA's most heartfelt aims. Key among these was that the MFA and all its players and officials should adhere to FIFA rules and standards. FIFA was football's ruling world body, and its rules and regulations applied to international member countries – not to a bunch of prisoners playing football on a godforsaken island off the coast of South Africa – but their will to adhere to its standards was a measure of just how seriously the footballers on Robben Island took their task of developing the sport on the island.

It was purely by chance that the prisoners managed to get hold of the FIFA rules. Thanks to pressure from the inmates and the International Red Cross, a small library had been established in the prison. It consisted of just a few shelves of randomly chosen, dog-eared books. Among the mainly pulp fiction and copies of the Bible was a slim volume containing FIFA's rules and standards.

One of the first tasks of another committee of prisoners was to expand the library by gaining the right to have books donated from university libraries and to borrow books from other libraries on the mainland.

Some of the MFA's objectives as listed in the constitution had an almost evangelical zeal. The MFA constitution spelled out the need to 'spread the word' and popularize soccer on Robben Island by arranging talks, lectures, and exhibition matches in which the better players would explain the rudiments of the game. It also pledged to put on special events that would serve the interests of both players and spectators, such as veteran games and matches between cell blocks. To encourage excellence and fair play out on the pitch, each season, it planned to select a Football Player ('Soccerite') of the Year.

The constitution contained a long list of rules and regulations, including how complaints should be made, the procedure for choosing representative sides and the way in which the league would organize its programme and knock-out competitions. There were sections dealing with the players' club registration and – one rule that attracted a lot of attention among the prisoners – the transfer of players from one club to another.

In the outside world, players had legally binding contracts which made them employees of their clubs. Player movement was completely controlled by the clubs. Players had little control over transfers and the substantial amounts of money that could be involved. On Robben Island, the players could decide for themselves if they wanted to move on to another club. In that sense, the players enjoyed more freedom than most professional footballers. The founders of the MFA were experienced enough to know there had to be some restrictions, lest there be no stability in the clubs. One restriction stipulated that the player had to request a clearance certificate from the secretary of his club before a transfer could be permitted. The founders of the MFA anticipated that clubs would try to poach players from one another, and this was a way of preventing it.

At the same time, however, it didn't really make sense for freedom fighters to deny one another the basic liberty of playing for whichever club they wished. The MFA resolved this problem by stating that no club could refuse a certificate of transfer for more than fourteen days 'without valid reason' and, if it did, the player had a right to appeal to the MFA's Protest and Misconduct Committee (PMC), which, after proper investigation of the circumstances, had the power to adjudicate between the club and the player. It was the only committee whose functions – ranging from dealing with players who were sent off the field by referees, through the unauthorized use or possession of association property, to threats of violence, actual violence, or insults to the officials of the association by players – were detailed in the constitution. The PMC also had the responsibility to act 'as tribunal with final judgement' in appeals by members against the actions of their clubs.

These rules represented something quite remarkable on Robben Island. The men, themselves imprisoned by a judicial system that granted them few, if any, rights, were ensuring that there was a full range of appeal available to football players. The prisoners were making sure that they created a system within which the sport would operate that was fair, equitable, and based upon the twin ideals of justice and democracy – in other words, one that was the absolute reverse of apartheid.

There were other committees too – for discipline and pitch maintenance, for first aid and fixture lists – but it is no coincidence that the committee that had the broadest mandate in the constitution was the PMC. It had a unique place in the life of the island, held far more frequent and much longer meetings than any other committee of the association – and generated more paper in its reports and minutes than all the rest of the committees combined.

Writing paper of any kind, pencils, pens, and ink were precious commodities. The prisoners needed stationery for their lessons, their letters, and to conduct the business of various organizations. They found ways to economize on paper by using sheets of different sizes and by making their handwriting as small as it could be and still remain legible. They turned paper products such as the brown bags that held cement into writing paper. The fact that the men were more than happy to donate so much of their precious paper to the PMC proved just how important getting organized football up and running was to them.

Of course, the prisoners being united in their aim did not automatically mean that there would not be disputes and disagreements. The draconian regime on Robben Island had not transformed the men into docile and unquestioning yes men. If one important purpose of establishing the right to play football and formulating a league structure was to reintroduce an aspect of self-determination and independence of thought into the men's lives on the island, it was only natural that they would encounter the same kinds of disputes and difficulties with football there as they would have outside. It was with this in mind that the MFA created another organization crucial to football – the Referees Union.

All over the world, in casual matches, footballers act as their own referees, but this was never an option for the Robben Island footballers. The philosophy of the MFA was absolute in this regard. It established the Referees Union (RU) on the back of the simple

statement: 'No referee, no organized football.' It was yet another indication of how seriously the men took the organization of the sport.
While the mottos chosen by the clubs themselves were colourful in
their imagery and playfully boastful – Manong FC's, was 'The vulture
is hungry'; the Rangers','Score is silver, art is gold' – the motto of the
Referees Union was both noble and realistic: 'Service before self.'

The Referees Union had its own constitution, its own officials, and
its own standards of conduct. Applicants who wanted to become
referees had to pass a written examination based on FIFA guidelines
and a practical examination to demonstrate that they knew how to
officiate on the pitch. The RU organized lectures and classes in the
cells and made books and publications available for potential
candidates.

The world over, referees and match officials are chosen to oversee
matches with no connection to their own hometowns but, of course,
this wasn't possible in the closed community of Robben Island. The
night after a match, a referee could find himself sleeping next to a
player he had sent off; the following day he could be breaking rocks
with a supporter whose club had lost on a disputed penalty or taking
classes with a captain whose team had been the victim of a strange
offside call. The pressure on referees was therefore enormous.

One of the good things about football was that it diverted the men
from the frustrations of life in the prison by exciting their passion
and inspiring loyalty among players and supporters. However, this
also meant that complaints made against the referees could be all the
more vociferous. For all the prisoners' rhetoric about how character
building and unifying football was, the sport could provoke passionate emotions that divided supporters and players, and it was the

referee who had to arbitrate – and to bear the brunt of the men's ire if a decision went against them.

The MFA recognized the problems and attempted to forestall potential difficulties by establishing a firm policy that no unofficial approaches could be made to the referee by anyone wishing to complain, in the cell block or any other area of the prison. A complaint had to be formally lodged with the relevant committee.

Marcus Solomon wasn't put off by any of these difficulties. He became one of the first men to step forward to train as a referee. For him, it was simple: you couldn't have football without a referee; someone had to do it; and he was more than happy to help out. Later, he would train and evaluate other referees and serve on disciplinary panels handling many of the trickiest cases that came before the PDC.

The MFA needed strong-minded men like Marcus. It was a matter of pride to the prisoners to show the authorities they were capable of self-regulation, that they could remain in control of themselves and others even when passions ran high, that they were able to deal with problems and broker solutions in their own community. The role of the referee was therefore vitally important.

Another area in which the men wanted to prove that they could run things properly was in the written side of the association's administration. If they were going to take the trouble of writing letters and using up their valuable supply of paper, there was no way they were going to be slipshod or even casual about it. All the correspondence between the MFA, the clubs, and their members had to be done by the book, written in an extremely formal style, almost according to a template. Anyone mentioned in a letter or in the minutes of committee meetings was referred to as 'Mr' and given their surname. Known and addressed only as numbers by the staff – or, more commonly, called by abusive racial or otherwise demeaning epithets – the use of surnames was the men's way of reasserting their dignity and individuality. The standard ending was 'Yours in sports', to signify that, whatever the differences of opinion expressed, the men remained united solidly behind the enterprise as a whole. Perhaps the most unusual characteristic of the correspondence was the universal usage of interior addresses, both of the sender and the recipient. If Tony Suze received a letter from the officials of the MFA, it would be formally addressed to Mr Anthony Suze, Cell C1, Cell Block Four, Robben Island.

Why did the men not make their arguments and settle their disputes face to face instead of committing everything to paper? After all, they lived together, worked together, even showered together and, particularly in the quarry, to relieve the tedium of the backbreaking work, they seized the opportunity to talk about anything and everything. The answer was not hard to find. Once something was written down, it was there for ever. The writer could not disown it; the recipient could not dismiss it. The men also were wedded to doing things 'properly'. If any of them had been the secretary of a club in Pretoria, he would not have thought to go to the home of the Secretary of the FA to discuss a football-related matter. If there was a right way to do it back home, that was the way it would be done on the island.

Nine clubs – Gunners, Ditshitshidi, Rangers, Hotspurs, Dynamo, Bucks, and Black Eagles having been joined intially by Manong FC and later Mphatlalatsane – were now lining up for the launch of the

MFA's first real season, each fielding a team in all three divisions: A, B, and C.

The football initiative was hugely popular. An incredible number of inmates had signed up and registered to play. Rangers boasted a playing squad of forty across their three teams, Bucks of thirty-eight, but, for both quantity and quality, right from the very beginning it was Manong FC was top of the league. Thanks partly to their non-partisan selection policy, they had an astonishing fifty-nine registered players.

Each of the nine clubs appointed their own committees to run affairs, trained men in first aid, appointed coaches, and selected players. Soon, nearly half the political prisoners on Robben Island were directly or indirectly involved in football.

Once they had their players and the clubs' administration was up and running, the football fraternity on Robben Island had more practical issues to deal with. First of all, if they were going to play proper league football, they wanted to look the part. Obtaining proper football kit for all of the players was a priority. On their initial approach to the prison authorities, they had offered a pragmatic justification – they did not want to damage their everyday clothes – but the real reason went a lot deeper: running on to a pitch in proper kit would give the men back something that they had lost – a taste of how their lives had been before they were transported to the island.

The colours their teams should play in became a matter of animated debate. Some wanted to adopt the strips of the clubs they had supported back on the mainland, others the colours of foreign favourites such as Manchester United, Real Madrid, and Wolverhampton Wanderers. In the end, the Gunners decided that their strip would be black and white, Ditshitshidi that theirs would be maroon and white. Rangers went for royal blue and gold, Hotspurs, green and white. The other teams had chosen their colours, too: Dynamo, maroon and black; Manong, maroon and gold; Mphatlalatsane, green and gold; Bucks, black and gold; and Black Eagles, navy and sky blue.

It was one thing deciding upon what colours to wear, though, and another getting hold of the kit in the first place. The International Red Cross gave some money towards it and so, too, although hard pressed financially, did members of the men's families back on the mainland. Reading between the lines of the heavily censored letters they received, and listening to the news from recently released Robben Island prisoners, they had come to understand just how important football was to the men.

Now that they had some funding, the players took things one step further, drawing detailed sketches of the design they wanted, indicating which colour should go where. Of course, the problem of how to actually source the kit then presented itself. It wasn't as if the men could just wander into the nearest sports outfitters. Through the Red Cross, they negotiated with the chief warder to place orders through sports shops in Cape Town. Each club placed its own individual order and then – waited and waited. All too often the prisoners were ripped off by the shops on the mainland, paying in advance and receiving sub-standard kit in return. The order would be short, the colours or sizes wrong, and the footballers weren't really in a position to register a complaint.

The MFA decided to try another approach: they went to the chief warder again. Not only did he agree to discuss the problem with them, in itself an indication of the new regime's more liberal approach, he also came up with a possible solution, suggesting that the MFA should in future co-ordinate all the clubs' different orders so that retailers were dealing with one, relatively lucrative client. It was a rare instance of inmates and staff positively co-operating.

There were other practical problems to address before they could start playing league football. The pitch was nothing but a patch of rough ground adjacent to the cell blocks. If it was going to provide a decent playing surface, something would have to be done. The prisoners entered into negotiations with the prison authorities to borrow a heavy roller, and used it to improve the camber and condition of the pitch. And not only that. The prisoners toiled long and hard to install a cement water tunnel and drain to prevent the ground becoming a mudbath in the heavy rain that frequently whipped across the island. The prisoners had also found a way to get the pitch into peak condition in dry weather: they had discovered a concealed water tap in the ground, just next to the pitch. Without the warders realizing, the men were regularly watering the football field.

Tony Suze made new iron supports for the goals, and his fellow prisoners Nlwana, Mbatha, and Chirwa replaced the nets. Their hard work saved the MFA at least thirty precious rands (at today's value, slightly less than £2), money which could now be used to pay for other equipment. The pitch had come a long way in two short months. Even the guards couldn't help but be impressed. An area that had been nothing but scrubland had been transformed into a lush, green playing field.

With everything ready, the men really were close to launching the league, and the prison cells crackled with expectation. Training was intense and, in order to get the necessary hours in, the prisoners in the A teams engaged in a potentially risky practice called 'camping'. Players in each team were scattered across all of the main cell blocks and, once the cells had been locked down for the night, it was clearly impossible for them to get together to train, so they would swap places as they lined up to be taken back to the cell blocks after working in the quarry. In this way, all the players from a particular team would manoeuvre themselves to be sleeping in the same block for a couple of nights before the match. This subterfuge soon became known on the island as 'border crossings' – a term that suggested hope, escape, and freedom, a journey to a better place.

When players were required for a 'camp' the cell-block cleaners would sometimes leave a note and then swap the prisoners' bedding between cells. The prisoners could pass messages between study groups and correspondence classes, and they managed to set up a communications network in the quarry, too. Individual work parties often toiled hundreds of yards apart, so the men had to devise a means of passing messages, orders, and instructions between themselves. The men made use of the warders' discarded matchboxes and cigarette packets as mobile letterboxes for 'dead drops'. The prisoners were constantly on the look-out for them and became adept at retrieving, filling, and dropping them discreetly. Those who transported the rocks in the hated wheelbarrows could also relay messages and spread news.

During the camping sessions, the men would train, discuss tactics, and talk about the strengths and weaknesses of their upcoming opponents in great detail. Was such and such a player perhaps carrying a bit of an injury? Was a specific player one- or two-footed, strong or poor in the tackle, positionally naïve or tactically gifted?

As the guards patrolled the cell-block corridors ordering the prisoners to sleep, the men would crowd close together and whisper. Like professional teams everywhere, the players and their coaching staff would put together a game plan – and then a plan B, and C. Should they play with wingers, a more defensive formation, or a packed midfield? Field two strikers – or three?

These camping sessions were obviously against prison regulations. Inmates were assigned to a cell and even the mat on which they were to sleep within that cell. To be found in the wrong block at lock-down meant immediate punishment. However, because of the prison regime's policy of rotating guards around the jail so they would not get too close to individual prisoners, the warders seldom noticed that the men had switched cells. The evening roll call was nothing more than a head count and, if there was the correct amount of prisoners in each cell, the warder considered his job done.

In December 1969 the first season of the MFA kicked off. Problems soon surfaced out on the pitch. Though the players had been training hard and getting fit in the cells, they were all short on match practice. This was most apparent in the impact areas of the game, tackling in particular. Mis-timed tackles and lunges carried the risk of injury, and the clubs' coaches began to put in extra work with the players to improve their timing. With five days' hard labour in the quarry a week, the last thing a player needed was to be injured. Any knock picked up through playing football was viewed as a self-inflicted wound by the prison regime, and no excuse not to work.

By mid season, Manong was getting into its stride and already five points ahead of its nearest rivals, the Gunners. At ten o'clock on a bright, sunny Saturday morning, 4 April 1970, the players strode out in their distinctive maroon and gold strip to take on Hotspurs' green and whites. Mark Shinners was one of the linesmen and a true football fan. He was more than happy to be officiating at an A-division match that day.

The players were up against the clock. Allotted a morning and an afternoon session for football, the MFA had to pack in six games across the three divisions every Saturday. As a result, and because of its remit to offer sport to as many as possible, the games were restricted to just thirty minutes – fifteen minutes each half, with an immediate turn-around at half-time.

Hotspurs entered the game at the bottom of the division and, along with the Dynamos, were already four or five points adrift of the seven other teams. This was always going to be a tough match for Hotspurs, and they were pinned back in their own penalty area for much of the first half. Manong peppered their goal with shots and headers, and then, after ten minutes, Tony Suze broke the deadlock with a ferocious volley from just outside the penalty box. There wasn't a goalkeeper in A division who enjoyed playing against Tony. He had the reputation of possessing the strongest and fastest shot on the island and, when it hit, it hurt. Just before the whistle went for half-time, Manong scored a second through striker Nkatlo.

The second half became a procession as Hotspurs tired and became more and more demoralized. Manong scored a further three goals – a second for Nkatlo and one each for Tshabalala and Tabane. Despite the inequality of the teams, the match was played in good spirit and there were few fouls but, for Hotspurs, it was yet another indication that, along with the Dynamos, they were a long way behind the other sides in Division A in terms of quality players. It was a problem both sides would need to address at the end of the season.

In Division B, the players were still working hard to improve standards. At 2 o'clock on 18 April Mark Shinners found himself refereeing a second-tier game between Ditshitshidi and Rangers, both mid-table clubs. He had to blow the whistle for numerous offsides, and chances on goal were minimal in both halves. As soon as the ball came anywhere near either penalty area, defenders lofted it straight into touch rather than looking up and casting around for different passing options. Neither strike force displayed much co-ordination and each played too far apart to threaten the defences. The only genuine chance for a goal came in the second half, when Ditshitshidi was awarded a penalty. Perhaps not surprisingly, it was missed. The game ended in a 0–0 draw.

Down in C Division, the players made little attempt to apply tactics to their games. They were just happy to be out on the pitch having a good run-around with the sun on their backs.

Now that matches had started in earnest, the grim, grey confines of Robben Island were abuzz with talk about football. The only other subject that inspired quite so much conversation and debate was politics. Initially, only a small number of fellow prisoners were allowed to leave their cells and stand on the touchlines to watch the games, but they returned to the cell blocks with passionate, blow-by-blow reports of the action, as in depth as those of any football journalist. The MFA soon realized that, in order to involve as many men as possible in their project, it needed to persuade the prison regime to allow more men out to spectate. This became the focus of the next campaign.

For the first half of the season the response from the guards was that there weren't enough staff to police larger crowds, but then, one Saturday morning, one of the senior warders surprised everyone. When some of the more junior guards trotted out their usual response as to why more spectators were not allowed to watch the games, he replied confidently that the prisoners were more than capable and disciplined enough to martial their own games. It spoke volumes about how the authorities were coming to view football on Robben Island – and about at least one senior official's changing attitude towards the prisoners. He had recognized their self-discipline and organization, and his attitude began to trickle down, with some of the warders beginning to trust the prisoners to arbitrate among themselves. Gradually, more men were allowed out to be spectators.

The A matches were supported by hundreds of inmates pretty much every week. The spectators proved themselves to be as fanatical as any crowd, and some real characters began to emerge in the pavilion – the 'pavvy'. One of them was Edgar Gamboye, who stood head and shoulders above the rest of the crowd in terms of height, and could make himself heard above them all too. He always supported sides that were either totally or predominantly made up of fellow ANC members and would yell, in his booming, voluminous voice, things like, 'Slit their throats! Kill them! This is not a game for cissies!'

And Gamboye was not the only one to carve out a place for himself in the stands. One prisoner, nicknamed Blue, sent his beloved Ditshitshidi team out on to the pitch with the plea to 'win for your friend, Blue', and loved to give supporters of rival clubs the pre-match warning: 'Tomorrow you die.' He was hardly a star footballer himself, but Blue loved to play the game, too. He never rose above playing in the C division, but that wasn't important. No veteran of the MFA would ever forget him or how much he contributed to the atmosphere in the pavilion.

Mark Shinners, a skilled and mentally tough footballer, was the first to admit that the impassioned support of the fans had a real effect on the players out on the pitch, but not always a positive one. He complained to fellow players about the 'cheerleaders', who would sing chants to rile the opposing team and its fans, saying how much they wound him up. Shinners was sometimes so distracted by shouts from fans or cheerleaders that he made mistakes on the field.

The teams soon had keen supporters in the isolation cells, too. Although they were denied the opportunity to watch the football, information was regularly fed back to them about who had won which match, who had scored, and how the games had played out, so the men in B Section, including ANC leaders such as Walter Sisulu and Nelson Mandela, could still follow the news. They took great pleasure in being included in what was going on and came to share the awareness of how important their breakthrough in being allowed to play and set up their own league was to the men. Some of them became huge fans of individual clubs.

Football mania continued its spread throughout the prison. Common-law inmates now supported specific teams, and those who worked in the kitchens, the library, the boiler room, and the hospital would do special favours for the players. Tony Suze was awoken one day at 4 a.m. by one of the cooks singing loudly about Manong FC and chanting, 'The vultures are hungry,' while preparing breakfast. The cook also passed drums of hot water through a window into Tony's cell block, something that Tony and his fellow political prisoners were not allowed to have.

Support for the teams throughout the prison was fervent. The first part of the week was consumed by minute dissection of the previous Saturday's match and, on Thursdays and Fridays, the men would be caught up in discussing the coming weekend's fixtures – just as they would if they were back living in the normality of the outside world. Anticipation reached such a pitch at some points that the tension seemed almost physical. Sometimes, the week before a big match, fans and players couldn't bring themselves to talk to their best friends if they were on the opposing side. There was just too much at stake.

Of course, the men still had obstacles to overcome in running the league, challenges that just wouldn't arise for football associations anywhere other than on Robben Island. Chief among these were the constant requests the executive committee of the MFA had to make to the clubs and individuals to contribute writing paper – a commonplace commodity but one upon which the whole football enterprise depended.

During the season, the executive committee put in its order for the following year, requesting that it be sent as soon as possible. It consisted of three hundred sheets of foolscap newsprint paper, one foolscap hardcover notebook, one blue Bic pen, and one sheaf of foolscap carbon paper. The amounts may seem paltry, but the MFA had to conduct lengthy negotiations with the prison authorities before finally being granted even this limited supply of stationery. In the meantime the MFA continued to depend on whip-rounds and appeals to individual prisoners for paper in order to keep the administrative side of the football association running.

The men's thirst for practical footballing knowledge became insatiable. The MFA wrote officially to the prison's chief librarian Silva Pillay, requesting 'as many copies as possible of instruction, guide, and rule books'. Shortly afterwards he submitted a list to the committee of eighteen titles which might be of assistance to the Referees Union, clubs, and individuals, among them books by prominent figures in British football such as Jimmy Greaves, Malcolm Allison, Bobby Charlton, Tommy Docherty, Jimmy Hill, Denis Law, and Sir Alf Ramsey.

These joined the small collection of books already in the prison library; supplementing two already prized volumes: the FIFA handbook, which laid out precisely the rules of the game, and *Soccer Refereeing* by Denis Howell.

Up until 1970 the most borrowed book in the prison library was Karl Marx's *Capital*, whose acquisition was approved by a (presumably not particularly bright or well-read) censor who thought a book about capitalism might 'teach the communists on the island the error of their ways'. The second most popular was Howell's classic text for football referees, which had a massive influence on the island's players and officials. It set down in unambiguous black and white exactly how to apply the rules of football out on the pitch.

Though most of the prisoners did not know it at the time, Denis Howell was a strong and vocal opponent of apartheid in sport. In addition to being a football referee, Howell was also Labour MP for Birmingham Small Heath. In the mid-Seventies, he became the UK's first Minister of Sport. A tireless crusader for 'sport for all' and fairness in sporting issues worldwide, he would have been happy to know that his *Soccer Refereeing* was so important to the men on Robben Island.

Back on the pitch, standards were fast improving. Thanks to continuing pressure on the part of both the prisoners and the International Red Cross, the food given to the prisoners began to get better too. Increasingly, meat, fish, and fat were added to their meals, not in huge amounts, but enough to raise their calorific intake and give the men more energy.

In addition, the men had become adept at poaching food. Down in the quarry, they would search for birds' nests and eat the eggs. One day, Tony Suze managed to catch a guinea fowl. It was smuggled back to the prison kitchen and handed over to Freddie Simon, who as well as being a strong and skilled footballer also worked in the kitchens. Freddie surreptitiously cooked it and added it to the following day's rations. The prisoners learned always to be on the look-out for anything that might be edible. Some became adept at trapping their constant companions on the island, making roast sea gull into a coveted delicacy.

Freddie Simon was to become one of the most popular players on the island. A common-law prisoner who over time was persuaded by other prisoners to support the ANC, he soon became a very active member of the party. He had a great sense of humour and was inclined to see the lighter side of life. He was always looking for fun and, as a football player, loved the limelight. His first links to the political prisoners were through football. Freddie was transferred into the cells with the political prisoners, but he continued to work in the kitchens, a job for common-law prisoners only.

He made an important contribution by helping to solve one of the political prisoners' biggest problems – how to smuggle supplies out of the kitchens in order to have something to barter for food and other luxuries. Simon used this opportunity to smuggle fat and sugar out to the political prisoners, to add taste and calories to their meagre diets. No wonder he was a popular man.

The improved diet, more sophisticated training methods, and growing self-confidence among the footballers led, in the course of the first season of league football on Robben Island, to vaulting new standards of play out on the pitch.

Though Manong was running away with the first season championship in A division, competition between the teams immediately below them, such as Gunners, Bucks, Rangers, and Ditshitshidi, was becoming ever more fierce. Games were hotly contested. At one match in May between Rangers and Ditshitshidi, Pro Malepe officiated as referee, and Tony Suze and Harry Gwala acted as linesmen. The match tested all three officials' mettle. The two defences had become expert at moving out in a line to leave the opposition strikers offside, and numerous attacks broke down at either end because of this tactical awareness. The final score, after an extremely tight encounter, was 2–1. In fact, most league games were decided by the odd goal – except that is, when Manong played.

The club won the first official championship by a mile. The consequences of its policy of political integration could not be ignored. Tony Suze, who had been the author of the constitutional clause that broadened the political base of Manong, was the first to admit that this had contributed hugely to their being the first team to romp home with the championship.

One of Manong's players was ANC member Lizo Sitoto. Big and strong, before being sent to Robben Island, Lizo had played rugby but, when PAC member Tony saw how he handled and kicked the ball, he shrewdly recruited him as a goalkeeper for Manong's A team. Many other players followed suit, signing up for clubs regardless of their direct political affiliation.

There were prominent figures in all aspects of football on the island. One such was Harry Gwala, who made being a referee almost into a calling. Harry was in his mid-forties when he was sentenced in 1964 to eight years. He was a teacher and trade-union organizer and a member of both the ANC and the Communist party, and renowned among the prisoners for his skill and ferocity as a debater. Despite the passion with which he held his own political opinions, men turned to him for advice and knowledge whatever their political convictions.

He was always immaculately turned out; some players reckoned he secretly had an electric iron in his cell. Everyone respected him but, at the same time, he could provoke fury among players and fans alike with the hardline approach to right and wrong he brought on to the pitch. 'Uncle' Harry Gwala was famous in the community for his insistence on the most rigid interpretation of the rules and the authority of the referee to interpret them on the spot.

His knowledge of the history of the game across the world was almost encyclopaedic, and he delighted in sharing it with comrades. He talked enthusiastically about the standard of football in the USSR, about great footballers in Hungary, Poland, and elsewhere, not just in the West. The men had only ever discussed football in Britain, with the possible exception of Real Madrid, and one or two Italian clubs.

He lectured the men on what he called the greatest team (Hungary, 1954) never to win the World Cup or the Hungarian player Ferenc Puskás, reminding them that there was a whole big wide world of football out there. People just like them, no matter what their nationality, background, colour, race, or creed, played the world over, and Harry Gwala made the men feel a part of this global community.

On 1 June 1970 Manong FC was crowned inaugural champion of the Makana Football Association's A division, closing the season seven points clear of their nearest rivals, the Gunners.

A DIVISION	P	W	L	D	F	A	Points
Manong	14	12	1	1	28	1	25
Gunners	14	7	3	4	14	9	18
Bucks	14	7	4	3	14	12	17
Rangers	14	5	4	5	10	13	15
Ditshitshidi	14	4	6	4	14	12	12
Mphatlalatsane	14	2	4	8	10	17	12
Dynamos	14	2	9	3	6	17	7
Hotspurs	14	2	10	2	7	22	6

Beaten just once during the season – 1–0 by the runners-up – Manong had scored twice as many goals as any other team, and the three top goal-scorers in the A division all belonged to the club. Nkatlo clocked up ten goals, Tshabalala scored nine, and Tabane seven.

The season had been altogether tighter in B division, with just four points separating the top clubs. The Gunners' second string ended up champions, with Manong's B team a disappointing third from bottom.

B DIVISION	P	W	L	D	F	A	Points
Gunners	14	7	2	5	13	5	19
Mphatlalatsane	14	4	1	9	12	8	17
Rangers	14	6	3	5	10	7	17
Ditshitshidi	14	4	3	7	10	7	15
Bucks	14	4	5	5	13	15	13
Manong	14	3	4	7	9	10	13
Hotspurs	14	3	6	5	6	11	11
Dynamos	14	1	8	5	5	15	7

Sadly, there is no longer any record of the final table of results for C division.

MFA officials awarded Manong a handmade wooden shield to mark its success as A-division winners. The players were euphoric – but not for long. When the ceremony had finished, guards stepped in and, offering an immediate reminder of what life on the island was all about, they confiscated the trophy. The prisoners had won a few new freedoms and, five years previously, the reality of their having negotiated and won so many concessions from the prison regime would have been unthinkable – as would the notion of any sense of co-operation between inmates and guards. Things had come a long way, but the prison bosses were still keen to remind them just who was in control on Robben Island.

5

Football Establishes Itself

'All that organization meant nothing if you didn't have that little round thing rolling around on the ground every week.' Mark Shinners, Prisoner 493/63

A gentle breeze blew off the Atlantic and across the island as Lizo Sitoto walked out into brilliant sunshine, his football studs clattering across the concrete floor of the compound. Manong team-mate Tony Suze was alongside him, the sun glinting on his maroon and gold strip. The men exchanged firm, confident handshakes and wished one another luck for the game ahead. The date was 1 August 1970 and the match was an early fixture in the league's second season. Although Manong was still the leading team, today it was playing against Rangers, and Lizo knew enough to expect a bruising encounter.

The Rangers captain was a tough, no-nonsense ANC activist called Jacob Zuma, known to be as uncompromising on the football pitch as he was in the political arena. The son of a policeman who died when he was just a child, Zuma had become involved in politics at an early age, joining the ANC as a seventeen-year-old in 1959. Three years later he was a committed and active member of the military wing. A year after that he was arrested, along with forty-five other young recruits, while training in the Western Transvaal. Convicted of con-spiring to overthrow the government, Zuma was handed a ten-year sentence, to be served on Robben Island. Now, nearly forty years later, Jacob Zuma is chairman of the ANC.

Experience told Lizo that he would have to be on his guard because Zuma would, as ever, be putting himself about in the penalty area, at corners and set pieces. Zuma was a tough footballer who played as a defender mainly at right back and centre half, and his team was disciplined, hard to break down.

Before reaching the pitch, Lizo paused for a moment to take in the scene. His team-mates were running out on to the lush green grass to join the Rangers players, who were resplendent in their royal-blue and gold kit, and homemade banners were being waved by the crowd. For a moment he didn't see the razor-wire fences and watchtowers, or the armed guards who patrolled the perimeter of the pitch with their Alsatians, only the vivid team colours, and the expectant grins on the faces of the players and the fans in the pavvy. He heard the men on the touchline boasting jokingly about their respective teams, laying bets, and laughing together in the sunshine. Some spoke in dialects and native languages he didn't fully understand, but he understood the happiness that animated their faces. Match officials shouted for the two teams to line up ready for kick-off. Lizo pumped himself up, enthusiastically clapping his hands together, and ran out on to the pitch. He felt 'like a bird that had been in a cage for a long time and had been released to fly into the sky'. His romantic notions ended when the match officials shouted for the two teams to line up and kick off the match. It was time for the goalkeeper of the best club on the island to start paying attention to his work.

Lizo's expectations had not been misplaced: the match was a tough one, played with an intensity now standard on the Robben Island football pitch. There were fewer misplaced passes than in the matches played during the previous season and the game was played at a higher level. Though lasting only thirty minutes, the match illustrated how tactically sophisticated the teams were becoming. For much of the game, any move made by one team was countered and matched by the other.

Tony Suze was doing his best to make ground against the Rangers defence down the right wing and get over the odd well-placed cross, but he and the rest of the Manong attackers were being largely squeezed out of Rangers, final third by a well-drilled defence led by Jacob Zuma. Although Manong were still top dogs on the island, a handful of the other teams, such as Rangers, had begun to up their game. Just before half-time, Tony did at last manage to get away from his defender and whip over a hard, hanging cross. Manong striker Shabalala connected with his head, and the Vultures found themselves 1–0 up.

The second half was closely fought, too, but despite forcing a series of corners towards the end of the match, Rangers couldn't claw back Manong's one-goal advantage. Another game had ended and Lizo had kept yet another clean sheet.

As Lizo jogged off the field, Manong fans patted him on the back and chanted his name. Picking his way through them, Lizo felt a tap on his shoulder. It was one of the older guards, who smiled and said, 'Well done.' Those two simple words made a real impact on Lizo. Six short years ago, such an exchange between a prisoner and a warder would have been inconceivable.

On a human level, football had begun to mellow a good number of the guards. Less hostile warders had become more indulgent towards the footballers, even beginning to lend their support to a particular team. On Saturday mornings, some of the warders would wander around the cell blocks to find out what the day's fixtures were. If they'd been detailed to guard a Manong game or any match featuring the A-division sides, it put a spring in their step for the rest of the day.

Many of the warders were young, single men working shifts of twelve days on Robben Island, interspersed with two days off. There were few recreational facilities and there was little to do in the barracks. For many, working at the prison was a thankless posting, and watching the football provided entertainment and a focal point to the week.

Isolated on the island, many guards took to drinking, heavily and alone, in their single rooms. Although they decorated them with posters and pictures, and had radios, record players, and books – if they could read – the rooms could almost be mistaken for prison cells. To add to this feeling of isolation, there was little sense of solidarity or mutual support among the guards, unlike that which was growing among the prisoners. In all the years that political prisoners were incarcerated on the island, there is not one recorded incident of an inmate committing suicide. Some guards did, however, take their own lives.

Over the years, and thanks to the increasingly powerful negotiating skills of the inmates, the relationship between the prisoners and their captors had become less full of conflict. Beatings and abuse were still carried out in the quarry but had become much rarer. Staffing rosters gradually grew more relaxed and there was less rotation of the guards, so the men now found they could have the same guard in the quarry for months on end, and thus a relationship, of sorts, could be formed.

Increasingly, the guards became caught up in the prisoners' activities. Many of them were poorly educated, a lot of them functionally illiterate, and they were fascinated by the amount of time and energy that the prisoners put into studying. The political prisoners coaxed and cajoled them into joining their studies, to devote time to improving themselves and furthering their careers. Soon, guards even sat with the men, albeit awkwardly, learning to read and write, and went on to pass exams, themselves becoming honorary students in the 'university of struggle'.

Now that the guards were beginning to consider the inmates as human beings, the prisoners swiftly grasped the opportunity to improve their life on Robben Island by cleverly and patiently cultivating better relationships with their captors.

Individual prisoners would target guards they seemed to get on with and try to build a personal bond or even friendship with them. Building these relationships served the prisoners in a number of ways. If another prisoner was being given a hard time by a guard, that guard's inmate friend might be able to negotiate to make life better for his comrade.

Sometimes, improved guard–inmate relationships led to some quite extraordinary and poignant moments. One morning, Tony Suze was cutting stones when a guard ambled across the quarry towards him. He gestured towards a corrugated-iron hut where the guards sheltered from the weather and beckoned for Tony to follow. Once inside, and with the excited enthusiasm of a small boy, the warder showed Tony a mono record player and a disc he'd recently bought. With a glint in his eye, the guard put the record on the turntable and told Tony: 'Listen to this. You'll love it, man.' It was the first music Tony had heard from the outside world in nearly six years. Apart from hearing other prisoners sing old resistance anthems, it was the first song he'd heard since 1964: Percy Sledge's soulful ballad, 'When a Man Loves a Woman'.

The prisoners also strove to improve relationships with the harshest guards, choosing to target those considered most hostile, the ones who meted out regular beatings, for a variety of reasons. If these warders could be 'humanized', the prisoners reasoned, their attacks would decrease and conditions would improve. Equally, these, in general, older guards exerted a strong influence over the younger warders. If their attitudes could be changed, it was hoped there would be a trickle-down effect. In addition, a hard-line 'friendly' guard could be of great use to the prisoners in terms of smuggling out unofficial letters and information. They were the warders whom the prison authorities would never suspect of helping inmates.

Perhaps the most remarkable success story concerned the notoriously brutal guard Sergeant Delport, the scourge of the quarry. An older, towering, red-faced Afrikaner, he viewed the political prisoners with utter hatred and was notorious for his violent sadism. In their early years on the island, the men quickly grew to be particularly careful and cautious around him. Swift to anger and quick to use his truncheon, he didn't need any reason or excuse to beat a man into unconsciousness. Mark Shinners referred to Delport as the 'chief tormentor'. He was a nightmarish figure and was in complete agreement with apartheid's ideals.

The four downward-pointing chevrons on the sleeve of his uniform jacket signifying long service gave some clue to the reasons behind Delport's dark fury. Time and again, he had been overlooked for promotion. His unquestioning loyalty to the apartheid regime was never in doubt, and it soon became clear to the prisoners that Delport's lack of success was down to his inability to pass the warders' examinations. He could read and write, but his lack of reasoning and academic skills continually let him down.

One morning when he came to open up the cell blocks he was in a particularly black mood. Unable to stop himself, he confided to the prisoners that once again he had been passed by for promotion. In order to open the lines of negotiation, the prisoners offered their sympathy, praised his loyalty and abilities as a guard, and acknowledged that the prison bosses didn't appreciate him. Then they quietly suggested to Delport that they could help him win promotion. He would probably remain a sergeant for ever, unless he did some studying – with the prisoners.

Remarkably, Delport sat down beside the men he reviled and began to study. With the help of the prisoners, who taught him maths and how to improve his vocabulary, he passed his matric (school-leaving certificate). In the next round of promotions, he was appointed from the rank of sergeant to lieutenant.

Having studied and shared time with the men, this most hard-bitten believer in the harshest application of apartheid slowly changed his attitude. He transformed from a brute into one of the most approachable and helpful of warders. In the years after freedom came to South Africa, Delport encountered some former prisoners and even apologized to them for his earlier actions on the island. The former prisoners have no doubts about the sincerity of his words.

Men on the island positively thirsted for news from the outside world. Here again, friendly guards could help. Though the political prisoners were consistently and officially denied the right to read newspapers or magazines, some guards would deliberately leave their discarded newsprint lying around the prison. The inmates also developed other ways of keeping abreast of the news. Some common-law prisoners in the other cell-block sections were allowed newspapers, and these became the object of much barter – and theft.

Common-law inmates and guards joked with one another that you could trust the political prisoners with your valuables, your money, anything ... except your newspaper: turn your back for a second and, as if by magic, it would be gone. One of the reasons the political prisoners welcomed the Sunday visits of clergymen from the mainland was that perhaps he would bring a newspaper with him and therefore the opportunity to steal it.

Some criminal prisoners worked as domestic servants in the guards' quarters outside the jail. Under instructions from the political prisoners, they would search through waste and dustbins, retrieve old newspapers and bring them back into the prison to exchange for reading and writing lessons. It wasn't purely news of the political situation the men hungered for. In the stolen and smuggled newspapers, they would read the often out-of-date match reports of their favourite football teams back on the mainland, avidly follow league tables and results, and learn who had been transferred, injured, or scored the goals.

When new prisoners arrived on the island, they were virtually interrogated by existing inmates desperate to wring every last piece of news out of them. It didn't matter how big or small; they were hungry for any facts or stories about life back home and the outside world in general and, as soon as the news was told to one group of prisoners, it would immediately be transmitted around all the sections of the jail containing political prisoners. Desperate for news, Walter Sisulu told a fellow prisoner that the punishment of not having a newspaper was beyond description.

Rudimentary crystal radio sets were made from wire, razor blades, and strips of metal. A common-law prisoner scavenged an old pair of broken headphones from a dustbin in the warders' village, and these were repaired by the resourceful Sedick. Once complete, the radio was hidden among the rocks in the quarry. While the guards were patrolling other areas, the inmates would struggle to tune in to even the barest of crackling reception from mainland radio stations in an attempt to glean some ever-valuable news about what was happening in the outside world.

The news the prisoners heard from the South African mainland, however hard they had sought to hear it, was not welcome. Black morale was at a low ebb. White South Africa was undergoing an economic boom, still propped up by its army of poorly paid, subjugated black and coloured workers. The regime's friends in international business, now satisfied that South Africa had crushed dissent in its own lands and then coaxed the world community to look the other way, were pumping yet more finances, investment, and resources into the country.

In mainland South Africa, the few remaining foot soldiers engaged in the black struggle were under constant surveillance and curfews, their movements severely restricted. Black resistance and dissent had been driven largely underground by the Bureau of State Security (BOSS), the sinisterly named new South African intelligence service, and the ever expanding arms of the apartheid military and police. Beyond this, however, there was some news of events on the international front that brought unexpected hope to the men on Robben Island, and much of it came through sport.

Two black American athletes, Tommie Smith and John Carlos, made a hugely powerful silent protest against racial discrimination at the 1968 Mexico Olympics. Smith won gold in the 200 metres and Carlos took the bronze medal. Stepping up on to the podium to receive their medals, they waited until the American national anthem began to play and then, with their heads bowed, each raised a black-gloved fist.

Smith raised his right fist to represent black pride and Carlos raised his left to represent black unity. Together, they formed a symbolic arch of unity and power. The silver-medal winner, a white Australian, Peter Norman, silently supported his fellow sprinters by staring straight ahead and wearing the same badge, that of the Olympic Project for Human Rights, that Smith and Carlos had on their jerseys. Norman's action was remarked on by the prisoners when they saw the photo. Here was a symbol that solidarity across racial barriers was a possibility. On Robben Island, the news buoyed the men up for days, and oppressed black people throughout the world celebrated it.

There were to be other body blows dealt to the apartheid regime between 1969 and 1971, the years when the Robben Island Makana Football League was establishing itself, and these too were primarily delivered by events and individuals within the sporting world.

The most significant one for the prisoners involved a quietly spoken South African-born cricketer named Basil d'Oliveira. A legend in Cape Town cricket, he scored over eighty centuries and once hit two hundred runs in an hour, but this major talent was denied the opportunity to play for his own country: Basil d'Oliveira was coloured. Desperate to play first-class cricket, he moved to Britain in 1960 and began playing very successfully for top county team Worcestershire. Six years later, and to the pleasure of true cricket fans the world over, d'Oliveira officially qualified to play for England. He made his test-match debut almost immediately.

Sedick Isaacs was particularly jubilant at his success, because he had known d'Oliveira from childhood. When he discovered the news, during one lunchbreak in the quarry, he proudly announced to his comrades that his 'neighbour' had been selected to play international cricket for England.

In the winter of 1968, England was due to tour South Africa. Given his impressive form, d'Oliveira should have been a shoo-in for the squad, but there was considerable speculation as to whether or not England would be allowed to enter South Africa if he was in the team. The English cricket board, the MCC, was determined to go ahead with the tour and, in an act that enraged sports fans and anti-apartheid supporters alike, they left d'Oliveira out of the squad. Following this, the *Daily Mail* published an extensive opinion poll which revealed that two out of every three questioned deplored the omission of the naturalized South African and believed he'd been dropped because he was coloured. As legendary British BBC cricket commentator John Arlott bluntly asserted at the time, no one of open mind could possibly believe he had not been selected to play for valid cricket reasons.

A storm of protest erupted. A senior delegation from the Anti-Apartheid Movement met with Minister of Sport, Denis Howell, to voice its outrage at the decision. As they left the Minister's office, the delegation was informed by waiting journalists that an injured England player had now been replaced in the tour squad by d'Oliveira. The South African response was immediate. At a National Party meeting in Bloemfontein, Premier Vorster delivered an incendiary speech baldly informing the England team that it was no longer welcome in South Africa. He drew loud applause from his audience of hardcore supporters but condemnation from the rest of the world. The MCC formally called off the tour, and South Africa found itself isolated even more from the sporting world.

When the prisoners on Robben Island learned of the news through their usual unofficial channels, they were ecstatic. Vorster had made a bad political mistake. His knee-jerk reaction had effectively placed South Africa's apartheid regime under a magnifying glass the world over, forcing its international supporters to express increasing concern about the nature of the system. This was a sporting boycott that apartheid, through its stubborn and almost deliberately provocative behaviour, had brought upon itself.

The British public had barely recovered from the events of the d'Oliveira affair when the all-white South African rugby team arrived in Britain. Similarly to the Cricket Council, the Rugby Board had ignored all requests for the cancellation of their tour. They would soon reap the consequences of that decision – each match on the tour was dogged by nationwide protests and mass demonstrations. Pitches

were invaded by protesters and, off the field, pickets were held outside the South African team's hotels. The British press estimated that
over fifty thousand protesters followed the tour from ground to
ground.

During the course of a miserable, embattled Christmas spent
far away from home in hotel rooms under siege from protesters,
ordered not to stray outside because of fears for their safety, the
demoralized players voted to return home halfway through the tour.
However, with the characteristic tunnel vision of those who supported apartheid, their management ordered them to continue.

Other international rugby players were quickly getting the message
that it was impossible to separate politics – and injustice, oppression,
and racial prejudice – from sport but, while many international
sportsmen and women were making a stand against apartheid, the
men running English cricket again revealed how determined they
were to hold to their stance to keep politics out of sport. A deeply
conservative body run by deeply conservative men, the MCC proved
that it had learned nothing at all from the bitter uproar that had surrounded the Basil d'Oliveira affair. The following year, 1970, the MCC
invited the all-white South African team to tour Great Britain again.

The driving force behind what became the Stop the Seventy Tour
organization was Peter Hain, a University of London student whose
family had fled South Africa to avoid imprisonment for its activities
in the anti-apartheid movement. By coincidence, the Hains had a link
with football on Robben Island. They had helped find and pay for the
attorney who represented Dikgang Moseneke, Mark Shinners, and
the others who were sentenced with them.

A widespread sense of outrage manifested itself in huge opposition to the tour, and tens of thousands of British anti-apartheid supporters and revolted cricket fans began to mobilize. Even before the South Africans arrived, county-cricket grounds the length and breadth of the country were covered with anti-apartheid graffiti; a hole just over a yard deep was dug in the middle of the Leicestershire pitch. Anti-apartheid campaigners threatened to physically disrupt games.

When African, Asian, and West Indian countries threatened to boycott the Commonwealth Games in Edinburgh unless the tour was called off, Harold Wilson's Labour government finally stepped in. It formally requested the Cricket Council to call off the tour on grounds of broad public policy. For the first time, the government had been forced to come off the fence in its relations with Britain's then third biggest trading partner, South Africa.

The cancellation of the 1970 England tour led directly to South Africa's exclusion from test-match cricket. New Zealand refused to play them and, in September 1971, the Australian Cricket Board called off the scheduled South African tour of South Australia. Effectively, the white international South African team had to disband – there was no one left to play against.

In May 1970, having already been excluded from the Tokyo and Mexico City Olympics, South Africa was excluded from the Olympic Games Movement altogether, becoming the first country in the history of sport to suffer such a humiliation. Later the same year South Africa was kicked out of tennis's Davis Cup, and it was no longer used as a venue on the Grand Prix tennis circuit.

The men on Robben Island were much heartened – whites-only

apartheid South African teams were now excluded from international competition in every sport. In the fight against apartheid, sport was showing South Africa's big business partners and the western governments who happily collaborated with them a new path, one that embraced ideals of morality and justice. The sports ban did not extend to individual sports. Tennis players and golfers like Gary Player continued to proudly represent South Africa on the international sports scene.

The more news Sedick Isaacs heard, the more he yearned to be back on the mainland taking a direct part in the resistance against apartheid. His ingenious mind began to explore an outrageous idea – escape.

In the entire history of the island as a prison, escape had been virtually impossible. Like its American counterpart Alcatraz, it had been well chosen as a place of incarceration. Even if prisoners did find a way out of their cell blocks, they then faced the problem of finding a way through the high, double-corridor razor-wire fences unseen by the armed guards who manned the watchtowers twenty-four hours a day.

If they were lucky enough to get that far, and out of the prison compound, would-be escapers then had to get off the island. Boats were always moored up on the island's jetties, but these were heavily patrolled and guarded around the clock. The thought of swimming back to the mainland was absurd. It was a seven journey through stormy waters full of man-eating sharks and some of the most restless currents on earth.

Few prisoners ever even contemplated escape; the odds against were just too high. Instead, they focused on finding ways to use their time on the island as part of their role in the struggle. But Sedick was a scientist, with a bent for thinking unconventionally and, though he was quietly spoken, his reputation for single-minded stubbornness was well earned. Even to attempt was probably madness, but Sedick was 'feeling lucky'.

The first part of the master plan was informed by his unsuccessful attempt to escape Pollsmoor Prison back in 1964. This time, he realized there was little point in laboriously trying to dislodge prison-cell bars, because the guards would soon discover any 'escape work' in their regular, and always thorough, cell searches.

Outside in the compound, Sedick knew that it would take far too long to cut through two lines of tough razor wire. A barrage of strong spotlights straked the perimeter of the prison throughout the night, and there was no way a group of prisoners furiously trying to chop through two separate fences would not be spotted. That approach would almost certainly be signing your own death warrant as, in the unlikely event of an escape attempt, the guards had orders to shoot to kill.

Sedick's solution to these problems was audaciously simple – he would get someone to forge a master key, first to get him and his fellow escapees out of the cell block without raising the alarm, and then through the main gates.

Lizo Sitoto and Tony Suze were two of the handful of prisoners who were invited to take part in the attempt. They helped Sedick to take detailed measurements of the locks on the cell and then took them to a prisoner called Japta (Bra Jeff) Masemola, who had worked as a blacksmith on the mainland. Masemola got a kitchen trustee to smuggle a knife to him, and he fashioned it into a rudimentary file. He made a basic blank key from scrap iron found on the beach next to the quarry. Over a period of time various versions of the key were smuggled into the cell block. Masemola would furtively pass the latest to one of the would-be escapers, under cover of work in the quarry, he would try it in the lock, and then indicate where it would need regrinding.

The smuggling back and forth of the key was no easy task, as the prisoners were strip-searched each day on their return from the quarry. In addition, the conspirators were taking an enormous risk either that the key would stick or they would be discovered. Tony and the other inmates would be on the look-out for guards, while Sedick slowly inserted the key into the lock, trying not to make any scraping or clanking noises.

It took two weeks, and it was done. Masemola had made a dummy key that would not only open the locks of the cell block but also the main gates of the prison. So confident was the prison regime of the impossibility of escape, all the locks operated on a master-key system.

The next problem to overcome was how to get off the island. Trying to steal a boat was far too dangerous. Sedick decided that they would make one. For once, the turbulence of the sea surrounding the island proved beneficial. The debris of wrecked ships regularly washed up on the beach next to the quarry and, over time, the men managed to salvage planks and large sections of wood. While other prisoners worked hard to help meet the would-be escapers' quotas, Sedick and his team slipped furtively out of the quarry and into a shielding outcrop of rock to work secretly on fashioning a wooden frame for their boat.

When they had done this, the men located and stole two empty, discarded 44-gallon fuel drums that had been dumped next to the quarry. They lashed these on to the bottom of the wooden platform and hid their makeshift craft amidst a jumble of rocks next to the sea, away from the quarry.

The would-be escapers undertook an exercise regime in order to build up their stamina for the trip. If they were going to cross the Atlantic Ocean from the island to the mainland, they would have to be fit and strong. Sedick took their heartbeats after each exercise session. The training was relentless. Even though Lizo and Tony were already pretty fit from playing football, Sedick pushed them harder and harder.

It seemed that luck was on their side. With contributions from fellow inmates, the men hoarded what food they could and they also managed to gather together some spare clothes from sympathetic common-law criminals who worked in the laundry. However, just days away from the date of the planned escape, Sedick's luck ran out. Something happened in the prison, unrelated to Sedick and his fellow prisoners' plotting, but it led to the guards discovering the escapees' plans.

In return for food and favours, one of the common-law prisoners had informed the warders that there was an illegal radio somewhere in the political prisoners' cell blocks – one of the crystal sets that the men had secretively pieced together in the quarry. A lightning shake-down was launched and, as well as finding the radio, they discovered Sedick's counterfeit master key. The escape attempt was stymied.

Before Sedick was dragged away, he did manage to derive some satisfaction from seeing the key turn smoothly when the guard tried it in the lock. Bra Jeff was moved to a different section of the prison, and all the cell-door locks were changed. Sedick took the blame; his punishment an additional nine months on his sentence and a year in solitary confinement.

On the surface, day-to-day relations between staff and prisoners had improved over the years, but Robben Island was still a jail under the control of an utterly ruthless apartheid regime. Sedick had been a thorn in the authorities' side for too long and, now they had him in solitary, the prison guards took the opportunity to exact their revenge. Sedick was manacled in chains in a tiny bare grey cell and regularly beaten and tortured. Hung upside down and thrashed with batons, he vomited blood on to the concrete floor and, awoken from troubled sleep in the darkest hours, punched and kicked. Sedick was originally given one book to read, the Bible, but a Koran was added to that. He kept himself busy by trying to commit both books to memory and by creating a series of mathematical and logic problems. Fellow prisoners also smuggled in some poems written by other inmates. Over the next twelve months of painful and solitary incarceration, Sedick kept himself sane through these mental exercises and his indefatigable hope for the future of a free South Africa.

6

The Atlantic Raiders Affair

'We lost to a hopeless side and we had to get some concessions for the sake of our pride.' Benny Ntoele, Prisoner 287/63

In the prison kitchens, Freddie Simon was on the look-out for food to smuggle out. Now that the daily diet had improved a little on the island, thanks to pressure from prisoners and the International Red Cross, the men were occasionally given eggs and vegetables, and more of the fish and chicken that went into the drums of maize porridge was proper meat rather than fat, bone, and gristle, so the pickings were a lot richer.

They needed to be. Manong FC was holding a clandestine victory party, an extraordinary and unheard of event in the prison. It was to celebrate its triumph in the championship. Other prisoners had helped out with supplies too. A couple of guinea fowl had been caught, and a dozen or so sea gull's eggs had been foraged from the beach, but Freddie and his friends in the kitchens, sympathetic common-law prisoners, had been charged with providing the lion's share.

On the evening of the party, in June 1970, the smuggled food was distributed to the team and their guests across the various cell blocks, and there was a great deal of backslapping. How loud the celebrations became depended on which of the guards were on duty: some enjoyed supporting football on the island and turned a blind eye, but others were far less sympathetic, and would come down on the party like a ton of bricks. In the cell blocks they patrolled that night, the inmates kept the noise levels down.

The Manong players had made a point of inviting fellow prisoners to join in with their celebrations, and most took it in good humour – there were certainly few enough reasons to celebrate in Robben Island Prison. Some, however, saw the invitation as nothing more than a chance for Manong to show off. In their eyes, the club was getting above itself, and its arrogance was beginning to extend well beyond the pitch. Manong FC was talking itself up, the players saying just how much they themselves rated their skills and how far ahead they were of any other team on the island. They had a point: the statistics proved it, as did the consistently expansive style they'd employed throughout the season.

As they chattered and congratulated themselves and each other, the seed of an idea began to develop. Manong's players decided they weren't being given the competition that their talents deserved. The solution they came up with would indirectly trigger a chain of events that would come close to destroying everything that the Makana Football Association was trying to create and cause disharmony among those in the prison community that would continue to rankle for thirty years.

One evening soon after the victory party, Tony Suze and a handful of fellow Manong club members sat down to compose a letter to the football association. They wrote that the team had been thinking for a long time about the quality of football on the island; it had improved, but the club wanted to encourage an even greater performance at the top level and suggested that a team be selected specifically to play against Manong. The implication was clear: only a group of the best players chosen from across all the other teams would be fit to compete against Manong Football Club.

The MFA responded in measured tones, letting Manong know that, if any special match were to be played, the offer would come from the MFA. Privately, senior MFA officials such as Dikgang Moseneke and Indress Naidoo were disconcerted by the condescending attitude of some of the Manong club's members.

The letter sent by Manong didn't achieve the result it was aiming for, but it did focus attention on one thing that was becoming difficult to ignore: Manong's dominance was indeed becoming a problem. It was head and shoulders above the other teams, and this was not only making a mockery of the association's desire to offer meaningful sport at all levels of ability but was also, in some quarters, affecting the general level of enthusiasm for football.

By November 1970, the fight to win the A division's second championship seemed like an extended instance of *déjà vu*. Seven games into the season, six wins on the board, Manong was once again streets ahead at the top of the table – and this despite the absence of their star player, Tony Suze, out of the game due to a damaged knee, an injury sustained in a collision with the Ditsitsiri goalkeeper in an A-division match almost two months earlier.

The tone of the letter from Manong had annoyed the executives of the MFA, but they took the point that interest in football was lower than in the past. The MFA decided to take a dramatic step to revive enthusiasm by introducing a new knock-out cup competition. Players were to form their own teams from within their own cell blocks. Rather than creating a more level playing field, however, this decision was to have the unintended consequence of highlighting even more starkly the players' differences in ability and creating a situation that threatened the existence of the MFA.

As well as the Manong players, some of the best footballers from the other clubs lived in cell block C4. These players came together and formed a club, the Atlantic Raiders, for the new cup competition. It was made up of the cream of the island's players, all from the top five clubs in the league table, including Tony Suze, Freddie Simons, Benny Ntoele, Moses Masemola, and Ernest Malgas. It was never clear if the Atlantic Raiders represented cell block C4 or if they were a group of footballers who just happened to be sharing a cell together. This seemingly trivial distinction would cause a huge amount of distress for both the MFA and the island community over the next few months.

The Atlantic Raiders took it for granted that they would win the new competition. They had a greater ambition: they wanted to show the rest of the island how good they were as individual players and how spectacular they were as a team. Their intention was not just to win, but to win with flair.

There may have been a degree of hubris in their intent, but these were committed footballers playing matches behind razor wire after a week of punishing hard labour in a stone quarry. They had few opportunities to express themselves or to experience a sense of achievement. Football had given them a rare outlet. In terms of their own sense of self-respect, what happened out on the pitch was of massive importance.

In the first round the Atlantic Raiders were drawn against a team called Blue Rocks. Normally, betting in the cell blocks, with cigarettes and tobacco, was frenzied before big matches, but not this time. Only a fool would bet against the Raiders. Blue Rocks was a makeshift team of older, less talented players. One of the Raiders described their opponents as 'nobodies'. To make an analogy with the broader world of football, it was as if Manchester United, playing at full strength, had been drawn against the team from the local pub. The question was not whether the Atlantic Raiders would win, only by how many goals.

On the day of the match, the Blue Rocks players looked on with unease as the Raiders warmed up. Individually, the players had skills and tricks in abundance and, more than anything, they exuded total and complete confidence. Tony Suze was particularly pumped up, having just recently returned from two months on the sidelines. The assembled pavvy settled down to watch the match, certain that it was going to be a walkover. Even before kick-off, everybody was feeling sorry for Blue Rocks.

The match started at 1 o'clock on 21 November 1970. Playing conditions were perfect: intermittent sunshine and blue skies. Against all the odds, a Blue Rocks breakaway in the first few minutes of the match ended up in a scrambled goal. The Raiders players protested passionately that the goal was clearly offside and had involved a handball – and then the fun began. The older team was jubilant, and determined to hang on to their advantage.

They took up a 10–0–0 formation that brought new meaning to the phrase 'defensive rearguard action'. Blue Rocks packed their penalty area, and any Raiders ball that came into them was immediately hacked out into touch or as far up the field as possible. There was little pretence at playing football – with a totally unexpected goal in the bank against the best team on the island, Blue Rocks had decided their tactics: dogged survival. It wasn't pretty by any standards, and infuriated the footballing purists on the Atlantic Raiders team. As the crowd's cheers for the Blue Rocks grew louder, the Raiders players' tempers began to fray.

After repeated barracking, and renewed complaints from Raiders players about the alleged missed-handball decision, the referee decided he'd taken enough abuse and stormed off the pitch. A new match official was hastily brought on. In the chaos that ensued, it was never clear who had appointed the referee or even if he was qualified, but no one was paying any attention to that at the time. What was important was the spectacle that was unfolding and the possibility of a memorable result. After a lengthy delay, the match continued. Puffing and blowing as they threw their ageing bodies in front of wave after wave of Raiders attackers, the unlikely heroes of Blue Rocks hung on to win 1–0.

For the crowd, the whole thing was priceless. The old men of Blue Rocks had turned the best players on the island into a laughing stock. The Atlantic Raiders, however, were incensed. They surrounded the match officials, and continued their protests all the way back to the cell blocks. Their self-esteem had suffered a damaging blow. After all, they had a certain status in the prison as talented footballers, and were admired and supported by hundreds of other inmates. On top of that, the goal should not have been allowed. The Atlantic Raiders decided to make their complaint official.

The next day, they came out with all guns blazing. The opening sally was a strongly worded letter sent to the MFA by Tony's good friend, Sedick Isaacs, now out of solitary and the non-playing secretary of the Raiders club. The letter displayed both Sedick's talent for wordplay and his bent towards litigation.

Knowing the FIFA rules as he did, Sedick was well aware that the Makena Football Association's constitution required that any complaint had to be registered immediately after the irregularity had been 'observed' – in other words, straight after the match. The Raiders captain Freddie Simon should have filed a protest when the whistle blew on the Blue Rocks game but, with all the angry post-match arguments and frustration, he had neglected to lodge his complaint.

Sedick's means of getting around this inconvenient truth was to refer to the Oxford Dictionary, which defines 'observe' as 'become conscious of'. The case for the Raiders was based on the assertion that it had taken them a matter of days fully to understand or 'observe' the gravity of the injustice inflicted upon them. In any case, they thought the issue was so important (and by extension, that the Raiders were so important) that any time limit should be waived by the MFA.

Sedick then turned to the facts in question and placed the blame on the referee for not applying the offside rule correctly and ignoring a handball violation. He accused the referee of treating the match as a joke and ignoring the decades-old protocols of organized football. After the referee had cost the Raiders a goal, Sedick wrote in the letter, he 'unceremoniously' walked off the field, leaving chaos in his wake. He had done everything he could to hurt the Raiders. Such conduct had to be addressed, and Isaacs claimed that FIFA regulations (Holy Scripture to the island football community) in this case demanded nothing less than a full replay of the match.

The letter expressed the Raiders' hope that the issue could be settled amicably but then took on a more threatening tone, warning the MFA that the Raiders were briefing a panel of men to act as their advocates. They wanted fair treatment and were prepared to go as far as it took to obtain it. When the officials of the MFA read the letter they were concerned that the Raiders were acting like lawyers, not sportsmen. They had no way of knowing that what the Raiders had in mind was something much more dramatic and unsettling than raising a mere legal challenge to the actions of a referee.

There was much more at stake for the Atlantic Raiders than that. The best players had been embarrassed. They had lost to what Benny Ntoele described as a 'bunch of nothings' and they didn't know how to cope with that. It didn't help that so many of their comrades on the island were so obviously delighted to have seen them lose to a team that had, comparatively, no talent and, apparently, no chance of winning. The Atlantic Raiders were going to fight their case to the end.

Given the raised passions, the best thing for all concerned would have been a cooling-off period. The Raiders would have had a chance to regain their composure, and officials could have looked further into the debacle with the referees. Unfortunately, just as the Raiders' letter was making its way to the MFA officials, the fixture list for the second round of the cup competition was delivered to each cell. The men in cell block C4 were outraged. There it was in black and white: Blue Rocks would be playing the Carlton team in the next round. It was obvious that there was no question of the match between the

Atlantic Raiders and Blue Rocks being replayed. Tony, Sedick, and the rest of the Raiders were furious.

For their part, the officials at the MFA could not understand why they should bend their procedures just to mollify the damaged pride of the Raiders. The MFA thought that any dispute would be handled in the course of events, while the Raiders thought that the issuing of the fixture list meant that the MFA had rendered a decision on their protest before even reading it.

On 28 November the Raiders fired off another letter to the MFA, this time accusing it of 'gross irregularity', of violating its own rules, and ignoring any evidence that supported the claims made by the Raiders.

Each action taken by the MFA seemed more dismissive than the previous one. The Raiders were convinced that the MFA had no intention of giving their case a fair hearing. Furthermore, their cell-mates in C4 began to think of it as a struggle that should involve the whole of C4, not just the Raiders. It was becoming a matter of us versus them, 'them' being the executives of the football association the prisoners had fought so hard to create.

The Blue Rocks *v* Carlton game was scheduled for that coming Saturday, 5 December. The Raiders were, however, determined to get some satisfaction from the MFA. On 3 December Isaacs wrote a letter demanding a meeting before the second-round cup match was played. The letter concluded with a phrase that became the topic of fevered conversation among the prisoners for months: 'failing which, full methods of duress shall have to be employed'.

The last sentence of the letter was both ambiguous and threatening. It left MFA officials worried about what the Atlantic Raiders might have in mind. Instead of seeking a meeting with the Raiders as a whole, on the eve of the Blue Rocks *v* Carlton game, 4 December, they called the captain, Freddie Simon, and vice-captain, Lucas Mahlonga, in for an interview, and asked them repeatedly what that phrase in the letter meant. What were they planning? The men refused to enlighten the MFA. Uncertain about what the Raiders might do next, nonetheless the football association was not about to be black-mailed. Its officials pointed out to Simon and Mahlonga that they would be held directly responsible for anything that might happen.

The next day, Mahlonga withdrew from all team activities. He of course knew exactly what his comrades were planning, and he was starting to have serious misgivings.

Late in the morning on 5 December, the giant-killing Blue Rocks players trotted happily out for their second-round match in the new cup competition. They were pleased to see a big crowd of prisoners ringing the touchlines but, very quickly, they became aware that most of them weren't there to support Blue Rocks or, indeed, Carlton. Word had got around the cell blocks that something extraordinary was about to happen.

As the Blue Rocks players began to warm up, eight members of the Atlantic Raiders, including Tony Suze, Freddie Simon, and Benny Ntoele, strode out on to the pitch and lay face down in the centre circle. Both players and fans were stunned. This was an unprecedented and highly charged act of defiance – and a dangerous one at that. Up in the watchtowers, the guards had become aware of the protest and were starting to get twitchy. The seriousness of the situation slowly dawned on both the players and the assembled prisoners.

The true spectators, who had been looking forward to the week's match, were angry. They felt cheated. Not only that, there might be a brawl, a riot even and, if that happened, the Raiders' protest could turn really nasty. The guards on Robben Island had never been backward in resorting to violence and, under such provocation, anything could happen – and it could result in a total ban on football on the island. What were the Raiders doing?

The men understood that the Raiders players were making a peaceful protest but, equally, they knew that the prison authorities needed no excuse to wade in with batons and guns if the situation escalated. The protesters just had to hope against hope that those circling the pitch would control themselves. They were relying on their comrades who ringed the pitch to show the restraint that had become almost second nature to the prisoners. At any rate, what the Raiders were doing was a highly risky strategy.

The football officials present had three options. They could agree to negotiate with the Atlantic Raiders (unacceptable, as it would mean giving in to coercion and was against all the principles of sport). They could remove the men from the pitch by force (even more unacceptable, as it violated the iron-clad principle among political prisoners not to engage in physical conflict with one another, and it would give the guards an excuse to intervene). The MFA leadership chose the third course: they did nothing.

The stand-off lasted for forty-five tortuous minutes. The prison seemed to hold its collective breath, waiting to see what would happen next. Eventually, the Raiders gestured to one another and left the field together. The crowd dispersed, the warders shepherded the prisoners back to their cell blocks, and that was the end of the football on Robben Island for the day.

The protest and its aftermath became the talk of the prison. Heated debate and discussion raged throughout the quarry and across the cell blocks. Was it just sour grapes on the part of the Atlantic Raiders or did the club have a legitimate complaint?

Benny Ntoele admitted years later that at the core of their protest, lay wounded pride. The Raiders had lost to a bunch of *mahala* (incompetents). They were the best players on the island and they had lost in the first match of the season to a hopeless side on a bad decision. They had to do something, if only to restore their dignity.

On 8 December officials of the Makana FA called a secret meeting behind a cell block to discuss what to do next. They decided to punish the first referee for leaving the pitch but at the same time make it clear that nothing could possibly excuse the actions of the Raiders. The leadership of the MFA initiated disciplinary proceedings, which would lead to a formal indictment of the protesters. A tribunal would be established to pass judgement and, if the men were found guilty, to establish the penalties.

The Raiders were typically combative in response and once again demanded a meeting with the MFA's executive. The MFA received a memorandum signed by Tony Suze and witnessed by Sedick Isaacs sent on behalf of cell block C4 – not on behalf of the Atlantic Raiders.

Suddenly, the dynamic of the situation had changed. Tony, Freddie, Sedick, and the others had turned a dispute between football players and the disciplinary committee into one between a body representing authority (the Makana Football Association executive) and a group of prisoners who shared a common life in cell block C4.

The letter claimed to make a few simple points on behalf of the men of C4. They had the best interests of soccer at heart and were anxious to have a peaceful settlement of the dispute. The Raiders were not prepared to take responsibility or blame for what had happened but, by stating that they were looking forward to the re-fixtured Carlton *v* Blue Rocks game, it was clear that the men of cell block C4 were implicitly accepting that there would be no replay of the Raiders *v* Blue Rocks match. There would be no further demonstrations. The men were looking for a face-saving way to end the dispute: what they needed was some sign from the MFA that it recognized that the Raiders had a legitimate complaint. It was a diplomatic and non-committal letter. Sensing an opportunity for compromise, the MFA agreed to talk.

The meeting took place on the evening of 11 December in cell block C4. Four members of the MFA executive, including the chairman, Dikgang Moseneke, smuggled themselves into the building.

An observer was also brought in, Ike Mthimunye, someone who was respected throughout the community. The fact that they had invited an observer showed that both sides were keen to ensure that the larger community would be given an objective report of what happened. An interpreter was also on hand, to enable non-English speakers to follow the debates. Twenty-one prisoners had gathered to challenge the MFA quartet, which created a highly charged and intimidating atmosphere.

Tony Suze chaired the meeting and declared at the start that, in this cell, all inmates were free to talk. The temperature of the meeting rose. The controversy was no longer between just the Atlantic Raiders and the Makana FA. Frequent recesses had to be called to let tempers cool.

Pressure had begun to build on the Raiders and their friends throughout the prison. Other clubs and their players, officials, and fans were giving them a rough ride, disapproving of their actions. Tony Suze, Freddie Simon, and Benny Ntoele, among others, felt that the Makana FA had cast them in the role of villain and were hanging them out to dry. One thing that everyone did seem to agree on was that football on Robben Island was in a chaotic situation.

Benny Ntoele, who had became a spokesman for cell block C4, opened his statement to the meeting by saying that the actions of the association made him think that it did not care about them or want to listen to their complaints; that was what had forced them to take such extraordinary action. All the Atlantic Raiders wanted was justice.

Chairman Moseneke restated the MFA's position: the Raiders had not used the proper method to lodge their protest. This brought angry responses from the cell members, who accused the MFA of hiding behind bureaucractic formalities.

Another speaker, not one of the Raiders, expressed the fear that football might be disrupted for everyone on the island – and after so many people had worked so hard to provide the opportunity for all to enjoy it. He couldn't understand how the association had let things get to this point. When he said that the hostility some of the prisoners felt towards cell block C4 was the fault of the MFA, it brought an angry reply from Moseneke.

He pointed out that it was the Atlantic Raiders who had tried to use hair-splitting definitions and legalistic ploys to draw attention to their protest. It was they who had handled things badly and they would have to take the consequences.

Moseneke wanted everyone to understand that the pressing issue now was not the result of a football match, it was the illegal action members of the Atlantic Raiders had carried out on the pitch on 5 December. He conceded that mistakes may have been made in the administration of the first match, but that didn't excuse the subsequent actions of the Raiders. He insisted that the association had done everything in its power to avoid the implementation of 'duress' when it had called in the captain and vice-captain for interview.

Tony replied angrily that it seemed to him that the leadership of the association had almost deliberately baited the members of the Atlantic Raiders into showing what they had meant by 'duress'.

The meeting was closed with a statement by Ike Mthimunye, the observer. The demonstration had 'disturbed the peace here on the island' and 'reactions were very high'. It seemed to him that the association and the Atlantic Raiders were facing one another 'with swords drawn'.

The discussions had ended in deadlock. For the next seven days, there was a distinctly tense atmosphere in the quarry and the cell blocks, with antagonism and bad feeling bubbling away on all sides. The Atlantic Raiders affair was fast spiralling out of all proportion.

A week later, the men met once again with the MFA in cell block C4. There was some effort to deal with the events that had taken place in the original match but, now, the dispute with the MFA had turned intensely personal and extended beyond issues concerning either the match against Blue Rocks or the demonstration on the pitch. While the dispute had simmered on, the MFA had tried to diffuse tensions within the prison by organizing a series of friendly games. Prisoners in C4 now claimed that the MFA had not chosen them to play in these friendlies because they had shown their support for the Atlantic Raiders.

The men also claimed that someone on the executive of the association had been going around the prison describing the inmates in
cell block C4 as 'ruffians'. Since there had not yet been a hearing on
the charges made against them, the men felt they were being singled
out for castigation without due process. This called into question the
possibility of a fair hearing.

In addition, the C4 cellmates accused the association of duplicity,
of trying to use some of the provisions in the constitution to punish
the demonstrators while ignoring other parts which might support
the claims made by the Atlantic Raiders. Moseneke did his best to
assure the assembled men that he regretted any aspersion that may
have been levelled against anyone in C4. Speaking for the association,
he reminded the meeting that the executive was made up of fallible
men.

One prisoner, Mr Chilsane, probably captured the mood of the
men in cell block C4 by sarcastically responding to this by saying how
'happy he was to get the statement that the association members are
not demigods'. In a more conciliatory tone, he told the chairman that
the association should recognize that the decision of the Raiders and
their supporters not to stage any further demonstrations showed that
their main interest was the continuation of football on Robben
Island. If the association could meet them part way, the problem
could be solved.

The discussion turned to how the judicial inquiry into the conduct
of the Atlantic Raiders would proceed. Challenges were raised as to
the impartiality of the men who would judge the case. Anxieties were
expressed about the method in which evidence would be gathered,
and whether the Raiders would have adequate time to formulate a

robust defence. At one point Mr Chilsane asked for permission to leave the room because his emotions were running so high he was afraid he might resort to violence, should the MFA continue to play with words.

Matters had come to a head. The whole purpose of the meeting had been to find a way to bring about some agreement between the two parties and now the situation had been aggravated further.

Moseneke recognized the need to let the process work itself out in an orderly fashion that would seem fair to everyone. He decided that the only way to handle the situation at this stage 'might be to refer it to a higher body'. In both meetings speakers had made reference to an underlying issue that was making it difficult to reach any kind of compromise: the association wanted the Atlantic Raiders to admit that it did not respect the association; the Raiders were demanding respect for their grievances. Now that each side was fighting for abstract principles such as pride, respect, and reputation, it had become that much harder to settle anything between the parties.

Days after the meeting, the higher body (a specially chosen panel of the MFA) ruled that the Atlantic Raiders players were guilty of bringing the game into disrepute.

The decision made it clear that the executive had nothing against protests per se (indeed it pointed to the civil disobedience of the Black Sash anti-apartheid organization in South Africa as a model the Raiders could have used) but felt that the men could have conducted themselves in a less inflammatory fashion. For example, they could have marched along the field, or moved on to and then off the field. Instead, they lay on their bellies. The pavvy was disturbed and the whole day's football greatly disrupted. That was not sportsmanship.

Each of the men was given a one-month ban from playing football.

The MFA hoped that this ruling would bring the Atlantic Raiders affair to an end but, to its chagrin, the Raiders dug in their heels and refused to accept the verdicts or the sentences. They immediately launched appeals, with Sedick and George Moffatt (a prisoner who went on to have a distinguished career as an attorney) acting as their lawyers.

Big Mo Masemola sent an impassioned letter to the Appeals Tribunal of the MFA. It became the model for the way in which most of the Raiders would formulate their individual appeals. In it, he raised procedural issues, and then reminded the committee that the trial had been delayed so long, he had missed the opportunity to play in a number of select side matches. Surely that was punishment enough – and one that had been levied even before he had been tried for his offence.

He wanted the tribunal to remember the circumstances surrounding both the match and the demonstration. The match had been the opening one in a new competition, and it had seemed that no one knew exactly how matters should be resolved. Why should a sportsman such as himself have to suffer because the Makana FA had not planned for potential problems? Furthermore, if the referee had not acted in an unprofessional manner, none of the subsequent events would have arisen.

Masemola claimed to be as much a victim of circumstances as the perpetrator of an offence. He was appealing against both the imposition of the sentence and its severity. He would be satisfied if the MFA would set aside its sentence in the interests of justice and restoring harmony to the community.

He concluded with sentiments that would have found an echo throughout the community – 'this is a place where sports is a necessity, not a luxury'– and ended the letter with the phrase that was the hallmark of most of the sports-related correspondence between prisoners, words that were taken seriously: 'Yours in sport'.

The Atlantic Raiders affair would roll relentlessly on for another three months. Sedick Isaacs and George Moffatt put together lengthy arguments and submitted detailed reports to the Appeals Tribunal. As a man with such a mischievous sense of humour, Sedick revelled in the verbal jousting and legal point-scoring.

In an interview nearly forty years later Tony Suze asserted that, for Sedick, it was an adventure, a kind of spontaneous dramatic play, one without a predetermined ending. The whole affair engaged, absorbed, and involved people in an intense and passionate way, and that was one of the reasons for prolonging it. In some ways, it was an intellectual game, but with a serious intent.

Dikgang Moseneke abandoned his role as Chairman of the MFA to assume that of Appeals Tribunal prosecutor. To this day, Dikgang's comrades like to remind the Deputy Chief Justice of the Constitutional Court of South Africa that the Atlantic Raiders presented him with his first opportunity to write a detailed legal brief. He put forward a strong case and ensured that the court focused on the specifics of what had happened, giving a close reading of the relevant provisions in the constitution of the MFA.

Sedick was lead counsel for the defence. In addition to numerous references to the constitution of the Makana FA, his arguments included everything from references to FIFA regulations and the Magna Carta to Justice Blackstone and the constitution of the United

States. He knew he was on sticky ground and chose to adopt a classic defence lawyer's strategy: if the facts are not in your favour, then challenge the law or the jurisdiction of the court.

One of Sedick's ploys showed marvellous originality and audacity. He presented a list of reasons why the members of the panel should excuse themselves and stand down. He concluded that the whole Robben Island community was against the Atlantic Raiders and, since the members of the tribunal were all members of the Robben Island community, they were not fit to adjudicate the matter.

Later in to the appeals, the Atlantic Raiders started on a parallel line of attack against the association and its affiliated clubs. Again, it was just the kind of action that suited what Tony Suze described as Sedick's 'special sense of humour'.

The secretary of the Makana FA received a beautifully written note. It was a bold attempt by the Raiders to join the MFA as a bona-fide full-time club. In normal circumstances, the secretary would have been delighted to receive an application from a prospective new team, but this was an outrageous demand, calculated to further muddy the waters.

The MFA sat on the note, unwilling to consider the application until the tribunals had finished but, a week later, they received another message from Sedick and the Raiders. The letter was headed with the newly selected and somewhat provocative Jolly Roger emblem of the Atlantic Raiders FC and was a formal application for affiliation to 'your esteemed organization'. Sedick submitted a list of players for membership. The first names were those of all the men indicted by the Makana FA for their centre-circle demonstration.

The letter was a model of precision and met every standard set down by the association for new clubs seeking membership to the MFA. The men had applied for cards to release them from their old clubs. The letter listed the officers of the club, its colours, and emblem. The motto was 'still to be chosen'.

In the letter the Raiders also suggested that the new club enter into friendly matches with MFA clubs and cheekily asked for a copy of the association's constitution – this request from men who had spent weeks arguing with the association about arcane provisions contained within that very document. They already knew it inside out.

The final paragraph of Sedick's letter reeked of irony. He hoped that the application would be most favourably considered because the Raiders were anxiously looking forward to assisting the MFA in the task of promoting football and contributing to the recreation of the community.

The formality of the letter was appropriate and the sentiments everything expected of a new applicant but, given the circumstances at the time, it must have enraged the MFA. How, though, could it respond, other than to accept the application? After all, the Atlantic Raiders were following the constitution to the letter.

What was going on in the creation of this new club? A joke, a way to raise their spirits? Or was it what one member of the executive of the association felt was an effort to form their own league? None of these. It was a combination of bluff and blackmail, an attempt to get the respect they thought they were owed and to have the punishments of the team members reduced. The men wanted to put the episode behind them but to come out of it with their pride intact.

Underlying this approach was the calculation that the Atlantic Raiders were in a position to put pressure on the association because of the quality of their players. Their clubs would not want to lose them. It was also assumed that the clubs would not want to see the creation of a virtual picked side as a single club. It would dominate the league even more than Manong had done, and the whole reason behind the new cup tournament had been to bring some relief from a league where one club was so superior.

The MFA was wrong-footed and stalled on making any kind of decision. This played into the hands of the Atlantic Raiders. If they had overdone it by staging the demonstration, it now seemed that the MFA's delays over granting permission to join the association were leading many of the prisoners to believe that the Raiders were indeed being victimized. Cranking up the pressure on the MFA even further, the Atlantic Raiders Football Club even announced that its maiden friendly match would take place on 31 January 1971.

It would never be played. The MFA had a surprise in store for the Raiders. It told the ever-meticulous Sedick that it had discovered a clause in the constitution that decreed that an application for admission could not be accepted while competition games were in progress. The only way to get around it would be for the Atlantic Raiders to rally enough clubs to vote to waive that clause – and any hope of that ended when the delegate for the Rangers FC had condemned the unsportsmanlike conditions under which the Raiders had been formed. He was not alone in his feelings.

The Atlantic Raiders' efforts had failed. The pressure they had tried to put on the existing clubs didn't work, as everyone knew that none of the Raiders players would want to wait until the following season to play another competitive match. Football mattered too much to them. In practical terms, waiting for the Raiders to become a club would cost them more time off the pitch than would accepting their punishment.

While the legal arguments played out, there were other, more important pressures brought to bear on the Raiders. Fellow prisoners appealed to them to end the crisis. The most telling of these was the efforts of the non-playing Chairman of Manong (the club that meant so much to Tony Suze) to convince Tony to do something to 'lead the men back to football'. The elderly chairman was noted for his wisdom and ability to act as a conciliator and those talents were evident in his conversations with the much younger Tony.

On 14 February 1971 the Raiders reluctantly and finally gave in. Sedick wrote a letter to the MFA stating that the Atlantic Raiders had 'peacefully passed away'.

He requested that a waiver be granted to allow its members to join their former clubs as soon as possible and concluded that the decision of the ARFC to disband had been taken in the light of complaints that it had been interfering with the standard of football. The Raiders were facing the reality of defeat and trying to salvage their dignity.

As the months had passed, it was clear that everyone was tired of the problems that had started with the giant-killing victory of the Blue Rocks. A compromise had to be reached; something had to be done to remove the wedge that had been driven between many of the men and to repair the damage that had been caused to the enjoyment of football on the island.

The prisoners were being denied the pleasure of playing and watching football, and even the warders were missing the weekly matches. The guards were going up to the players they knew and asking impatiently, 'What's going on with you people? When are we going to see some football again?'

Implicit within the guards' confusion about why the players had stopped playing competitive matches was the fact that the prison regime knew little or nothing about the heated debates and meetings that were going on behind closed doors. Ironically, and as vexed and problematic as the Atlantic Raiders affair had been, this did illustrate quite how successful the prisoners had been in taking full control over an important area of their lives within the prison.

Finally, the various parties came to a pragmatic, face-saving agreement. The Appeals Tribunal of the Makana FA would change the sentence. The one-month ban from football would be suspended for six months, on condition that the men did not commit an offence involving violence and/or disobedience to association orders. The MFA also insisted that the Raiders players submit letters of apology to the association, as laid out in the trial court judgement.

One by one, the players acquiesced and penned their letters of apology. After five testy, bad-tempered months of to-ing and fro-ing between the two sides, the Atlantic Raiders affair was over. Its repercussions, however, would continue to resound for a long time to come. The consequences were felt not only in what was to happen in the Robben Island sporting community in the immediate years to follow, but also decades later, in the memories of those who had been involved.

Marcus Solomon, who put in a lot of time on the disciplinary committee, was appalled by the actions taken by the Atlantic Raiders. He still finds the lack of respect shown to the association, its establishment the result of so much effort by the men in the prison as a whole, upsetting. In a conversation that took place in 2000, one of Tony Suze's closest friends from childhood and a fellow prisoner told him that, though he loved him like a brother, he still hadn't forgiven him for all the trouble caused by the Atlantic Raiders affair.

The 1970 annual Makana FA report summed up the impact of the affair on football on Robben Island:

> The very best of exhibition matches brought us the worst of sorrows ever told. Here our football society was shaken to its very soul. Literally all our bodies were shaken, involved, and immersed in this historic event. The individual referee in charge of the match was under fire. The Referees Union was declared the most inefficient body by The Raiders. The Protest and Misconduct Committee was insulted and cartooned in a manner unparalleled in our football history here. The Executive turned out to be the Prosecutors and the persecutors in the eyes of The Raiders ... the 'pavvy' was heaving with thick points of anger. And last yet not least, individual relationships with Raiders demonstrators were inconceivably strained. The volume of paper, time, and meetings on this issue alone is unbelievable to hear ... this matter has been settled and I leave it to you to learn from this catastrophe, which should never recur.

The Atlantic Raiders affair was one of the most dramatic episodes in the history of football on the island. The actions taken by the Raiders and the reaction to them demonstrated the men's passion for football, and their all too human resistance to the harshness of the regime to which they had been subjected on the island. Years in prison had not turned them into passive, rule-bound robots or paragons of virtue. Men such as Sedick Isaacs and Dikgang Moseneke had retained and even honed their intellectual talent; others demonstrated a single-minded resolve to do what they believed was right.

Thanks to the series of hearings, the numerous tense meetings, and the dozens of memoranda and letters that were exchanged, hundreds of valuable sheets of foolscap paper were expended on the Atlantic Raiders affair. The transcript of the appeal proceedings alone took 129 pages, as it had to be produced in triplicate in order that all involved parties had access to it.

The most intriguing question is why the whole thing took the course it did. The men clearly had disrupted a match to the point that a week's programme of football had to be cancelled. What could be a more cut and dried case of violating the principles of sportsmanship and the rules of the Makana Football Association? On the other hand, why did it take so long to mete out the punishment that the Atlantic Raiders so clearly deserved?

Perhaps the answer is not so hard to find. Every one of the men on the island had been convicted by a judicial system whose major purpose was to protect a regime dedicated to the persecution of the majority of its citizens. It would have been impossible to convince any of the men on Robben Island that this system represented anything that even approached fairness and due process.

The behaviour of the Atlantic Raiders was a real annoyance and, for a while maybe, even a threat to the good-hearted continuation of football on the island, but there was an unspoken agreement among the prisoners that they would grant one another the rights the system outside the prison had denied them. The principles of justice had to be observed.

The behaviour of the Atlantic Raiders was a major annoyance, In retrospect, the events surrounding the Raiders has some qualities of farce. At the time, some of the men involved did see the humorous aspects of it, but they were a very small minority of the community. How it played out also showed the striking changes that had taken place amongst the prisoners. Two leaders of the Raiders were Tony Suze, a political prisoner dedicated to the PAC and Freddie Simon, a common-law criminal who had become an ANC member after his imprisonment. Any co-operation between men like them would have been unimaginable even a few years earlier. Football had brought them together and their wounded pride had made them allies in an ongoing drama.

For a while, the Raiders' actions and the responses to them represented a genuine threat to the good-hearted continuation of football amongst the prisoners. The desire to play football collided with the unstated assumption amongst the prisoners that they would grant one another the rights of appeal that the system outside the prison had denied to them. The principles of justice had to be observed even if that meant frayed tempers and postponing the pleasure of playing and watching football. The time and effort involved in resolving the case against the Atlantic Raiders is not as remarkable as the fact that the prisoners had developed a set of bureaucratic structure that enabled them to get past the problems caused by the Raiders and to keep the Makana Football Association intact.

7

Growing Older with Football

'It's impossible to think of the island without recreation. It was an essential part of life.' Indress Naidoo, Prisoner 885/63

Commanding Officer Piet Badenhorst pushed open the rickety door of the hospital prison and, as the patients and orderlies fell silent, paced up and down the ward glaring purposefully at the prisoners in the beds lining the walls.

He asked each patient in turn how he came to be in the hospital. Some talked about injuries sustained in the quarry, others had flu or gastric problems. Badenhorst's eyes lit up when one inmate described how he had picked up a leg injury in the most recent round of Saturday-morning football matches. This was what the new commanding officer wanted to hear. All the rights the prisoners had so relentlessly fought for were about to be challenged.

Piet Badenhorst had been appointed commanding officer of Robben Island Prison in December 1970 and had brought with him a new team of warders. He was a hardliner and boasted to prisoners that he had been sent to clean up the island, which, as far as he was concerned, was out of control, the prisoners allowed far too much leeway.

It was now April 1971 and this was by no means Badenhorst's first visit to the hospital. He had come in several times to conduct an informal survey of the men who were sick or had been injured badly enough to have been excused from their work details. His claim was that the recent increase in numbers was caused by one of two factors – the willingness of the prisoners to sham injury just to avoid work or the destructive effects of hard-played football matches.

In either case, Badenhorst saw the inability of men to fulfil their work quota as a challenge to discipline within the prison and an affront to the courts that had sentenced them for their crimes. He was not going to tolerate it. If the only way to return good order was to bring an end to organized sports on Robben Island, then so be it. The prisoners must bear the consequences of their actions.

Badenhorst flexed his muscles by issuing a series of directives aimed at reining in the control the prisoners had over their own world of football. Henceforth, they were under orders to clean their cells and wash their clothes every Saturday morning. Inevitably, this would cause serious delays in getting out on the pitch, and matches would be cut short or not take place at all.

New restrictions were placed on the fans, too. The pavvy had developed into a place with a carefree, almost carnival atmosphere and Badenhorst was determined to destroy this. Guards were ordered to maintain strict discipline among the spectators – and 'strict discipline' could be interpreted in whichever way they wished.

In the prison as a whole, the quality of the food began to deteriorate, studying privileges were withdrawn, and the behaviour of the warders became more vicious. Inmates were banned from singing freedom songs in the quarry and random beatings were once again common. It was as though the clock had been turned right back to the bad old days of the early Sixties.

The footballers were outraged, and the MFA had to move quickly to prevent individual prisoners from staging their own unorganized protests. The association had learned through long experience that the only effective way of negotiating change with the prison regime was for the prisoners to demonstrate complete unity.

The executive asked that each club collect written complaints and make them known to the MFA. The association would then arrange a meeting with the chief warder to seek an explanation for Badenhorst's attitude.

One of the fundamental issues at stake was whether playing football had been granted as a right or a privilege. The leadership of the MFA was determined to enforce what it regarded as an absolute right but, as they rolled up their sleeves, ready to do battle, a series of events on the island led to significant changes in the prison.

In May 1971 a group of Namibian inmates, which included prominent South West African People's Organization members, such as Toivi ja Toivo, were placed in the B-section cells alongside the isolation prisoners. They started a hunger strike, in protest at having been arbitrarily denied meals in the previous months, and soon Mandela, Sisulu, and others joined in. Late one night a gang of warders swarmed into the cells housing the Namibians and set about the prisoners. Toivi ja Toivo was punched by a warder, and immediately retaliated. He, along with twenty-eight other Namibian prisoners, was severely beaten.

The following day, Nelson Mandela and Walter Sisulu made official complaints and, some weeks later, three high court judges visited the island to investigate the incident. A month after that, Badenhorst's tyrannical reign on Robben Island ended, and he was transferred back to the mainland along with his guards.

His short regime had served as a salutary reminder to the football community on the island that they should never take for granted any of the rights they had fought so hard to gain. Unfortunately, Badenhorst's time as commanding officer had also left another legacy: certain guards had felt inspired and empowered by his get-tough policies and, on an individual basis, continued to harass the prisoners. The fixture list was regularly interrupted by these warders, with or without orders from their superiors.

In one instance, two teams took the field at 1.30, eager and ready to play, but were then sent back to their cells and informed there would be no football for them that day. No reason was given. On other occasions matches were delayed or cancelled after claims by the authorities that the men's cells were not satisfactorily clean, or whole blocks were locked up for the day because of minor infringements of prison rules.

In the midst of the football season, the players had repeated problems with one particularly disagreeable warder called Lieutenant Van de Westhuizen. He was not as crudely brutal as many of the warders and did not participate in doling out any physical punishment personally, although he may have enabled others to do so. What made him particularly objectionable in the eyes of the prisoners was that they now expected a degree of fairness and predictability in the treatment they received from the officials who ran the prison and, with Westhuizen, their expectations were frustrated.

At one point he summarily closed football down for the day on the grounds that, during the course of the week, he had visited the prison early one morning before unlock and found a number of prisoners in their beds, despite the fact that the bell had been rung. He had confronted the prisoners at the time and taken their meal tickets – standard procedure for the punishment of individuals – then immediately afterwards had announced that there would be no sports that weekend for the entire prison. He went to every cell block and, with great relish, made the same statement to each set of disappointed men. That Saturday, rather than playing football, the offenders, plus a group of innocent prisoners, were marched down to the quarry to work.

The executive of the Makana Football Association raised this example of collective punishment in a stern letter to the commanding officer, decrying Westhuizen's actions as unjustifiable on the grounds that, as he had already identified the culprits, there was no reason to punish the entire prison. The letter called to the commander's attention that this was the fifth occasion on which football had been interrupted without reasonable cause – and in most of these instances Lieutenant Van de Westhuizen had been the warder responsible.

The letter went on to remind the commander that the purpose of sport was to promote the spiritual and physical wellbeing of the prisoners and that there was no reason to punish those innocent of an offence. When football had been established in the prison community nearly five years earlier, the prisoners had not been told that the threat of its withdrawal would serve as a form of punishment. (They had, however, been aware that this might happen, and it had indeed featured in the debates they had had about the advisability of accepting the right to play football in the first place.)

The letter also served to illustrate the complicated nature of the relationship between the prisoners and the authorities in Pretoria who controlled much of their lives. Two weeks earlier, the prisoners had received a questionnaire from headquarters asking how well the organized sport on the island was going and to what degree the prison commander assisted in setting it up and consolidating it.

There is no firm information about the timing of the distribution of the questionnaire, but it is safe to conjecture that it had something to do with external interest in what was happening on Robben Island. In its response the MFA summed up the prisoners' position that 'sport is intended for recreation' and also reminded the authorities that hundreds of rand had been spent on sporting equipment from its own pockets.

After many years of discussions, protests, confrontations, and negotiations, the prisoners assumed they had reached some kind of working relationship with the prison authorities. Less than a year earlier, they had received assurances from the prison's chief warder for administration that individual crimes would be punished but there would be no collective punishment encompassing the inno- cent. He had also agreed to do his best to safeguard the men's football privileges.

Something else was going on, however, during the dispute trig- gered by Lieutenant Van de Westhuizen. He literally held the keys to the future sporting activities of the prisoners, and the men he commanded carried the rifles and truncheons with which they could enforce his commands. The only recourse open to the prisoners was to try to exert some pressure on his superior and to develop a negotiating strategy to accomplish that.

They assured the commanding officer that they did not doubt for one moment the sincerity of the department in modernizing the administration of the prison but they were concerned by the 'unfortunate, sudden turn' things had taken under Westhuizen. If they were not given a guarantee that recent actions would not be repeated, they would have no choice but to suspend their sporting activities, with immediate effect. They would not resume until they had some assurance from the commanding officer that the withdrawal of the opportunity to play football would not be used as a weapon against them.

The letter recognized that, under abnormal circumstances, for instance when the prisoners got out of hand, the commanding officer would retain the power to suspend all privileges in the interests of restoring order and discipline, but they challenged him, and Westhuizen, to demonstrate that such conditions had existed at the time the lieutenant had taken his action. The letter concluded by saying that the prison community as a whole had full confidence in the commanding officer.

This correspondence was a model of diplomacy. It paid appropriate respect to the inherent powers of the commanding officer and recognized the need for order and security within the prison. They were prisoners; he was the head of the institution. At the same time, the letter reminded the commanding officer that his superiors in Pretoria believed that organized sport run by the prisoners themselves served the broader interests of government policy.

Only at the end was there mention of the bargaining chip the prisoners thought they held – the ability not to play sport. It was clear that, however much the prisoners cherished the time they were out on the pitch as players and on the touchlines as supporters, there was something even more important to them – the ability to exercise control over at least a part of their lives. Hopefully, the situation would not reach the point where football had to end, but everyone knew that the prison community would support such an action if it became necessary.

The response came. The prisoners received no assurances from the commanding officer that the practices undertaken by Lieutenant Van de Westhuizen would cease. In response, the MFA called for an immediate suspension of football. It lasted eleven weeks.

Throughout this period there were constant negotiations and, eventually, the commanding officer relented. The prisoners were able to re-establish a full programme of football, having won a guarantee that the authorities would not use the sport as a tool for collective punishment in the prison community.

A combination of solidarity in the community and the knowledge that the South African regime thought that its provision of sports for the prisoners enhanced its stature internationally had given the prisoners the requisite tools to exercise their skills as negotiators. If the continuation of sports was an important element in forging a sense of community on the island, it was equally important for the prisoners to be able to mobilize themselves and use the threat of suspending football in order to demonstrate that the community did exist and that it was able to defend its rights.

While the prisoners were able to fend off the latest challenge from the authorities, there was a potentially greater problem facing the MFA, one over which the prisoners could exercise no control.

Competitive sport is unlike virtually any other activity. Nonathletes expect to get better at their chosen field of endeavour as they get older. Their ability develops in rough proportion to the experience and wisdom they have gained. It is just the opposite in sports. Men and women reach the pinnacle of the activity at a very young age and then undergo an often rapid decline. In professional football, it is not unusual to see a man approaching age thirty thought of as old or even 'washed up'.

The lifeblood of soccer has always been the constant flood of hopeful, young would-be players being coached and trained, ready to break into the game. An intolerable situation for a manager would be to see his best players leaving the club when they might be at the peak of their skills and to be unsure that there were any promising young players getting ready to join the club. Like so many other aspects of life on Robben Island, the ability to maintain a solid playing roster for a football club presented special problems.

From 1971 onwards, some of the best players left the island. Their team-mates missed their skills and the contribution they made on the pitch, as well as the enthusiasm and skill they exhibited during the gruelling training sessions. When Sipho Tshabalala left the Gunners FC, he wrote a poignant letter of farewell in which he thanked his team-mates and the officials of the Makana Football Association. His 'indebtedness ... for my performance during my short stay here is beyond any description' and he hoped they would 'continue to stand firm with courageous determination'. The best goal keeper in the MFA was leaving, but even his team-mates had to share in a sense of joy in the reason for his departure. They were losing a flamboyant shot stopper and he was gaining a new life outside of prison. August 1, 1971 marked the date of his release after serving a seven-year sentence on Robben Island.

Situations like that of Tshabalala were becoming increasingly common after 1972. A rugby club gave Indress Naidoo a farewell certificate that reminded everyone of its debt to him 'for a historic victory' in a cup competition and conferred 'membership ad infinitum' on him. We can be certain that he had no desire to take up again active membership in the club that had meant so much to him. Another club praised Joseph Tyhala for all of his services to sport and congratulated him 'as he now leaves to enter a new walk of life'. Football and rugby players were losing team-mates, students were losing their tutors, and audiences were losing their favourite musicians and storytellers as the population of the island began to diminish.

The normal pathways to future development were not remotely available to the men who ran football on Robben Island. They certainly did not plan to recruit new players from outside even if they could. The systematic and brutal efficiency of BOSS and the South African police meant that by the early seventies, pretty much all of the hardcore activists and freedom fighters on the mainland had been killed, or incarcerated on Robben Island. This meant that just a trickle of new prisoners were making their way across the stormy waters to Robben Island. As a consequence, few young new footballers were arriving in the prison.

Early clues to what this meant for football on the island were contained within the document that Sedick Isaacs sent to the Makana FA during the Atlantic Raiders affair – namely, in the letter which asked if the cell block C4 team could apply to become a bona-fide member of the island FA.

In it, Sedick Isaacs listed the names of the men he would like registered to the FA as Raiders players. Next to each name, Sedick listed their respective ages:

Name	Age in years
Hoho, A	38
Mpongoshe, L	35
Chiloani, A	33
Simon, F	32
Philhe, D	40
Masemola, M	30
Ntoele, B	30
Tabana, L	32
Suze, A	29
Komptani, N	32
Malgas, E	36
Isaacs, S	29
Fini, K	28

Any club (especially one just formed) whose youngest player is twenty-eight years of age has a problem. The men who formed the foundation of the Makana FA were getting older. And these weren't pampered professionals, but players who had also endured ten years of backbreaking hard labour and poor diet. Though they would never admit it, many of the older players were starting to slow up, feeling the aches and pains more, finding training harder – some needed much longer breaks between games. This was increasingly a serious problem that the Makana FA had to address, if the hard-won right to play football on the island was to continue. Club officials expressed their worry about the fitness of the players and the concern that there might someday not be enough fit players to run a proper league. In some cases, the usual suspects were blamed – the incompetence of the referees. One chairman summed up the problem, 'there is much concern about injuries ... the referees must be more vigilant to impress on players the necessity of careful marking lest we have more injuries and no soccer in the future'.

Things were back to normal with the authorities and the interrupted league programme was resumed. The shutdown had cost the 1970–71 MFA season all but six truly competitive games in Division A. Manong headed the table once again, posting four wins, a draw, and a narrow 1–0 loss to Ditshitshidi. The B division managed eight games, with Ditshitshidi's B team ending the season as champions, unbeaten in all eight games – seven wins and a draw.

One club fielded two teams in the competition for the first time, both in B division – Dynaspurs B1 and B2. Dynaspurs (DFC) had been created from the remnants of the Hotspurs and the Dynamos – two clubs which had struggled to match the quality of the other teams. They had each had small squads, and it made sense to amalgamate. The DFC now had some very good players on its teams, including Molefe, Singh, George Moffatt, and Freddie Simon, the one-time Atlantic Raiders captain, but the Dynaspurs were more important for men whose names usually appeared on the team sheet of the B division – Marcus Solomon, Steve Tshwete, and Indress Naidoo. Steve Tshwete became the first chairman of the new club.

From the beginning, though, DFC had its fair share of problems, some of which were unique to the circumstances in which football was run on Robben Island. One of them was highlighted in a complaint made by a prisoner called Mr Roxo, who had come out of six months in solitary confinement to discover that the club he played for, Hotspurs, no longer existed. He didn't subscribe to the merger and therefore did not consider himself a member of Dynaspurs.

Since news was smuggled into the isolation cells regularly, there was some doubt as to whether he could have remained unaware of the merger while in B Section but, in any case, Dynaspurs officials claimed that Roxo had been told as soon as he returned to the main section and that he had given his full support.

The dispute became a procedural, quasi-legal issue when Roxo made a formal appeal to the MFA that he be released from Dynaspurs. After several weeks, he got his wish and became a member of the Bucks Football Club.

As the season ended, a new commanding officer, P. J. Fourie, arrived on Robben Island, and the prisoners sensed that a window of opportunity was opening. Though hardly a liberal, Fourie looked upon football as a way of maintaining order within the prison. While the men were happily playing their games, he could worry less about the possibility of work stoppages and hunger strikes. He didn't want any trouble.

The MFA realized that this was a man it could do business with. It was time to turn up the heat in their two-pronged battle to gain more recreation time outside and to have a second pitch laid so that the number of fixtures could be expanded.

The men's assumptions about Fourie had been correct. After four years of trying, the leaders of the MFA finally managed to persuade the prison authorities to let the men out to play on Sundays as well as Saturdays. The MFA also got permission from Fourie for the second pitch.

In many ways, league football was entering its heyday on the island. As well as benefiting from a more co-operative prison regime, its internal organization had now become a well-oiled machine. Everyone had kit and their own boots; the all-important committees were well run; match and referees' reports were dutifully filled out for each and every game. The MFA's lofty ideals of establishing sport for all, irrespective of ability, was benefiting hundreds of prisoners every weekend.

However, not all was sweetness and light between the respective clubs, their players, and match officials. A very human instinct – the desire to win – was causing problems. As standards of play had improved, matches in all three divisions were becoming increasingly competitive. Every prisoner had a chance to participate in sport on the island, whatever his level of skill or fitness, but put a football in front of him, and a man wants to win. Situations flared up, tempers became frayed, and sometimes games boiled over. In Marcus Solomon's opinion, too many players were trying to win at all costs and it was beginning to undermine the high ideals of the MFA.

Already a prominent referee, Marcus had been working tirelessly to train up new match officials. Along with his fellow refs, he had persuaded top players such as Tony Suze, Mark Shinners, and Lizo Sitoto to take up the whistle and patrol the line. They hoped that the experience might help the players view the game on the island from a different perspective. The real idea behind it was so that the footballers could learn from the Atlantic Raiders debacle, and to re-address the whole notion of why football was so important to everyone on Robben Island.

At the turn of the year, Marcus had also accepted the job of acting chairman of the new Dynaspurs club, while Steve Tshwete, the chairman, was serving time in solitary. Solomon now had a platform to say something dear to his heart. Marcus had been immensely troubled by the Atlantic Raiders affair and felt that its events pointed to a much wider malaise within the game on the island. Delivering the annual report to the club, he pulled no punches.

In it he questioned why there were so many moans and groans when teams lost matches, so many protests and criticisms, and why the MFA and the Referees Union were receiving so many complaints. Increasingly, he wrote, he was coming across more and more incidents of bad behaviour and a win-at-all-costs mentality – and he believed it was because so many players now lacked that element which serves to make a good footballer: sportsmanship. Clubs had become obsessed with winning in order to gain points and were losing the correct attitude towards playing the game that was so vitally important to Marcus. For him, football was more than just a game – it was a way of testing men's values.

The most passionate of the island's players or their fans would not perhaps have agreed with Marcus's analysis of the importance of winning but he was not alone in his concerns about the way in which football was developing on the island. Officials of the clubs and the MFA were particularly concerned about the pressure players were putting on each of their club's selection committees, whose brief was to pick teams in such a way as to give all the players equal time out on the pitch in competitive games. Often, in terms of footballing ability, that meant that a club might not, technically, be fielding its strongest side. The better players, however, were now challenging this practice. Tony Suze, for one, would often tell the Manong selection committee to 'go easy on the socialism, we want to win this week'.

The MFA also had growing concerns about the increasing number of instances of sharp practice and the emergence of prima-donna behaviour among the players. Marcus's own club, Dynaspurs, was mired in a major disagreement with the Bucks. Dynaspurs had not been the most popular club on the island since its inception – some of the other clubs had opposed the amalgamation of the Hotspurs and the Dynamos, and a number of players felt it had been arrogant to field two teams in the B division.

When Steve Tshwete returned to take up the chairmanship, he was stunned to discover that five very prominent Dynaspurs members, some of them holding key positions in the club, were demanding clearance to leave and join the Bucks. According to Tshwete, none of these men had ever shown any dissatisfaction with Dynaspurs. The DFC executive finally concluded that the Bucks Football Club had adopted a policy that concentrated on recruiting from its club.

Relations had already become strained between the two clubs as a result of arguments over irregular practices, and Tshwete had voiced a fear that the situation was sliding into anarchism. The solution had been to approach the executive of the MFA to act as arbitrator. After long discussions and testimony, the hostilities came to an end with a recognition by the DFC that not all of the accusations of recruiting against the Bucks had been accurate but, equally, it was clear that Bucks, like many other sides on the island, was now regularly trying to poach the best players and officials for its own club.

The specific dispute between the Bucks and Dynaspurs had been settled, but the underlying problem remained: the level of competition among clubs for victory was more intense than ever. The dispute between Dynaspurs and Bucks was symptomatic of an atmosphere of hostility and short temper that was showing up with greater regularity both on the field and in administrative meetings.

Arguments on the pitch were reported to be increasing, as was the number of charges levelled against players for insubordination to referees. A former member of Dynaspurs was investigated by the MFA for publicly stating that two officials, Singh and Solomon, were killing the club. Concern was shown by the executive over uncalled-for remarks by some prisoners (most of them members of clubs) to officials and players. The executive wrote to the clubs, asking them to make their members refrain from such abuse as it was ruining the sporting atmosphere.

The MFA condemned many of the clubs for being 'points happy' after discovering that half of the registered players in C division were being deprived of their rightful opportunity to play. Some of the best B-team players were regularly relegated into the C teams – and for one reason only: to win points. The same was happening in B division, with the better A-team players turning out as ringers to help win matches.

Everyone was after points, by whatever means. Boats of new prisoners arriving on the island were scanned for possible players, the best footballers immediately identified, and then doggedly pursued by representatives from each of the top clubs.

Referees and linesmen were coming under increasing pressure

and hostility from players, who made frequent charges of incompetence and favouritism against them. Perhaps this in itself was proof positive that the prisoners had replicated some of the aspects of their lives back on the mainland, but referees and linesmen were becoming ever more frustrated by the players' behaviour towards them. Over the twelve months of 1971, the MFA received no fewer than forty-seven match reports from the clubs complaining about refereeing decisions.

A complaint against Indress Naidoo was considered so serious that it was referred directly from the executive of the MFA to the Referees Union. It was filed by the Gunners following an A-division match against Rangers and contained a series of inflammatory accusations.

The Gunners claimed that whenever the ball touched the upper body of one of their players, Indress called handball. Whenever he allowed a free kick for Rangers, the ball was always placed three or four yards forward from where the offence had taken place. There was a clear handball in the eighteen-yard box by a Rangers player and, though Indress blew his whistle, he did not call a penalty.

The Gunners accused Indress of making many strange offside calls. The most bizarre charge ever made against a referee on Robben Island was part of the Gunners' complaints against Naidoo. They claimed that he had allowed the Rangers to use a laceless, heavier ball during the first half when they had the advantage of playing with the strong wind. The Gunners claimed that when they had the advantage of the wind, Indress made them play with a lighter ball, which was uncontrollable in the wind.

Partly because Indress Naidoo was such an important figure within the MFA, justice had to be seen to be done strictly and correctly, so

▲ Legendary striker Samuel Eto'o (left) and FIFA vice-president Jack Warner (right) on Robben Island, 18 July 2007. They kicked the first two of eighty-nine goals to celebrate Nelson Mandela's eighty-ninth birthday. This preceded the ceremony that marked the honourary membership of the Makana FA to FIFA.

▲ An aerial view of Robben Island with Cape Town and Table Mountain in the background. One of the most beautiful settings in the world was the scene of one of the most brutal prisons. The prison is on the left-hand side of the island.

▼ Sophiatown, Johannesburg. During the apartheid era, black, Asian, and coloured workers were compulsorily evicted from their homes so that each racial group lived in a different area, away from white districts. Here, 60,000 were removed and forced to load all their belongings into government trucks; many were taken to Meadowlands, now known as Soweto. Sophiatown was renamed *Triompf* ('triumph' in Afrikaans).

◄ Every aspect of life was segregated under apartheid, from marriage, home, education, and work to trivial activities like taking a bus or taxi.

▲ Manual labour for Robben Island prisoners not only included working in the quarry, but also building their own cell blocks, two of which can be seen here.

◀ 'Dias', the boat that took prisoners from Cape Town to Robben Island. Today it ferries the staff of the Robben Island Museum (a UNESCO World Heritage Site) back and forth across the bay.

◀ Marcus Solomon in 2005, sitting in the quarry pondering over the thousands of back-breaking hours he spent in there. In the midst of the labour, the prisoners organized education, discussed politics, and talked endlessly about football (soccer).

▲ Lizo Sitoto on the island in 2006. Sitoto was sentenced to sixteen and a half years in prison in 1965. A rugby player at home, he became a top class goalkeeper on the island.

▲ Antony Suze, 2006. He leans against the barbed wire fence that surrounds the prison. From childhood, Suze was a keen football (soccer) player. During his years on the island he was at the forefront of the campaign to play the game, as well as being the league's leading goal scorer.

▲ Four of the men whose tenacity and determination helped make the lives of hundreds of political prisoners more bearable (left to right): Lizo Sitoto, Marcus Soloman, Tony Suze, and Sedick Isaacs. They are standing in front of the tour boat 'Makana', which takes visitors to the island.

SCORE
IS
SILVER

ART
IS
GOLD

RANGERS
FOOTBALL Est. 1967 CLUB
Robben Island.

◀ Aside from playing football (soccer), club members also took great pride in the administrative tasks that surrounded their club. This is the logo for Rangers FC, one of the founders of the Makana Football Association

SOCCER!

GREATEST VARIETY!?

INTER-CELL MATCHES TO CLOSE

MFA SOCCER SEASON

DATE: 13TH OCTOBER, 1973.   TIME: 2 × 2 HRS

MORNING

BOOMS TRAAT ABAKHULU! V. WANDERERS

DIKWANKWETLA   V.   MAMBA

AFTERNOON

PULA AYINE!   V   BOMBERS

CABINET XI   V.   EXODUS

HAPPY SUMMER REST SOCCERITES!

Yours MMabuse 10/10/73
MFA SEC.

GEVANGENIS
ONTVANGSKANTOOR
RECEPTION OFFICE

▲ In addition to a full league programme, the Makana FA organized a number of competitions to allow the men to retain their enthusiasm for football (soccer).

DYNASPURS UNITED FOOTBALL CLUB

ROBBEN ISLAND
18TH JULY 1970

THE HON SEC
MAKANA FOOTBALL ASS
ROBBEN ISLAND.

SIR,

RE LEAGUE SEASON 1970-71.

EXECUTIVE COMMITTEE:

1] PRESIDENT MR S TSHWETE.
2] VICE PRESIDENT MR D PHITHI
3] SECRETARY MR I NAIDOO.
4] VICE SECRETARY MR G SINGH.
5] TRUSTEE MR N BABENIA.
6] EX MEMBER MR G MOFFAT

THE FOLLOWING PLAYER WILL PARTICIPATE IN THE FORTHCOMING LEAGUE:—

A DIVISION	B¹ DIVISION	B² DIVISION	
1] F SIMON CAP.	1] S MADHUMULO CAP.	1] A. KHONZA CAP.	21] G SINMANIKANTA
2] G MOFFAT VCAP.	2] T. HOSO V. CAP.	2] Z. NDALOSE V. CAP.	22] A MASHABA
3] G SINGH	3] F MLONDA.	3] W. FANTI	23] E MBELE
4] M. NDINGI	4] D PHITHI	4] D. MKABA	24] P. NTCHABELENG
5] H MAKGOTHI	5] S HASHE	5] N. ZWENI	25] W MOSES
6] L MOLEFE	6] S TSHWETE	6] G HENDRICKS	26] M. MACHULEMA
7] B. FIHLA	7] I NAIDOO	7] E MALGAS	27] N DIALU
8] A HOHO	8] V THOLE	8] R. NGWEMA	28] J DLAMINE
9] H PLAATJIES	9] W MABHOLO	8] M VIKILAHLE.	29] K NDOPISHUI
10] M. SOLOMON	10] S NAQOLA.	10] W. MAKINANA	30] J CHIRWA
11] ~~S NTENISU.~~	11] K ROXO	11] S. TSHUMU	31] ~~D ALOFOGICHI~~
11 G NAICKER	12] N DICK	12] J. MHLANTI	32] W XANDEMINI
	13] C. KETANI	13] R VANDEYAR.	33] S NGCONGO
	14] A. BAKABA.	14] M. NXUNGWANA	34] J. NQSONDLA
	15] S NTENISU [G.K]	15] W. HASHE	35] B. NGWEVA
	16] M. NGOBE.	16] H BHARTMINI	36] T. DIKANE.
		17] J. JANUARY	37] ~~L HAFFIER~~
		18] M. HLAYA	38] Z. BOYANE
		19] R. MBANA	39] K WEIGHI

February 1971, EXAMINATIONS.

Candidate	Theory 150	Practical 50	Total 200	Grading
Brander, S.	107	20	127	B
Tole, V.	78	18	96	B
Chiloane, P.	37	29	66	A.

5th JUNE 1971 EXAMINATIONS.

CANDIDATE	THEORY 75	PRACTICAL 50	TOTAL	GRADING.
S. Chibane	32	17		B
M. Masuku	35	21		B
G. Moffat	27	31		A
M. Mthembu	18	17		B
M. Shimmers	48	35		A:
M. Solomon	51	21		B A
N. Letsoko	40	18		B

31st JULY, 1971 EXAMINATIONS

	CANDIDATE	THEORY 75	PRACTICAL 50	TOTAL	GRADING
	P. Silwana	67	31		A
	P. Maphanga	36	18		B
18/9/71	M. Masuku		38		A
	D.M. Mmutle	63	34		A
	G. ZUMA		29 36		A
	S. CHIBANE		30		A
	D. Malepe		38		
13/5/72	S. Hanabahi		36		
	M. Shimmers		39		

▲ 'No Referees, No Soccer' was the motto of the Referees' Union. Each man had to pass a written FIFA examination before being allowed to referee league matches

◀ An example of how popular the game was, and how much importance was placed on record keeping and administration. Dynaspurs FC (the combination of Hotspurs and Dynamo clubs) fielded teams in three levels of competition.

SOCCER

MAKANA FOOTBALL ASSOCIATION
FINAL LEAGUE LOG

A DIVISION

	P	W	L	D	F	A	PT	LEADING SCORERS
MANONG	4	4	0	0	11	3	8	SUZE, A [MFC]
PIONEERS	4	1	1	2	5	4	4	4 GOALS
INKONJANE	4	1	1	2	5	5	4	
DINARE	4	0	2	2	2	5	2	
IS. TIGERS	4	1	3	0	2	8	2	

B DIVISION

	P	W	L	D	F	A	PT	
IS. TIGERS	4	4	0	0	8	1	8	TANANA, M
MANONG	4	3	1	0	5	2	6	[ITFC]
PIONEERS	4	2	2	0	8	3	4	
DINARE	4	1	3	0	2	10	2	4 GOALS
INKONJANE	4	0	4	0	0	7	0	

C DIVISION

	P	W	L	D	F	A	PT	
IS. TIGERS	4	3	0	1	5	0	7	GCINUMZI, T
PIONEERS	4	3	1	0	5	1	6	[PFC]
MANONG	4	2	2	0	3	2	4	
INKONJANE	4	0	2	2	0	5	2	3 GOALS
DINARE	4	0	3	1	1	6	1	

Issued by: S. Mabuse / MFA-SEC
6/8/73

Counter-signed: _____
S.C.C. SEC.

The R.I. Amateur Athletic Association

◯◯◯◯

THE R.I 72 SUMMER GAMES —
~ Program ~

Time	Track Event	Time	Field Event
8·00	100.m Heats	8·00	Putting the Shot X
8·06	1500·m Finals ✓	8·20	Stick pulling (knock outs) X
8·14	100-m Sack Race ✓	8·26	Discus· ✓
8·20	200-m Heats	8·50	Tug o' War
8·26	80·m Veterans Heats		Black Mamba vs Olympia
8·32	400 m Heats		Spartans vs Nyikema
8·40	100·m Potato and Spoon ✓		Black M. vs Spartan
8·46	100·m 3 Legged Race (heats)		Nyikema vs Olympia
9·10	Hurdles (heats)		Black M. vs Nyikema
9·20	100·m Finals ✓		Olympia vs Spartan ✓
9·32	100·m 3- Legged Race (finals) ✓	9·14	Blind-fold Object Location ✓
9·40	400m Heel and Toe Walk ✓	9·26	Passing the Soccerball ✓
9·50	80·m Potato and Spoon Race (Vet.) ✓	9·46	High Jump ✓
9·54	100·m Late for Work Race ✓	9·52	Weighed Cricket Ball X
10·00	200m Finals ✓	10·08	Long jump ✓
10·06	100·m Bucket Race X	10·20	Standing Broad Jump X
10·10	80·m Late for Work Race (Veterans) X	10·42	Triple Jump X
10·16	100·m Needle and Cotton Race ✓		
10·22	80·m Finals for Veterans ✓		
10·26	50·m Wheel Barrow Race X		
10·30	Hurdles Finals ✓		
10·36	80·m Needle and Cotton (Veterans) X		
10·42	800·m Finals ✓		
10·50	100·m Walk (Veterans) X		

▲ The Summer Games (or 'Robben Island Olympics') became an important feature of life on the island. Note the precision with which the event was organized and the variety of activities that took place.

◀ The league table for the first half of the 1973 season. As usual, Manong FC dominated the 'A' Division.

ATHLETIC COMMITTEE

AND

SPORT AND GAMES CO-ORDINATION (AD HOC) COMMITTEE

ROBBEN ISLAND
PRISON

Resolution

Whereas the Officer Commanding gave us permission to arrange Sport and Games Competitions during the holiday season and to buy prizes and refreshments,

And whereas the head of the Prison gave us every co-operation with respect to equipment, time off for preparation and play etc.

Therefore be it resolved that this inadequate token of gratitude be presented to the Colonel (the Officer Commanding) and the Lt (the head of the Prison);

Therefore, barring the inconveniences attempted by one or two warders both before and during the Sportsday, the occassion was a resounding success.

▲ This letter, given to the Officer Commanding of Robben Island prison, showed Sedick Isaacs' diplomatic skills and his ability as a calligrapher. The last paragraph is testament to his much-admired talent for pointed sarcasm.

the Referees Union investigated the matter fully, calling a number of witnesses, including players, fans, and Indress himself. It found the evidence inconclusive. The Gunners accepted the findings and agreed that the matter should be closed but, in a classic Robben Island political compromise, it was agreed that, although Indress was a competent referee, he had shown some prejudicial attitudes towards the Gunners and would not in future be asked to officiate in any of their matches.

There were so many requests for a change of referee by individual clubs that the MFA had to establish a new rule: requests would have to be made at least seven days before a match and contain 'live instances' of the referee's past behaviour to justify the request.

The MFA wanted to minimize the number of requests not only because of all the extra administration and yet more use of precious paper but because, once they acted upon a request, they were effectively ruling on the competence and/or integrity of the referees. This became a great source of unpleasantness and caused lasting bitterness and ill will within the footballing community on the island.

The Referees Union was aware that there were problems with some of its match officials and with some specific decisions made out on the pitch. After all, that was the nature of football. It had to take any complaint seriously, but it also had to support its referees. Without such support, refereeing at any level in any league would be transformed from a difficult task into an impossible one, and the confined nature of life on Robben Island was bound to make any situation concerning the disciplining of referees much more complicated than it would be anywhere else.

The RU was caught between a rock and a hard place: ensuring that all the clubs thought they were being treated fairly and competently by the referees and ensuring that individual referees felt appreciated in the difficult job they were performing. While the individual clubs often felt that the Referees Union was over-protective of its members, many referees felt deeply exposed.

This became particularly clear when no less a footballing luminary than Harry Gwala tendered his resignation as referee. Over the years, Harry had established himself as one of the most charismatic and influential prisoners on the island. His decision came as such a shock to the leaders of the Referees Union that there was a move to establish a commission of inquiry into the reasons behind it.

Harry's reasons were clear: he was sick of being accused of favouritism. The chairman of the RU had told Harry that questions had been raised as to whether his membership of Bucks FC or his political affiliation was influencing his performance as a referee. There was probably no prisoner on the island who would react more vehemently to questions about his integrity than Harry Gwala.

He felt strongly that referees had shown the ability to distance themselves from their clubs and he rejected even the hint that his decisions on the field were based on anything other than his clearest judgement and his understanding of the rules of football. Since everyone on the island agreed that Harry's knowledge of the game was unsurpassed, the questions about his integrity were withdrawn, and Harry tore up his resignation letter.

Not every referee, however, demonstrated the clear-eyed fairness of Harry Gwala. Sometimes a club's accusations of prejudice were borne out, adding further fuel to the fire that too many referees were biased and favoured certain teams above others.

Dynaspurs put in a complaint concerning the referee who had been chosen to officiate before playing their October 1971 B-division match against the Gunners. DFC players had heard the referee, Mr Tole, telling fellow prisoners in the yard that he would make it his duty to ensure that the arrogant Dynaspurs would lose any match he was up to referee. The MFA called a meeting with Mr Tole, who admitted making this statement. He was banned from officiating at any further matches that involved Dynaspurs and given instruction in how to abandon prejudiced attitudes.

To try and ensure total impartiality and further improve the standard of its match officials, the Referees Union decided to police itself even more rigorously. The most experienced referees were appointed as match observers and instructed to write detailed reports on the performance of the officials in charge of the games.

One of the enduring problems the RU had was in getting referees to take notice of what their linesmen were doing. A report on a B-division Rangers *v* Mphatlalatsane match in February 1972 emphasizes the point. The referee, Mr Letsoko, was accused of failing to meet his linesmen to discuss how they were going to run the game. As a consequence, the referee forgot all about his linesmen and ran the game as if he were the only one officiating at the match. On many occasions he didn't see them raise their flags for offsides or off-the-ball offences. According to the match observer, Mr Letsoko capped a dismal performance by blowing the whistle late for half-time.

Later the same month, a C-division friendly between Ditshitshidi and Dynaspurs suffered the same problems. The referee, Mr Kekana, and his two linesmen displayed 'poor co-ordination', with the ref taking no notice of his linesmen. As a result, many handballs and fouls went unpunished. The observer concluded that Mr Kekana's performance left much to be desired.

Another enduring problem for the Referees Union was to get its match officials to clamp down on rough tackling. A report on a Manong v Ditshitshidi game noted that the players were so desperate to win that a number of unnecessary collisions occurred, with both teams regularly going for the man and not the ball. A number of players were penalized for tackling from behind. Two men had to leave the field – one with a knee injury, the second with a crocked ankle.

On Robben Island, if a player was injured, his first concern was not whether he would be fit for the following match but whether he would be able to make it into the quarry to hack out his daily quota of rocks. If a player was unable to meet his quota, he was punished. Other prisoners would cover and help their comrades but, even so, labouring in the quarry at whatever pace when carrying an injury was a miserable and painful experience.

The will to win had become endemic. This tension between mass participation and the celebration of individual skills and a real desire to be the best would prove to be one of the most volatile and debated elements of the sport of football on Robben Island.

8

Two Football Codes on One Island

'We played touch rugby for just a few weeks – but soon it was the real thing.'
Steve Tshwete, Prisoner 350/64

Tony Suze and Lizo Sitoto exchanged grins as they jogged out on to the pitch together. Tony was smiling because Lizo was about to turn their sporting relationship on its head. Tony had taught Lizo how to play football. Now, Lizo was to become the teacher and his Manong FC friend the student.

They both wore their kit and boots, but the ball that Lizo held in his hands was oval and the football nets had been replaced by tall posts made from planks dragged from the beach. Tony was about to have his first lesson in playing rugby. A new sport was about to be introduced on Robben Island, and the existing football community would have an unusual new challenge to face.

The prisoners had always had the intention of, in time, trying to introduce sports other than football into the prison. Even before the original Matyeni Football Association was formed in 1967, a group of prisoners interested in sports had written a draft constitution for something called the Robben Island Sports and Recreation Association. The philosophy behind it was to encourage the spirit of sportsmanship and co-operation among the prisoners on the island across all manner of sporting activities.

The draft listed some of the proposed sports, which included football, rugby, tennis, volleyball, and softball. The draft constitution also stated the association's intention to popularize sport by arranging matches and organizing talks and lectures, ensuring that every player in every sport would adhere to recognized standards as prescribed by international rules, and to act as the liaison between all sporting bodies and the prison authorities.

The reason it had taken so long for any of these other sports to be established and played on the island was largely due to the successful introduction of football. It had taken years to win the right to play, and that had focused everyone's energies on football alone. It had been easier to ask men to take the risk of making a Saturday-morning complaint in order to achieve the finite goal of playing a sport they loved than for the broader issue of sport in general.

Once the MFA became established, hundreds of the men found themselves totally consumed by the day-to-day running of football, and there was little time to think about setting up other sports. Undeniably, the massive, unifying impact that football had had on the men on the island showed how much sport could mean. Now, with football well established, the time had come to get other sporting activities up and running.

To this day, many former prisoners disagree about the origins of rugby on the island. In the late Sixties, the odd friendly match took place, but more as a novelty than anything else. It was in the early to mid-Seventies that the sport truly came to establish itself, and two men were essential to its development – and that of other sports – on Robben Island: Sedick Isaacs, who was appointed the first secretary of the Island Rugby Board, and Steve Tshwete, its first president.

Sedick's motive in trying to popularize rugby was his belief that it would give prisoners the opportunity to learn new techniques and rules; it would keep their minds active. Ever conscious that well-exercised minds and bodies were more able to fight off the depressing effects of long-term imprisonment, Sedick was keen to offer the prisoners a more diverse range of experiences. He was convinced that, after a couple of years of playing and watching the same sport, the prisoners were running out of stories to tell one another. He also thought that by starting rugby afresh, the sport could learn a lesson from the early years of football and begin with clubs that were not based on political affiliation.

His partner in the enterprise, Steve Tshwete, was a man who, in years to come, would serve as South Africa's Sports Minister. He shared Sedick's view that rugby could be a valuable way to demonstrate how political divisions could be minimized through sports. More importantly than that, he was rugby mad and had been itching to play again for years. Tshwete was often asked by other prisoners why they should play the white man's game, the sport of the oppressor. His answer revealed how much everything in South Africa, especially the way South Africans interpreted their own history, was affected by the racist policies of the apartheid system.

Before he had been imprisoned on the island, Steve Tshwete had been part of a flourishing black rugby community in the Eastern Cape and surrounding areas. It boasted a number of leagues and competitions that featured high-quality rugby. Marcus Solomon and

Lizo Sitoto had both played to a high standard, but Steve Tshwete was truly gifted. They had all played rugby from an early age, and there was a long and proud tradition of the game among black people in the east of South Africa.

Steve was born in rural Eastern Transvaal and as a child worked in the fields with his parents. They had insisted that he get an education and, at school, Steve quickly became politicized. From his teenage years on he immersed himself in the political struggle, joined the ANC, and became active in various levels of the MK military wing. A natural orator, he was as at home trying to influence a crowd as he was organizing small groups of MK colleagues.

Sedick Isaacs and Steve Tshwete made an odd couple, different in almost every aspect of their personality and physical appearance. While Sedick was slight in build and quietly modest, Steve Tshwete was a big man, someone who seemed almost overpowering in his size and his energy. Sedick was softly spoken; Steve had a deep voice, a big, booming laugh, as well as a special talent for bringing opposing views together.

The two men shared an essential trait: both were determined that they would emerge from the prison stronger than they had entered it and they would do everything within their power to ensure that they and their comrades found ways to maintain the struggle while still in prison. They were also perceptive observers of what people around them were doing and what was important to them. It was this quality that, in later years, contributed towards Steve Tshwete becoming such a superb political organizer and Sedick a scientist and mathematician recognized throughout the world.

The two men had very different approaches towards sport. Steve

Tshwete had the enthusiasm and zest of a participant, one who loved being in the midst of the battle on the field. Sedick was not a sportsman, other than being an excellent swimmer. He was keen to keep the men on the island occupied and engaged. Steve was convinced that, given a chance, he could have been good enough to represent South Africa at international level; Isaacs didn't know how to kick a ball. Steve knew at first hand how much sport meant to the men on the island; Sedick studied psychology and was intrigued by the ways in which lack of activity while in prison could have a permanent negative effect on the men. They each had their own reasons for taking an interest in expanding opportunities to participate in sport on Robben Island.

Though chalk and cheese, the very differences in the personalities of Steve and Sedick made them an effective double act. In order to accomplish their goals they had to challenge both the authorities and their comrades. They had to convince the former that the chance to take part in additional sports should be a right for the prisoners and would not upset the good order of the prison. They had to persuade fellow prisoners that it was worth expending time and effort doing new things, taking a chance that they might discover something different that gave them pleasure.

The problems they faced in getting the prisoners involved in a new set of sports were similar those they had had to overcome when establishing league football on the island: lack of time, the need for facilities, the changing attitude of successive prison administrations, and the lingering vestiges of political divisions among the prisoners. This time, though, there was one additional difficulty – the reluctance of many comrades to become involved in something new for fear that it would diminish their opportunity to play football, and the un-willingness to try something that was unfamiliar. Both Sedick and Steve knew that football was god on the island, and they were careful not to alarm the men who were enthusiastic about football by letting them think that the importance and pre-eminence of their sport would be compromised in any way.

The prison authorities were intrigued by the men's request to play rugby. The warders had convinced themselves that the prisoners might be good at football since that was a primitive sport and all you had to do was kick, but rugby was a different story. You had to have tactics and planning and a variety of skills. Unable to think outside of the structures of apartheid, many of the guards believed that only a white man could master rugby.

The authorities had seen how well the prisoners had organized their footballing activities and saw no reason to refuse permission for rugby. Indeed, the biggest opposition that Sedick Isaacs and Steve Tshwete encountered was from those involved in football on the island.

The two football codes were both competing for a precious com-modity – the limited amount of free time available to the prisoners. Though there were now two pitches and the men were allowed out on both Saturdays and Sundays, the footballers jealously guarded the time they had fought so hard to gain.

Individuals felt strongly about the importance of their own foot-ball code. Many men felt the other was getting more time than it deserved and, naturally, disagreements occurred. Men involved in other sports generally felt that the footballers were unduly favoured, and this was nowhere more apparent, once the game was up and running, than among the hardcore rugby players.

They had waited for so long to play rugby and now they felt they were not being given their due. Players and officials made a number of allegations against the MFA, football clubs, and individuals, claiming that people were working towards the suppression and suspension of rugby on the grounds that rugby was getting in the way of football.

There were long and often fiery debates between the representatives of the two codes about the use of the pitches and the timing of fixtures. Many warders initially protested about having to supervise the prisoners' sporting activities over a two-day period when they were at their most short-staffed. Often, piqued and annoyed by these new demands on their weekend guard duties, the warders would find whatever petty excuse they could to deny the men time out on the pitch and keep them locked down in their cell blocks for entire weekends. Footballers felt that the introduction of organized rugby would only complicate matters.

A letter to the Makana FA from Manong Football Club in February 1972 addressed the problem of setting up matches but it also underlined concerns among footballers that rugby was muscling its way on to their patch.

Manong officials were worried that, if rugby was played first, footballers would be faced with the problem of re-lining the white markings on the pitch – and that would eat into the time left available for football.

Considering the relative number of players – there were hundreds of football players, just over a hundred for rugby – Manong believed it was unfair to divide the available time for playing sports by half. The Island Rugby Board said it was confident it could popularize the game and raise the numbers of players and clubs to match those of football. Manong scoffed at the idea, saying the claim was 'cooked up'.

Manong FC also expressed its anxiety that, because rugby was a tough, straining contact sport, anyone who played a match in the morning would be too spent, battered, and bruised to manage a game of football in the afternoon. A player of both rugby and football would have to decide which he favoured, and that might lead to further disharmony between the two codes.

The secretary of Rangers FC voiced his club members' concerns in another letter to the Makana FA. They proposed that each Saturday, Sunday, and/or public holiday should be devoted to just one sport. Football and rugby should alternate, and bad weather should be taken into account. The reason behind this was just the point made above: if the two codes played on the same day, players might be involved in both and, because some might not be able to pull out the stops equally in each sport, it might cause bad feeling in their clubs.

In the end, a compromise was agreed upon by the two codes. From early 1973 onwards, football and rugby were played on alternate weekends. This middle way, however, seemed to satisfy neither side, and disputes over playing time continued for years.

The actions of the prison authorities also served to inflame the situation. Should one code get extra time the following week if the cells were opened late when there was a game scheduled? How should delays caused by rain be handled?

The secretary of the Rangers Football Club saw the potential danger to all sports caused by the disputes between the two football codes. He warned that some individuals were not tolerating differences of opinion in a healthy, sporting spirit. Too many people were behaving badly both on the pitch and in meetings. 'They frequently used words like "sellout" ... and such tactics could only lead to estrangement and bad feelings in our community.' The consequences were grave, as many prisoners were serving long sentences, and sport and other community ventures were supposed to maintain group morale rather than be a source of division and disappointment.

One golden rule, however, was never broken – that the men must always show a unified, common face to the 'enemy'. No matter how much the prisoners fought among themselves, internal disagreements were always put to one side when it came to negotiating with the prison regime. This sense of solidarity and unity was never better exemplified on the island than when the authorities threatened to withdraw recreation time because of what they claimed was the laziness of the prisoners.

One cold, windy day in August 1972 a joint delegation of football and rugby officials was marched out of the prison compound by armed guards to meet with one of the chief warders in his office. He told them that the new commanding officer had expressed deep concern that the work rate of the prisoners in the quarry was unacceptable and was threatening to withhold recreation time until it improved. Instead of playing sport, as a punishment the men would be made to work extra hours.

The delegation asked why the commanding officer was considering such a blanket punishment. Couldn't his guards identify those individual prisoners who weren't meeting their workloads and deal with them accordingly? The chief warder told them that the CO did 'not want to see the place full of lawyers'.

The delegation returned to the cell blocks to deliver the news. The prisoners' response was decisive. With the agreement of men right across the island's sporting community, they decided to tackle the authorities head on. If the commanding officer intended to rob them of their right to play sport, then they would wrest back control of the situation by calling an indefinite halt to all sports activities, to take effect immediately.

A few weeks later, another joint committee, which included Steve Tshwete, Sedick Isaacs, Indress Naidoo, and other representatives, met again with the chief warder. There was an almost surreal quality about this meeting to discuss the 'current sport problem' with the chief warder on duty. In advance of the meeting, the committee had requested an appointment with the commanding officer. The chief warder informed the delegation that their current demand to see the colonel was 'construed as a threat [and] the Colonel is not going to allow himself as Officer Commanding to be threatened'.

The delegation firmly denied that it was threatening the commanding officer; it was merely requesting an unambiguous definition of the conditions under which recreation was allowed, and whether it was fair to use its withdrawal as a form of punishment.

The situation harked back to that initial debate held among the prisoners when they first won the right to play football. Now, having played for years, they were not going to have strings attached. What would happen, for argument's sake, they asked, if they played the third week of their league programmes, and then the CO decided to cancel the fourth? Such instability was not conducive to the good running of organized sports.

At the start of the meeting, the chief warder got to the heart of the issue – if they wished to meet the commanding officer to discuss the issue, first they must resume playing football and rugby. The situation was a curious stalemate: the prison CO was insisting that the prisoners play sport; and the prisoners were denying themselves the fun of playing until they received an assurance that, in the future, their recreation time would be guaranteed.

The prisoners knew they were in a strong negotiating position. The CO must have been thinking about reaction outside the prison, most particularly that of his political masters in Pretoria. It would be difficult to explain to his superiors there that a concession they had trumpeted to the West was now being spurned by the very men who were supposed to be benefiting from it. How would they explain it to the International Red Cross and to the regime's allies and opponents around the world?

They could say that it was the prisoners' own choice but, in order to make people believe this, they would have to explain the reasons behind the men's decision: the arbitrary punishments inflicted by the prison regime on the inmates. This, clearly, was unacceptable.

It took a few weeks. The CO withdrew the higher work quotas he had imposed and the attendant punishment of additional labour. Over the years, the prisoners had made scores of remarks about the importance of being able to organize and control the sport they were involved in on Robben Island. The action they had just taken in shutting down all sport rather than allowing it to be used against them showed the truth of their assertions.

Now that the external battle with the authorities had been won, it was time for the organizers of sport on the island to get their own house in order. Discipline was becoming a problem. Rough and violent play was more and more common, especially in rugby. The Island Rugby Board Committee minutes for 1972 warned that, instead of being a form of entertainment, matches had begun more to resemble a battle.

Rugby is a tough contact sport, and close-quarter play offered a perfect opportunity for prisoners with scores to settle to get their revenge on the pitch. In July 1973 a report was presented to the IRB about prisoner Mr Makhwethama.

Mr Makhwethama had been playing in a B-division football match when he accidentally collided with an opponent, Mr Playties. Playties didn't take kindly to this and approached Makhwethama after the match. He vowed to get his own back during the rugby match they would both be taking part in the following week. As both played scrum half, Playties would get plenty of opportunity to 'do for' his adversary. Things didn't rest off the pitch either: prisoners taunted Makhwethama 'day after day' about Playties' plan to pay him back.

The IRB got wind of the situation and decided the threat was not an empty one. Both the rugby and football clubs involved were warned in writing about what might happen, but the letters were never answered. The match was played and Playties stuck to his word. Makhwethama was injured so badly, it was weeks before he got out of hospital.

The physical nature of the game often led to fights and bust-ups. Tony Suze had always had ambivalent feelings about rugby – football was the sport for him – but, if rugby was what was on offer for some part of the time, he would play it and he would play it well. He was involved in a number of instances of full-on, rough play and was warned on at least one occasion that opposition players would 'get even' with him.

After one episode of foul play out on the pitch there was an exchange of words that nearly came to blows. Tony requested an interview with the executive of the IRB to ask permission to remain in his rugby club but to be allowed to stop playing because he didn't find rugby to his liking and got into too many arguments because of it.

The IRB bluntly pointed out that rugby, unlike tennis and cricket, was a tough game and should be understood as such. Some members of the IRB accused Tony of having no respect for his club, the spectators, or the game and demanded that he apologize and then give more appropriate reasons for his retirement from the sport. The matter was let drop. The incident was one of many instances in which normal human temper got in the way of sport's ideals.

Secretly, many rugby fans wanted Tony Suze to continue playing their code, because he was so good. An all-round sportsman, his natural skills, tactical astuteness, and pace soon made him one of the best rugby players on the island. Everyone wanted him on their team.

Lizo Sitoto would watch Tony twist and turn up the pitch, so quick and slippery he would leave players flailing in his wake. Steve Tshwete was another fan. Though, out on the pitch, the cocky, confident Tony would constantly wind Steve up, Tshwete had great respect for the Pretorian's abilities on the rugby pitch.

Tony Suze and Steve Tshwete shared a similar passion for their politics and their involvement in sports, but Tony was PAC and a football player, Steve ANC and rugby. They each had the same fiercely competitive nature and relentless drive to win. Each played the other's sport, and one confrontation between them became a legend among the prisoners. In any discussion of rugby on the island, sooner or later 'that drop goal' would come up.

Tshwete was famous throughout the island for his crunching tackles and, when he found himself playing directly against Tony Suze, he thought it was about time he showed this football player what rugby was all about. The ever-confident Tony could not hold his tongue and spent the first few minutes of the match bragging to Steve about just how fast and skilful he was. It was a red rag to a bull.

Tony was in his own half of the field, almost on the touchline, when Steve lined him up for a clattering tackle. He was going to crush him. With fast anticipation, Tony sidestepped and drop-kicked the ball. Steve reckoned it was just to avoid the tackle, because anyone who knew anything about rugby had to know you could never convert a goal from so far inside your own half, but the ball just kept going and going. It went straight through the posts.

That drop kick became known across the island, forming part of its sporting folklore. Years later, Steve would say he had never been able to forget it and that, even if he had succeeded, Tony would remind him of it whenever they met.

The guards, too, used to enjoy watching Tony, and others with long background in the game, play. They had had no idea that blacks from the Eastern Cape like Tshwete had played the game enthusiastically for years. The guards were amazed at the high standard on the pitch. Initially, they had come to the matches just to laugh, but many soon became regular and enthusiastic spectators.

During one match, Marcus Solomon became aware of two guards avidly watching a free-flowing move that ended in a glorious try. They applauded heartily. The guards were seeing the men as skilful rugby players, not simply as terrorists and communists. They were coming to accept that the political prisoners were human.

Rugby-loving warders suggested tactical tips to the captains of the clubs and a couple of the guards went so far as to offer their services as coaches. The inmates declined politely, but the offer revealed just how much the prison staff were becoming involved in the sport.

Many warders openly rooted for one side or another during games and frequently appealed from the touchlines about match referees' decisions – just like the spectating prisoners did. On some occasions guards took players aside after a match and implored them to lodge complaints against decisions that might have influenced the results.

The most dramatic intervention by a guard came when he became so upset at the way in which his favourite rugby team was being treated by the referee that he marched out on to the pitch in an effort to stop the match. The mini-protest lasted only a few seconds, but it was testament to how much rugby meant to the staff on the island, let alone the prisoners.

9

Something More than Football

'Our Olympics was the most emotional and happy day of the year.'
Vusumzi Mcongo, Prisoner 93/78

Now that rugby was firmly established as a sport on the island, Sedick set about introducing a dizzying number of additional sports in the hope of filling in the time between the football and rugby seasons and offering something to the men who showed no inclination or talent for either of the two versions of football.

Perhaps the most unlikely sport he managed to establish on the island was tennis. This classic country-club sport seemed out of place in a harsh prison setting, but Sedick was nothing if not unpredictable. It took months of correspondence between him and the commanding officer to get the process started – partly because not only was Sedick requesting that the prisoners be granted permission to play the sport, he was also asking for cement with which to build the court.

He was finally allowed to go into a storeroom with two comrades (one of whom was the irrepressible Blue) and scoop up whatever cement powder they could find on the floor. For this they were provided with a broom, a spade, and a wheelbarrow. Blue used his spade to cut into some unopened bags of cement that were there, and soon the three men were helping themselves to as much as they liked. After a while Sedick tried to restrain Blue in order that their theft wouldn't be too obvious, and the three men finally left the storeroom with a wheelbarrow full of cement.

The armed warder who accompanied them paid little attention, but the head warder who had to approve the exercise did not know quite what to make of it. He knew something was wrong but, as he could not think of any precise offence they might have committed and was embarrassed at having possibly been hoodwinked, he just told the men to get out of his sight.

The prisoners had no idea how to mix the proper proportions of sand, cement, and water, but somehow their new tennis court was laid in good order. With assistance from the International Red Cross, Sedick got hold of tennis racquets, balls, and a net from a sports shop in Cape Town.

The sport attracted a lot of participants from across a wide range of ages, and soon another court was required. This time, the prisoners were issued with pre-mixed cement, and the result was a court of much higher quality. The sport wasn't, however, attracting many spectators – until, that is, Sedick made it part of his most ambitious sports venture yet: the Summer Games. Sometimes referred to as the Robben Island Olympics, the Summer Games were to become Sedick's greatest sporting success, and a testament to his persever-ance, imagination, and organizational skills.

As with almost every activity on the island, those trying to establish the Olympics had initially to battle against great obstacles. Sedick knew that he would have to negotiate carefully and tactfully with the men involved in football and rugby on the island to ensure that there would be time available and commitment to his new dream.

He selected a team of six men, representative of each cell block and the major political factions, as the executive committee for the Games and asked them to survey the prison population about their attitude towards and interest in athletics. The response was unexpected. Some men tried to convince others not to participate because it would be yet another sport that took resources away from their first love, football. Others thought that athletics would favour the younger, fitter prisoners so, for the majority, there would be no point in taking part – they would be beaten out of sight. The committee even encountered some hostility towards them for asking the questions in the first place.

Surprised by the results of the survey, Sedick and his committee nonetheless set about tailoring the new activity so that it would be as inclusive as possible. Inspired by the Makana Football Association's A-, B-, and C-division categorization, they tried to address the wants and needs of all prisoners by making sure to arrange the competitions along lines determined by athletic experience, age, and proficiency. This last category was self-assessed.

The committee then approached the authorities to seek approval for the Games. It was to receive a surprising request in return. Chief Warder Fourie suggested to the prisoners that, since he had afforded the community the opportunity to play various sports, the athletics event in that inaugural year would be the proper time to christen the Robben Island playing field the P. J. Fourie Stadium. Permission was given for the Summer Games, and painters were instructed by Fourie to make the relevant plaque. It was, however, discreetly destroyed once athletics had become established, the prisoners reasoning that Fourie's little act of vanity had never been meant as an instruction but merely a request.

The next problem facing the committee was getting those who organized and participated in rugby and football to allow them time to use the playing area for practice and competitive meets. The two soccer codes were of course reluctant to lose any opportunity to play or train and, in this instance, it wasn't just a matter of turning over the field to other sportsmen: changes had to be made to set up lanes for running and jumping pits.

In order to tempt more men into the enterprise, Sedick and his supporters created a totally separate veterans' category, which did put to rest some of the prisoners' earlier anxieties. Other committees were established to help clubs train their members in order to improve performance. Eventually, the ever-persuasive Sedick had enough good will and help from fellow prisoners to launch the first Summer Games.

The long list of events for 1972 and 1973 shows how much planning and effort went in to setting up the event. The design of the programme produced to mark the occasion jumped off the page. It had been written by Sedick in the precise italic calligraphy he was practising at the time. The programme was headed 'The R. I. Amateur Athletics Association' and had as its logo a version of the International Olympic Committee's five-ring symbol.

The use of the five rings was Sedick's way of getting his comrades to see the importance of their own Olympics and to tie their events in with something they were familiar with from the world outside the prison. Given Sedick's talent for irony and sarcasm, it's possible that he chose to use the symbol with some malice aforethought.

The then president of the IOC, Avery Brundage, was very protective of its symbol. For him, what was at stake was much more than the protection of a lucrative international trademark. He thought of himself as the protector of the spirit of the Olympics, something he saw almost in quasi-religious terms. At the same time, Brundage was doing everything he could to ensure that white supremacist apartheid South Africa remained a nation in good standing with the Olympics. That nation's fervent anti-communism appealed to Brundage's political sensibilities, and the racial attitudes he exhibited in the United States would not predispose him to oppose apartheid. He, and his supporters, could say that they were doing nothing more than trying to keep sports separate from politics. In the case of South Africa that was impossible, since the politics of the nation determined the racist policies that ensured that the vast majority of its population would never have the opportunity to compete in the Olympics. The fact that the sports policies of South Africa contravened the Olympic ideals, as well as the regulations of the IOC concerning discrimination mattered little to Brundage and his supporters.

The greatest irony was that the prisoners on the island shared other ideals that Brundage championed: sport could be a positive force in building character, creating social change, and bringing people together in common cause. Brundage talked about how the Olympics forged new friendships between nations while presiding over an organization deeply divided by political and moral concerns. The Robben Island Summer Games, with their five-ring symbol, were using sport as a means of bringing together groups of men divided by bitter rivalries.

The Summer Games served as the culmination of the athletic contests that ran throughout the year on Robben Island, because some of the track and field events had a series of qualifying heats. The games were staged between 8 a.m. and 4 p.m., with track events scheduled to take place at six-minute intervals. An endeavour like this required lots of volunteers, to do everything from judging events to helping lay the sandpit for the jumps. For much of the year, the island was a bleak, cold place, and it is hard for us, perhaps, to fully comprehend how the prisoners must have felt to be taking part in their own Olympics, as athletes or spectators, on a bright, warm, sunny January day.

Many of the events would be familiar to everyone, for example, races ranging in distance between 100 and 1,500 metres. There was a separate category in the shorter races for veterans, men of forty-five years and above. The field events – shot put, discus, long jump, high jump, standing broad jump, and triple jump – took place in another part of the recreation area.

The day was punctuated with other events which Sedick had decided to incorporate into the Olympics, some of them revealing his dry sense of humour. A couple turned elements of everyday life on the island into sporting challenges, for example, the wheelbarrow race and the late-for-work race. Stick pulling and throwing a weighted cricket ball also formed part of the field events. Among the track events were the potato and spoon race (separate categories for veterans), the bucket race, the needle-and-cotton race, the three-legged race, and the veterans' walk.

One event that drew enthusiastic cheering from the crowd was the tug of war, which matched four teams in a round. Sedick clearly expected there to be decisive winners, as six contests had been scheduled into a twenty-four-minute period. If spectators admired the strength and team work of the tug of war, the event that followed – Find the Object Blindfolded – would give them a good chuckle.

After the first session of the Games, there was a three-hour break, followed by the distance relay, a gymnastic display, plus football and rugby displays.

Within two years, the Summer Games was such a hit with the prisoners that Sedick had to expand it to include a number of indoor games. There were four divisions of draughts and four of French draughts, three each of dominoes, chess, and bridge, and three each of both singles and doubles table tennis. The same compulsion to properly organize competitive sports that had been evident when football was established on Robben Island manifested itself across the board.

As much as the prison community looked forward to its annual Olympics, there would have been something missing had it not been for Sedick's negotiating efforts: prizes. There had to be some equivalent to the gold, silver, and bronze medals of the international games. The authorities did not allow trophies of any kind; although sport was now a reality they couldn't ignore on the island, the apartheid regime did not want prisoners to have permanent reminders of sporting success. Conditions for the prisoners had undoubtedly improved on the island, but the men were still there to have their self-esteem crushed, not raised.

Sedick decided to persuade the prison regime to allow prizes that would actually be of much more immediate interest to the athletes:

food – sweets, chocolates, and biscuits; luxuries to the men on Robben Island.

His intention was to buy these prizes in the same way that the leagues had bought football equipment: by making an appeal for money throughout the various cell blocks. To make this appeal, though, he had first to find a way of placating the anti-athletics camp. An easy solution quickly presented itself. The programme for the Summer Games already had to be weighted to include a certain amount of rugby, football, tennis, and volley-ball events, and this meant that the participants in those sports would also be eligible for some of the forty packets of biscuits, eighty bars of chocolate, and forty packets of sweets that would be purchased with the funds.

The commanding officer gave his permission on the condition that Sedick liaise with one of the prisoners' least favourite chief warders, Lieutenant van der Westhuizen. Since their earlier troubles with the guard the men had nicknamed him the donkey because of his slow stubbornness. Sedick now had to engage in talks with Westhuizen, to agree on how many events would take place and how many prizes would be needed.

Although Sedick later told fellow prisoners that negotiating with the lieutenant drove him to distraction, there were, however, definite advantages in dealing with a man who, in his opinion, was slow-witted and none too good at arithmetic.

Sedick had to sit down with the lieutenant in his office and count out the requisite number of packets of biscuits or sweets and, as he did so, he sensed an opportunity to get hold of extra prizes for the men. He counted off the packets in twos – two, four, six, and so on – but, along the way, he would quickly repeat a number a couple of times, so he'd end up with more packets in the pile

Lieutenant van der Westhuizen became more and more confused, and demanded that Sedick count the packets of biscuits out one by one. He obliged but, once again, stuttered backwards and forwards over certain numbers, so that the total amount of packets was still way more than the regime wanted them to have. The prizes, along with a programme, were handed out to the winners in a ceremony, but then the biscuits were taken back to the cells to be shared out among the men.

Secretly, Sedick made sure that the winners in the Games would still have a lasting reminder of their victories. Though denied medals or trophies, he personally drafted certificates for the men. The documents given to victors in the 1972 and 1973 Robben Island Amateur Athletic Association Summer Games were beautiful examples of calligraphy and bore the names of the chairman, Indress Naidoo, the master of the Field, P. F. Silwana, the Field Secretary, E. Ismail, and the Organizing Secretary, Sedick Isaacs.

Prisoners on the island were won over, and athletics became an established part of the sporting activities in the prison. Success though it was, however, the prisoners had long ago learned that everything they created for themselves had to move forward in order to keep people engaged. The executive felt that it was time to talk about future reforms, most of which centred around problems with the judges. The issues that came up were similar to those that were going on in football, which was just one more sign that sport was well enough established that any problems that arose could be openly discussed.

Among the proposed reforms was one that took into account the need for the judges to have a more thorough knowledge of the rules – an echo of football's ongoing battle to educate its match officials in the ways of the game. Judges had allowed outsiders to interfere – even, on occasion, to enter the field. They had not used their discretion, and sometimes attempted to coach athletes.

As well as improvement in the judging, more equipment was urgently needed. For most of the events, there was just one of everything – one javelin, one shot for the shot put, and so on. Retrieving these items after each and every throw was time consuming and, clearly, given so much use, they soon showed signs of wear or were damaged.

These issues aside, however, the executive could feel confident that it had succeeded in its aim 'in organizing these games, to entertain our population and thereby take [the prisoners'] minds away from the pain of imprisonment, to expand the scope of interest and sector of experience, to stimulate them into becoming general sportsmen and not stay narrow-minded soccerites or restricted ruggerites'.

The mix of sports on the island was now pretty comprehensive, but Sedick remained always on the look-out for novel and diverting ideas to amuse the men. Some never quite made it off the ground. The Makana FC received a letter from prisoner M. Speelman saying that he'd had a great idea that would cause a sensation among the island's football fans – namely, choosing a team of short and a team of tall players. Mr Speelman helpfully enclosed a list of short players on the island, including himself.

Not all of Sedick's own proposals were taken up by the prisoners. His biggest failure was an attempt to introduce basketball. Most of the prisoners were familiar with netball, a game they viewed as being for schoolgirls. That prejudice, combined with the sport's supposed non-contact quality, and the fear that the constant handling and bouncing of the ball might have an adverse effect on football skills, doomed the sport. Isaacs tried one more approach – he labelled the sport American basketball in the hope that that would reduce the feeling against it, but his amateur marketing failed and he abandoned the effort.

He read a book about volleyball, but didn't have much success with that either. Again, there was no contact in volleyball, and too many of the players didn't see it as a real sport. Some also objected that using an actual football might ruin that precious piece of equipment. The sport never achieved broad popularity, but it did become impotant to those who partcipated in it.

On one occasion, Sedick Isaacs, on behalf of the volleyball players, approached Dynaspurs United FC about borrowing some much-needed equipment. In a letter to the football club he begged for the loan of their size three football to use in matches. He helpfully reassured the club that volleyball is played with the hand or head and at no time is the ball kicked.

Some days later Sedick was forced to write another letter to Dynaspurs informing them that the football they had so generously lent had now been confiscated by one of DFC's players, Mr E. Malgas, while a volleyball match was actually in progress. He hadn't liked seeing their beloved match ball being knocked around in some game he thought was utterly inferior to football. Sedick angrily told Dynaspurs that the act had caused great inconvenience and disturbance to the promotion of this new game and registered a complaint.

Independently of Sedick, volleyball did become popular in the isolation section, where there were fewer prisoners available to take part in sports and no space for a game such as football. The sport showed its rough side there when Ahmed Kathrada broke a finger trying to defend a spike.

Sedick worked tirelessly to try and overcome the practical day-to-day difficulties of running so many different sports. Money and resources were extremely limited, kit and equipment hard to come by – every bit had to be ordered and paid for in advance from the mainland and, sometimes, because of bureaucracy or vindictive white store owners, it could take as long as a year for orders eventually to arrive on the island – and there was much begging, borrowing, and stealing between the various sports associations. Sometimes prisoners were very protective of their own sport's resources.

As ever, there was pressure on the cell blocks' limited supply of paper. Each sporting association continually appealed for more. In July 1973 the island's Sports Federation Council noted that it had an important meeting coming up and had only two sheets of paper left in the office. The council made urgent pleas to other sports for help and asked the International Red Cross for thirty emergency sheets to tide them over.

In the early years on the island, the prisoners had dealt with another paper shortage in an imaginative way. When they found ways to obtain tobacco, they had to figure out a way to roll cigarettes. Writing paper was both in short supply and, in any case, did not make very good paper for smoking. Someone came up with the idea of using pages from those books of which there were multiple copies in each of the cells. Bibles were plentiful and the paper of their pages seemed almost heaven sent for this particular purpose. As with every other activity on the island, this led to long, complicated discussions and debates – was it appropriate to use the Bible for such purposes, and which sections of the Bible were the most appropriate to rip out? Old or New Testament? Revelations or Ecclesiastes? Should it be the whole book or specific sections from many different books? The need for this kind of discussion was, in part, a reaction to how much time they had on their hands. But there were more important reasons. The prisoners wanted to ensure that they were including and involving everyone in decision-making. In effect, they were practising for the democratic South Africa of the future about which they all dreamed so passionately.

Whatever the problems, the hard-won right to play a variety of sports now complemented an ever broader spectrum of cultural activities in the prison. It would have been inconceivable to men imprisoned in the early days that, by the early Seventies, prisoners would be holding singing competitions and forming choirs and bands.

One prisoner, Nelson Nkumalo, fashioned a saxophone from dried pieces of seaweed. Others ran ballroom-dancing contests and some did tap dancing. Theatrical performances were staged, including a play about Rhodesia (now Zimbabwe) in which Sedick Isaacs took the part of former white Rhodesian Prime Minister Ian Smith. The most memorable productions were a glorious and inspiring staging of Handel's *Messiah* and another that set the story of the Sharpeville massacre to music.

From 1973, the prison authorities even gave the inmates permission to watch films. The first showing was memorable for many reasons. The film was shown at night in the recreation hall and the men had to be marched across the compound in darkness. For almost all of them, it was the first time they had seen the moon and stars since they had been imprisoned. The dramatic film became almost comedy relief for the prisoners and demonstrated how wide was the political gulf between the warders and the prisoners. The film was *The Green Berets*. Starring John Wayne, it followed the story of two tough US army detachments sent to fight in Vietnam. To the prisoners' amazement, the guards just could not understand why the inmates were all rooting for the Vietcong throughout the movie.

10

Football Struggles to Survive

'We needed football. Without it there would have been so much depression. It made you feel free in an unfree status.' 'Terror' Lekota, Prisoner 14/76

Strong winds were blowing off the Atlantic across the football pitch, and the skies were grey and overcast. It was a cold Saturday morning in April 1973, and the two teams about to play warmed up with a degree of extra vigour.

According to the league fixture list, the first game that morning was Tony Suze's Manong against Jacob Zuma's Rangers, an A-division match between two old rivals that would be keenly fought, to say the least. Following this encounter, Gunners were down to play Ditshitshidi in the B division. A full programme of league matches across the divisions was scheduled throughout the rest of the day and into Sunday – but none of these matches took place. The MFA had agreed to a number of hastily arranged friendly games being played instead, and for the most bittersweet of reasons: throughout 1973 and 1974, most weeks, the football association found itself fielding request after request from players for specially arranged friendly games to mark the departure from the island of football-playing comrades. Many of the footballers were coming to the end of their sentences, most having been imprisoned between 1963 and 1965. Inmates were leaving the island in droves. Between the early and mid-Seventies, nearly a third were released.

For many, leaving the island would, ironically, be one of the hardest days of their lives. They were saying goodbye to close friends and valued comrades. They had forged deep male friendships in the dark furnace of oppression and persecution. In extreme conditions, they had formed profound, sometimes life-saving support networks. In the outside world, men talk about looking out for their friends, but it is very rare for someone to have to go to the lengths the men on Robben Island did. Many committed and loyal friendships formed on Robben Island endure to the present day.

The men were desperate to get back to their families and loved ones but, even before they left Robben Island, many sensed that the transition from years in prison to life back home would not be straightforward. To take the boat back to the mainland and leave such an unbelievably close-knit set of friends was hard. How would they cope without them, those men who had helped and cajoled them through the rigours of working in the quarry, who had studied and played sport with them?

How would friends, family, and future workmates ever be able to relate to the experiences the men had had on Robben Island? How could they even begin to understand the enormity of what they had been through? Though the men were going home, in some cases after nearly a decade of imprisonment, for many it must have felt as if they were travelling to a foreign country.

Those who still had time to serve were happy that their friends were finally going home, but they also realized that their departure might spell disaster for the future of football on Robben Island. These men were strong characters, they had formed the formidable backbone of the MFA and its clubs. Suddenly, much of their acumen, dedication, enthusiasm, and passion had gone. The effect was bound to be demoralizing.

Throughout 1973 and 1974 Jacob Zuma, the captain of Rangers, and the old hardline communist referee Harry Gwala were released, along with Marcus Solomon, Mark Shinners, and Indress Naidoo. As well as being a tough defender, Zuma had played a very active role in the deliberations of the MFA and represented his club on various administrative bodies. Harry Gwala had been a virtual encyclopaedia of football history and rules for many of his comrades. He may have been inflexible once he had made a judgement, but he was generous with his knowledge, his advice, and his support, the latter being especially important when newly trained referees found themselves having to defend controversial decisions. Indress Naidoo had been active at practically every level of sports administration. His role as secretary of the MFA and as both a referee and executive of the Referees Union had placed him at the centre of things. Some of his colleagues joked about how he would do sports paperwork to the exclusion of everything else (especially studying), except chess and bridge.

Marcus Solomon had been a referee, a player, and an administrator. Although he came from a rugby background, he became a more than adequate football player in B division. His co-operation with Steve Tshwete was aided by their shared passion for rugby. He kept Dynaspurs going while Steve served a six-month spell in solitary, and Marcus had to navigate the club throughout all the upheaval of the

Atlantic Raiders affair. A man with a smile that lights up a room and a laugh that can fill it, he is to this day a man intensely passionate about fairness, moral standards, and justice. On Robben Island, he threw himself unreservedly into some of the most complicated and controversial activities involving refereeing and disciplinary matters.

As Marcus packed his few belongings into a small prison-issue cardboard box, he found himself torn by difficult, conflicting emotions. Desperate to get off Robben Island and see his family and friends again, he was also overcome by a sadness that lodged heavily in his chest like a quarry stone. He admitted to friends on the island that it was the saddest day of his life in the prison.

Mark Shinners left a memento behind for a close friend: the tennis racquet that he'd used for the past year and, with it, a note that read, 'Here you take it, I'm leaving now.' Unfortunately for Shinners, a few years later he got the tennis racquet back. He arrived on the island to start a second prison term shortly before his friend was released.

Replacing footballers and administrators of the calibre of Mark Shinners, Jacob Zuma, Harry Gwala, Indress Naidoo, and Marcus Solomon was not going to happen – and they were only the most noticeable of the losses. Many of the unsung heroes who conducted all the hard, back-room work in administering and running football had taken the boat back home, too. The departures had an immediate effect.

In the course of the Sixties South Africa's security services had been so successful in rounding up the great majority of active ANC and PAC members that the new prisoners now making their way on to the island amounted only to an occasional trickle. In the early to mid-Seventies, the boat from the mainland usually arrived merely with supplies and, very occasionally, a new inmate.

The Makana FA's annual report for 1973 highlighted the problem of the ever-dwindling prison population, noting that its own executive now consisted of just the vice-chairman, the secretary, and the trustee. The roles of chairman and vice-secretary were vacant, and the remaining trio were working furiously just to keep the association ticking over. It had taken years to establish football on the island; now its structure and organization were unravelling, approaching crisis point. The MFA secretary made a heartfelt plea for more committed involvement throughout the prisoner community. With numbers diminishing, every able-bodied individual was asked to contribute what they could – physically, intellectually, and materially – for the sake of football.

Some clubs were struggling to field teams in all three of the divisions. In 1973 Dynaspurs were forced to disband one of their B-division sides, simply because they were running out of players. A-division players were now regularly turning out in the B-division sides – no longer as a ploy to win more matches, but just to help them field full teams. Reluctantly, the MFA was forced to consider scaling down its activities. To counter the loss of its personnel, the Makana FA decided to reorganize and reshuffle its resources. The first, albeit reluctant step was to be realistic and reduce the number of clubs, not a move they approached with much relish.

The MFA's major worry was that loyalty to individual clubs might deter some sides from wanting to merge. Each of the clubs boasted fanatically devoted fans, and rivalry between them was intense. Proposing amalgamation was like asking the teams and supporters of Manchester United and Manchester City, or Liverpool and Everton, to forget all previous loyalties and hostilities and merge together.

Indeed, one of the major factors that had made football so popular on the island was that the passionate loyalties the men had felt back on the mainland for their respective clubs – such as the Swallows, the Pirates, and the Bucks – had in some way been replicated within the prison. You *were* Manong, or Rangers, Dynaspurs, Gunners, et al. You had your own club to shout for, to discuss with fellow fans, and noisily support. In many ways, it was just like being at home again.

In the end, the situation became so serious that the clubs, their members, and supporters were forced to adopt a new mood of realism. Games were being cancelled or postponed because teams were struggling to put out full sides. Eventually, even the most avid fans had to accept that a change had to come. They didn't like it, but they realized it was untenable to continue running the MFA leagues in their present form.

Gunners, Ditshitshidi, and Mphatlalatsane dissolved and then were resurrected as two new clubs, Pioneers FC and the Island Tigers. In a remarkable turn of events, Dynaspurs, the first and proudest of the consolidated clubs, merged with a rival club to become Dinare FC. Its new partner was Bucks, the club that Steve Tshwete had accused a year earlier of trying to poach Dynaspurs players. This came as a body blow to some of the club's loyal fans and caused new selection headaches in the remaining pool of players, a number of whom had 'let Dynaspurs down' and defected to the Bucks but, in the end, the need to maintain enough clubs to continue a regular fixture list overcame past antagonisms.

The MFA shrank to just five clubs – Manong, Rangers, and the new sides Island Tigers, Dinare, and Pioneers FC. At its height, the association had boasted nine thriving clubs, all with big pools of players and an army of willing backroom staff.

Reorganization was not just a straightforward exercise in shuffling players between teams either. As everything had to be done correctly, according to strict FIFA rules, each of the newly merged clubs had now to create its own individual constitution, every point of which had to be discussed, debated, and agreed upon. Money, donations, paper, and other stationery the previous clubs still held had to be pooled and accounted for. More than anything, the MFA needed to attract fresh blood to its administrative staff to formally and effectively run the new clubs. Here again, shrinking prisoner numbers caused problems.

Interest in the game was declining, and standards of behaviour both on and off the pitch were slipping. There were more and more complaints by officials about conduct. A trustee of one of the clubs remarked that both discipline and a certain level of neatness were integral to the game of football, and his members increasingly lacked both, which led to a lack of team spirit and was reflected in sloppy play on the pitch.

Players no longer seemed to care about the condition of their kit, the colours the MFA and the clubs had fought so hard for, first to gain permission to wear, then to raise money to buy, then to wait months to receive. The club shirt was of massive importance as a symbol of what the men had achieved. The colours had been sacrosanct. Now, some players were failing to wash and maintain them properly and, worse still, wore their shorts, and sometimes their shirts, in the cell and to work in the quarry. For those on the island who took footballing seriously, this was close to sporting blasphemy.

The MFA and the clubs were now finding it more difficult to haul in the donations needed to keep up their high standards, as players were increasingly reluctant to dig into their own pockets, but there was much more than money at stake. It seemed to the football hardcore that too many men no longer thought the game was important enough to make sacrifices for in terms of commitment of time, energy, and effort. A deep malaise had set in.

Even the condition of the main football pitch was suffering. In 1973 the MFA's annual report noted that the field had not been receiving proper maintenance. Once lovingly attended to like a beautiful garden, regularly watered, re-dug and re-turfed, the pitch was now infrequently rolled and the grass was often too long to host good-quality matches. The association was finding it harder and harder to find volunteers to work on the playing area. Only a few people could be bothered to turn out to help with the lining of the field – and, even then, it was the same faces every week.

The annual report also identified a growing reluctance on the part of the prisoners left on the island to become involved with the MFA. The skeleton committee was still struggling to fill its most important and senior posts and had to attempt to cajole prisoners into taking part, to twist their arms.

In some ways, it was easy to understand, given the many other activities the inmates had now won the right to enjoy themselves. With many existing prisoners anticipating release, they were thinking about their futures back on the mainland and committing more time to studying and distance-learning degrees. They knew how tough it would be to get work in apartheid South Africa and were seeking to gain every advantage they could before their release date. It was the rate at which candidates declined that came as a surprise to the MFA.

One hundred per cent of the candidates approached to stand as chairman refused to take up the position, and 50 per cent of candidates asked to be members of the committee turned the offer down. The MFA was forced to call an emergency meeting and, after much pleading and persuasion, the posts were finally filled.

It had always been hard to attract prisoners to refereeing, but now match officials were exceedingly thin on the ground. The relationship between the football association and the Referees Union had become fractious, so the MFA summoned representatives of the RU to an interview, to discuss their failure to cover some of the matches and to recruit new officials.

The meeting was a disaster. An MFA report described it as a war of nerves. The RU's conduct was insubordinate, arrogant, and embarrassing. One member staged a walk-out, then the secretary resigned – apparently taking with him all the most vital information about the day-to-day running of the RU. After his resignation, queries from the MFA were no longer answered, and football took another step towards potential implosion.

In 1974, for the first time since football started on the island, the MFA decided not to select a Player ('Soccerite') of the Year. The reason given once again served to show to what extent the prisoners' interest in football was on the wane. The association announced that, because of the lack of seriousness, zeal, and determination shown by the players in the A division, there was no 'legitimate choice'. After spending so many years battling to establish organized football in the prison, this came as a body blow to the original pioneers. There could be no stronger indication that the game was in decline.

In an effort to revitalize the sport, the MFA tried different approaches, some new and some they had attempted before. It set up a number of friendlies and select side matches. These were not set up as cup tournaments but were specially formed teams – at least one important lesson had been learned from the Atlantic Raiders debacle. Skills contests were put on, with teams playing matches that emphasized the elements of excitement and skill rather than the fundamentals of team work, in an effort to infuse the games with some artificial extra interest. It seemed that the high ideals which lay behind the generation of league football on Robben Island were in danger of being forgotten.

In 1974, a day was dedicated to what its organizers described as:

AN EXPERIMENT in sport:
Sportsmen who like to experiment with new ideas (the innovators) are invited to volunteer.

The day would include volleyball and a number of traditional track and field activities, but the new attraction was something called hand soccer. One can only speculate on what the reaction of Pro Malepe, Tony Suze, and other stars of the Makana Football Association would have been if this new sport had achieved a permanent place on Robben Island. The mere fact that it was proposed showed how desperate things had become.

Another sign of the changes in the attitude of the prison population towards sports was evident in the way in which the MFA itself was now operating. Its first chairman, Dikgang Moseneke, had delighted in the number of meetings that both the executive and the association held. The fact that they attracted a healthy attendance indicated that other men were interested in what was happening and that they would be willing to put in the effort to make league football succeed. It was important for there to be discussion at meetings but, in the end, firm decisions had to be made in order for the MFA to run effectively.

Moseneke had encouraged attendance at meetings as a means of communicating with the men. He was under no illusions about how to run an organization made up of so many strong-willed individuals and factions. He could be described as a consensus-building politician, who believed strongly that important decisions should never be decided by vote. Matters should be discussed thoroughly until all opinions became synthesized into one sound common decision. Stark votes did nothing but encourage division, disintegration, and block formation, which tended to crystallize with time into a factionalism the football community had worked hard to eliminate.

He also had enough faith in the goodwill of his comrades to believe that consensus could, and should, be reached about important matters before divisions could sabotage the enterprise. He understood that the prisoners had to present a unified front to the authorities on the island and to 'create structures', a phrase now often repeated by former prisoners in describing their successes on the island.

Now, MFA meetings had become more and more anodyne and focused on administrative matters, with overworked officials keen to agree quickly on the way forward on small, day-to-day practicalities. The joust and the debate, the bigger visions and discussions about ideals were no more. In 1973, the secretary of the MFA, Solomon Mabuse, bemoaned the fact that there had been so few special meetings called in the previous year. He dearly missed the substance and discussion that had characterized earlier meetings of the MFA – the passion, the verbal missiles, and the eloquent harangues. The sting had gone out of the delegates.

By the start of 1974 the sting had gone out of matches as well. Competition between the five new clubs was not intense. Good players such as Tony Suze still gave their all, but the men were older, the pace of the games had slowed, and the fans in the pavvy were less fervent in their support; once loud, boisterous, and frenzied, the level of noise generated on the touchlines had become quiet and subdued.

It was clear to the executive of the MFA that something drastic had to be done. The matter came to a head when the Makana FA received a letter from Dinare FC (the merged Bucks and Dynaspurs) openly questioning whether it might just be better for everyone concerned to cut their losses, abolish football as an organized sport, and merely play ad hoc friendly games whenever it was possible to fit them in.

A good number of MFA officials were crestfallen at the very thought, but it did make them even more aware that big decisions had to be made about where to go next. The MFA distributed the letter to all the other clubs, asking them to submit their own feelings in writing so that a major summit meeting could be held to discuss the future of football on Robben Island.

The written responses from the five MFA clubs muddied the waters still further: there was major disagreement on what should be done. Two clubs were in favour of dissolving and putting an end to organized league football; two were against. The fifth would only favour dissolution if an investigation by a newly set-up ad hoc committee was first given the opportunity to explore any other options and then report back to the MFA.

Some days later, the summit meeting took place and, for three exhausting hours, delegates from each of the clubs debated into the night, sometimes loud and heated, sometimes in quiet whispers when a new, less sympathetic guard came on shift.

All the clubs agreed upon the problems that football faced. The standard of play was in decline. A lot of the players were leaving the island. Teams had become lopsided, and there was no longer fair competition down through the three divisions. One club proposed that a redistribution of players might solve the problem. To support its proposal, it pointed to the popularity of the Summer Games, which had proved that a 'constant reshuffle could maintain interest'.

Manong took the opposite position, claiming that redistribution would not work. Supporters' interest in merged clubs such as Dinare and the Pioneers had proved to be lukewarm and, if sides were amalgamated or rearranged again, it would only serve to weaken further the men's sense of loyalty – and, more importantly, make them even less interested in the fortunes of football. In any case, it would be the equivalent of establishing representative or 'picked sides' and the MFA had had trouble filling those teams since the inception of the league.

Pioneers FC took a more direct approach. So far as dissolution was concerned, it believed that clubs who could no longer keep running should simply disband. In terms of the balance of footballing power, if a club felt it could not compete, it should dissolve and either avail its members to the MFA for redistribution, or themselves encourage members to join other clubs.

The opponents of dissolution believed that the current imbalance could be a potential source of more fevered competition because the weaker sides would always strive to beat the stronger – an argument similar to that continually put forward by the biggest clubs in the top leagues the world over for the past decade.

In fact, the longer the meeting went on, the clearer it became that the participants were talking about issues that might affect a football organization anywhere in the world. How hard should a league work towards creating some kind of competitive parity, and how much should a football organization focus on its complete season rather than tournaments or knock-out competitions?

When the meeting finally came to a tired close, the chairman summed up the situation. He spoke about the recreational value of football, its obligation to the non-playing section of the community, and the important role it played in the shaping of character. He feared that, in the meeting, the delegates had focused too much on specific points and had overlooked major issues such as 'encroaching age, forlorn and static stay in prison, and the constant outflow of players'. The secretary, Solomon Mabuse, then made a statement, reminding those gathered of the importance and complexity of the issues before them. If the clubs agreed unanimously to dissolve, the next step would be a massive one: the MFA would have to be totally dismantled and a new organization created in its stead.

The clubs were, however, unable to come to any agreement. The MFA proposed that, as a next step, it establish a commission to interview and survey a cross section of the footballing community on the island. The clubs agreed on this latter compromise, and the commission was mandated to report back to the MFA within four months.

No one was surprised when Sedick Isaacs was chosen to chair the ad hoc committee or that he did most of the work on the survey. Indeed, the subject was tailormade for him, touching on two areas of his specific academic competence – statistical analysis and psychology. His committee was charged with discovering what the inmates thought about football and what measures might be taken to solve the current problems.

The massive documentation for the prosecution in the Atlantic Raiders case had been the first legal brief put together by Dikgang Moseneke. His comrades like to say that he had 'cut his teeth' as a lawyer on Robben Island, and that it would stand him in good stead for his work in the struggle against apartheid on his release. Similarly, the detailed statistical survey on the state of soccer on Robben Island could be regarded as Sedick Isaacs' first statistical research publication and something that helped to prepare him for his life beyond the confines of the island.

With characteristic efficiency, Sedick and the committee under-took a survey of players from all of the football clubs in order to investigate the extent of the problem. Their task was to obtain a snap-shot of how men on the island now viewed the sport. What was their attitude towards playing – were they still passionate about the game or were they losing interest? How old were they, and how would they assess their own current level of fitness and ability to play? Did they enjoy the loyalty engendered by attaching themselves to one specific club, or would they be happy to play in ever-changing teams, based on the availability of players? How important was football to them?

Using a random sampling method, Sedick and his committee chose ten players from each of the remaining clubs and, over the next few months, buttonholed them in cell blocks, the quarry, and the exercise yard to canvass their views about the future of the game.

Although he made it clear in the executive summary of the report that the method had little statistical validity, the survey did provide important data about football and its participants.

The results were not encouraging. The most telling was that the average age of regular, active players was now nudging forty. Many were much older. Through their A-, B-, and C-division teams, Rangers had no fewer than sixteen players who were in their forties – and four of those were nearly fifty years old. Only two teams, Manong and Dinare, had any players who were still in their late twenties, and then only a handful. These were now, by far, the youngest footballers left on the island.

As the players aged, their level of fitness went into decline and they became more worried about injury. Injury meant difficulty in satisfying their quotas in the quarry and, as all the prisoners were now getting on in years, there were fewer young, fit, able-bodied men to pick up the slack.

The survey also revealed that the general feeling across the board was that too many players were bored with the ever-increasing amount of selected and exhibition matches the MFA had organized in trying to maintain the men's interest. The footballers themselves were thirsting for competitive games. The men relished competition and enjoyed directing their loyalty to one club. They hungered after the good old days, when there had been nine well-functioning sides.

Such nostalgia just ignored the reality of the situation. The merging of the clubs into just five had been inevitable. The problem was, though, that with so few clubs playing one another so frequently, the players and supporters felt overwhelmingly that they could predict with a high level of accuracy which team would win, by roughly how many goals, and what tactics they would employ. The habits and set pieces of individual players were now so well known that there was no sense of expectation. In the absence of new blood, the matches had become stale and predictable. How the MFA might resolve that particular problem was, however, hard to tell.

Sedick's investigation also supported the general sense that there was a huge gap in ability between the clubs and that the men involved thought this was a serious problem. Everyone surveyed recognized the importance to participants of thinking they had some chance of winning, and there was broad agreement that something had to be done on this score.

Setting up categories within the league had been the original means of approaching this difficulty, but it had led to another, ironic, somewhat intractable situation. The A division was the flagship of the MFA, attracting the most talented players; the teams played the best quality football, and it could claim time for matches. However, the survey identified soccer interest at its highest in the C division, which also contained the most players. Maybe Marcus Solomon's crusade for football for all had been more successful than he thought.

Perhaps most worryingly, many of the footballers reported that they were increasingly feeling the wearying effects of long-term imprisonment. The oldest were now struggling to get through the days of hard labour and tedious routine. Though the diet had improved from the earliest years, it was still limited and largely unvarying. And though the men's spirits had not been broken, they were tired.

Sedick paid special attention to these concerns. He had been reading books on psychology for a long time now, with the eventual goal of earning a degree. His special and impassioned area of interest was in charting, identifying, and analysing the ways in which precisely those factors cited by the men ground them down and caused such a lack of drive and enthusiasm. It seemed that, in asking him to help find the MFA a new way forward for football on Robben Island, the association had provided him with laboratory subjects for the very issues he had previously read about only in textbooks.

As the results of the survey came in, Sedick realized that the whole thing was about much more than just football. It was about finding a way to help the prisoners re-energize and rejuvenate themselves, be it through football or other means. Sedick could only wonder how much worse the problems the prisoners were experiencing would have been had sports not provided a buffer between them and the impact of imprisonment.

His job now, along with his survey team, was to suggest a way forward for all concerned. They came up with a raft of recommendations, recognizing that perhaps only some of them could ever, realistically, be implemented:

1. that a new football society be created where 'the law of supply and demand be given a chance to operate'. This meant having a brief 'no club period', in which new clubs would be formed
2. that new kit with new colours be provided, something to add a visible flair to the sport
3. that a new, smaller field be created. This was a concession to the reality of the increasing age of the players
4. that the MFA should retain the names of some of the clubs and seriously consider resurrecting the names of older clubs. This would both foster 'social cohesion' and serve as a link to past good memo-

ries. It was possible that the new club names were a reminder of the crisis that had brought them into existence

5. that further negotiations should take place with the prison authorities to ensure that trophies could be awarded and engraved so that victories would be permanently recognized. The committee recognized that winning did matter, as did recognition of that success

6. that the MFA should subscribe to a number of football periodicals and films. This was a way to introduce new ideas, to stop football becoming stale and predictable

7. that the MFA should do everything possible to enlist new members

8. that when reforms had been put into effect, a further survey should be taken to judge their effectiveness.

There was a general agreement in the footballing community that most of the reform package be adopted and tried out – but two of Sedick's ideas were rejected out of hand, and this said a lot about the pride and single-mindedness of the footballers on Robben Island.

They could not and would not agree to the concept of smaller pitches. Their reaction reminded Sedick instantly of his attempts to introduce croquet – a game that would have been perfectly suitable for prisoners of a more advanced age – a couple of years earlier. The prisoners had turned it down out of hand, simply because they identified it as a game for old men. It was true that reducing the size of the field would be an obvious concession to the lower fitness levels brought about by age but, although everyone might recognize the aging of the players as a problem, why go out of the way to admit it?

The players also rejected point blank the idea of having a no-club period when men could be swapped between given friendly or select teams without retaining any strand of club loyalty. Though there were now only five clubs, the players still held much store by their affiliation to them and the relationship it gave them with their fellow players and fans. Shared experience, solidarity, and unity in playing for 'the shirt' – just as with players and fans all over the world – was massively important to them. It was this passion for their respective sides that had helped make football such a success on the island and had even turned prisoners who previously had little interest in the sport into keen fans and committed students of the game.

The men in B Section knew how important the sport was to their fellow prisoners and gradually became ardent supporters of the game. Each weekend, results and short match reports were smuggled into the isolation cells, where many inmates would pore over the details, trying to visualize parts of the action. In the early years of the MFA, men in B Section had got an occasional look at matches, either when the men were exercising or through the windows of their cells. When the authorities realized that this breach in security had taken place, they made sure that it did not happen again. Men in B Section were not allowed near the playing field, windows were blacked out in their cells, or walls were erected to ensure they could not share in the pleasure of football with the other prisoners.

Ahmed Kathrada had been sentenced to life on Robben Island. As one of the ANC leaders kept permanently in the isolation section, he was not allowed to participate in sports with the prisoners in the communal cells. Prior to his imprisonment, he had shown very little interest in football but, over time, Kathrada's interest in football began to extend beyond the walls of Robben Island and even the boundaries of the African continent. In a letter written to a cousin in

1975 he asked if he could recommend a magazine in English that covered international football.

This softly spoken man, who had an almost courtly bearing, became a dedicated reader of *Shoot* magazine and a passionate supporter of Leeds United – particularly of its often argumentative hard-man skipper, Billy Bremner. A team that was often accused of being thuggishly efficient and a player who was famed for his aggressive play and lack of discipline became the firm favourites of this quiet revolutionary. He explained to comrades that he thought of Bremner as a radical who rejected authority.

A letter Kathrada wrote to another relative later the same year made it clear that footballing news from the outside world was now making its way on to the island quite soon after actual events took place, and in ever more detail. Kathrada's letter was sent shortly after Leeds United had lost 2–0 to Bayern Munich in the final of the European Cup in Paris. In it he expressed concern about the state of football in England, and his sadness as a Leeds follower. Kathrada was disappointed at the loss of the match, but what troubled him more was that Leeds United fans had run riot in Paris afterwards. He told his relative that the news of the behaviour of Leeds fans had 'burst upon the prisoners like a bombshell'. Kathrada concluded his lament about what had happened in Paris with a rhetorical question: 'We have always thought the English were so polite and even tempered. Have they changed so much or have we been wrong all this time in our opinion?'

That football had managed to involve so many prisoners in its culture on the island – even previous 'agnostics' like Kathrada, locked away in B Section – was a measure of its success. It would be a tragedy if the sport were allowed to melt away.

The Makana Football Association soldiered on, trying to put in place the new reforms, but it was soon to discover that the very success of organized football in the earlier years had contributed to it now having become a minority interest in the minds of the majority of prisoners. Not only did the game have far fewer participants on the island because of the departure of released prisoners, there was far more competition in the prison from the pull of other activities.

By the mid-Seventies, prisoners were not only engrossed in rugby, athletics, tennis, and organized indoor games but were now regularly being shown films and taking part in everything from ballroom-dancing classes to an ever broader array of college and university degree programmes. These had the advantages of being novel and not requiring the physical commitment of football. They could also be done from time to time, rather than demanding the almost around-the-calendar commitment that football did.

That constant schedule had been one of the greatest attractions of football when it started. It had been something to take the men's minds off prison life. But, by 1975, the inmates had other diversions and found more personal ways to cope with life in the prison. What had become increasingly clear was that, though football might still be important, it was now only a part of life in the prison, rather than a way of life in itself.

By 1976, and despite the new reforms, the diminishing number of willing able-bodied players, referees, administrators, and first-aid units was posing a serious threat to the future of organized football on Robben Island in any meaningful form. As the MFA continued to contract and fall in on itself, its remaining players, officials, and fans could never have predicted that, within one short year, football on the island would be totally rejuvenated. On the South African mainland, surprising and unexpected events were being played out which would cause a huge sea change in the fight to dismantle apartheid – and, ironically for the MFA – bring a fresh new supply of talented young footballers on to Robben Island.

11

The Arrival of the Soweto Generation

'*Biko's death leaves me cold.*' J. T. Kruger, Minister of Justice, Republic of South Africa

Laboriously crushing rocks in the quarry one day, Sedick Isaacs looked inquisitively over towards a huddle of guards who were exchanging angry words in Afrikaans. They were too far away for Sedick to hear what they were talking about, but their body language made him curious: they seemed detached and in their own world, jittery, a little afraid even. Sedick was good at reading people, and this was not the first time over the past few days that he'd seen warders looking concerned and deep in discussion. They were treating the prisoners differently, too. Sullen and moody, the guards had been meting out more arbitrary punishments than of late. The abuse they shouted at the inmates was more vitriolic and obscene and reminded Sedick of the guards' behaviour in the early days.

It was a weekend in June 1976, and all sports events had been cancelled. The guards were tight-lipped and utterly unwilling to discuss the reasons why, behaviour that was rare by then. The prisoners were being punished – but they sensed it was for reasons that had little to do with their actions. This strange new mood among the prison staff was the talk of the cell blocks. Over the years, the men had come to know the guards and could sense when there was something in the air. Sedick and his comrades were determined to find out the reasons behind this.

Ever since the prison opened, the authorities had made a constant effort to restrict the flow of news to the prisoners. After all, one major reason for Robben Island Prison's very existence was to isolate and demoralize them. They did not want the inmates to learn of any successes on the mainland in the struggle against colonial rule or the emergence of new opposition movements within South Africa. They also wanted to deny the prisoners any knowledge of the fact that some segments of the international community were finally beginning to take steps against the apartheid regime.

This clampdown, however, was different. The quarry, cell blocks, the canteen, and the hospital were regularly searched and ransacked for home-made crystal radio sets and contraband newspapers. Censorship of the few letters that were getting through to the prisoners on the island was fierce. Anything that remotely touched on politics or events back home was literally cut or blacked out so as to be virtually indecipherable. Some of the letters that came through contained little more than the address, the names, and the most mundane of platitudes. There were ways to counter the censorship by creating codes, but that was laborious and not very reliable. In any case, there were so few letters being allowed, they were not a good source of news.

The men had to figure out other ways to get information. Having newspapers smuggled into the cells by prisoners working elsewhere on the island was one tactic but, sensing that something extraordinary must be happening on the mainland, a small group of prisoners thirsting for news took an immense risk.

In one instance, comrades had created a diversion while two men crawled outside the perimeter wire into 'the killing zone' in order to rummage through a pile of rubbish, looking for newspapers. They were taking the chance of being shot or, at the very minimum, going into solitary confinement, but they felt it was worth the risk. The men returned safely to the compound with a newspaper and, back in their cell block, eagerly flicked it open – to discover that their precious acquisition was years old. They had risked their lives for a brief lesson in history.

They resorted to a more basic means of obtaining newspapers – theft, from guards, or from visiting clergymen – and through this, prisoners began to piece together some parts of the jigsaw. They were amazed even by what little thay had managed to glean about a series of events that had rocked South Africa's mainland.

Largely unbeknownst to the prisoners on Robben Island, an important new inspiration had begun to take root among South Africa's black youth throughout the late Sixties and Seventies. Hugely influenced by Malcolm X's Black Power movement in America, young people in the townships were fast developing a sense of possibility and pride and experiencing a renewed and impassioned determination for change. The essence of the movement in South Africa, as well as its tactics were proudly and definitely home grown. These aspirations of a younger generation of black South Africans found their voice in the Black Consciousness Movement.

Inspired by a young medical student named Steve Biko, the movement took as its motto the phrase first popularized by the legendary Muhammed Ali: 'Black is beautiful.' Young blacks looked increasingly across the Atlantic Ocean, not just to the determination to dismantle segregation but to the ever-growing confidence of black Americans. Biko's creed for the Black Consciousness Movement in South Africa was based upon a passionate desire to raise levels of self-respect and a sense of direct involvement in 'the struggle' among black youth.

To educate and politicize them, senior Black Consciousness Movement members secretly went into schools and colleges around the nation's townships to give talks and lectures. Some senior teaching staff viewed this development with alarm, worrying that the students under their care would now attract the unwanted attention of the security services and the secret police. Others turned a blind eye and encouraged the visits, for they, like the students, knew a change had to come.

At the heart of the movement's beliefs was that the young must learn black pride, that despite decades of being made to feel as if they were third-rate human beings by the suffocating propaganda and control of the apartheid regime. They had to start asserting themselves, believing in themselves, and presenting themselves as equal to whites.

An undercurrent of active resistance was beginning to spread around the nation's black schools. Soon the apartheid regime would offer South Africa's black youth the opportunity to test their growing self-confidence.

The government brought in new laws designed to forcibly encourage more black people to speak Afrikaans. This, of course, was the hated language of the oppressor. Hitherto, black schools had largely taught in English and indigenous languages. The Afrikaans Medium Decree now required black schools to teach nearly half their lessons in English, the other half in Afrikaans. Teaching in indigenous languages was allowed only in a couple of minor subject areas.

Already struggling in a woefully inadequate education system starved of resources and facilities, young black children were now being set up even more for failure. Many of them knew precious little Afrikaans, and the withdrawal of classes in indigenous languages would serve to distance the young from their culture and heritage. Few black teachers in the townships could speak Afrikaans either, leading to the ridiculous situation that teachers were forced to teach, in a language they didn't understand, children who, equally, did not understand. It was an act that was aimed at further disadvantaging the already disadvantaged.

The enactment of this new law coincided with the release of some facts and figures by the apartheid government which indicated the huge gulf between educational provision for whites and non-whites. In the Cape region, 490 rands were being spent annually on every white student, in comparison to the 28 rands spent on each black scholar. Less than 2 per cent of black teachers had been educated to university level. White children were educated on a national ratio of thirty children to one teacher; black children, fifty to one.

It was no surprise that, with young students already struggling in an unfair system and now having a major new obstacle thrown into their path which would suffocate learning and destroy any possibility of advancement, the new law caused deep resentment in black residential areas throughout the country.

As exam season approached, students and their families were crestfallen. They had worked hard, but now that the examinations were set in a language they barely understood, how could they possibly pass?

Students of Orlando West Junior School in Soweto walked out of their classrooms and went on strike. Soon they were joined by children from many other Sowetan schools. Students formed an action committee – the Soweto Students Administrative Council – and decided to show their unified support against the Afrikaans Medium Decree by holding a mass protest rally.

On 16 June 1976, thousands of black students set off from their schools to converge on the Orlando Pirates football stadium. Older children were asked to shepherd the little ones home, to keep them safe and away from any potential trouble. Though the action committee had largely kept its plans from parents and had not wanted to involve adult school staff, many of the teachers were so impressed by the well-organized, orderly, and peaceful nature of the rally that they too joined in. Singing songs and hymns, chanting, and carrying placards that bore slogans such as 'To Hell with Afrikaans', they marched peacefully from their different schools towards the football stadium.

It would not be long before the protesters heard the rumble of armoured cars, the regimented clip-clop of mounted police horses, and the marching feet of the military, who had set up barricades in the roads around Soweto to prevent the students getting into the Orlando Pirates stadium.

In a chilling echo of Sharpeville, police officer Colonel Kleingeld claimed that a handful of students had begun to throw rocks. Reports at the time said that Kleingeld had shouted out orders for the crowd to disperse – but, because he didn't have a loud-hailer, his words went completely unheard by the greater majority of the students.

The police fired tear gas into the crowd, and total pandemonium ensued. Worried that they were becoming surrounded by thousands of panicked students, police officers began to shoot at random into the crowd. As bullets whizzed around their heads, the students did begin to panic. Reports claimed that protesters grabbed and killed a police dog and then set it alight. Police continued to fire. The first person to be shot and killed was an unarmed thirteen-year-old schoolboy, Hector Peiterson.

South African photographer Sam Nzima snapped a picture that would travel around the world and become a terrible iconic image of just what the apartheid regime was capable of doing to its own people. It showed eighteen-year-old Mbuyisa Makhubo, his face contorted in anguished horror, running towards a press car, a dying Hector Peiterson gathered up in his arms. Racing alongside him was Hector's big sister, Antoinette, equally distraught. Hector was driven to the nearest clinic, where he later died.

As the shooting continued, horrified young children watched as over twenty of their classmates died on the ground. Their horror soon turned to rage and, although faced with guns and bullets, the crowd began to fight back and the situation escalated alarmingly. The police came under a hail of stones and bottles. Cars and public buildings were set on fire. Soon, uprisings were cutting a swathe through Soweto. Plumes of smoke rose above the township and army helicopters buzzed above the crowds. Rioting spread to other townships, mostly orchestrated by young students. They targeted shebeens (locally owned, often unlicensed places that sold cheap alcohol in townships) and beerhalls in particular, asserting they were places that rotted the resolve of black adults, dulling any will to fight against their situation.

There were arson attacks on the University of West Cape and an Afrikaans school in Cape Town. For urban whites, the trouble was alarmingly close to home. The government responded by flooding military and police into the townships. Convoys of troop carriers and armoured cars criss-crossed the black homelands in a bid to control the uprising. It took them three long weeks and, during that time, hundreds died and thousands were injured.

The streets of Soweto reverberated to the sombre sounds of funeral cars and weeping mourners as mass burials took place across the township. In December 1976 an investigation by American publication *Newsday* concluded that 332 people had died in the Soweto uprisings – and an additional 435 in related episodes nationwide. Other unofficial sources suggested it could be many hundreds more. Over three thousand youngsters were arrested and interrogated.

For the men on Robben Island, this remarkable series of events represented a seismic shift in the battle against apartheid, filling them with a mix of joy and dread – joy because a new sense of active resistance had clearly been rekindled on the mainland, dread because most of the prisoners had wives, girlfriends, family, and friends living in the townships. They worried about the unconfirmed (to them) news that hundreds had been killed in the uprisings. Very soon they would get the full story, first hand.

The young black people sentenced as a consequence of their actions in the Soweto uprisings and their aftermath poured on to Robben

Island in their hundreds. Their passionate youthful militancy created a totally new and challenging dynamic within the prison.

Long-serving prisoners were desperate to hear news of home and details of the protest. They were keen, too, to show the new prisoners how to survive life on Robben Island. As the 'elders' were to find out, however, the Soweto generation had its own ideas about how to deal with time in prison.

The older inmates had spent well over a decade fighting and negotiating, often against all the odds, to win rights and concessions that had now made the prison a more human and humane place to live. The new arrivals were different in so many ways. There were greater numbers of younger prisoners, few of them had had any political experience before their imprisonment, and even fewer had any background in organizing anything. One thing they did have, though, was a spirit of defiant rebellion coursing through their veins.

They brought with them a passionate loathing of the apartheid state and its machinery of repression. They had seen their friends murdered and beaten while South Africa and the rest of the world looked on. Efforts to talk or negotiate with the police and the security officers had led only to death and imprisonment. When they arrived on Robben Island, these young men had no intention of setting aside their hostility towards the authorities, just because they were now prisoners.

Tony Suze and his fellow older prisoners were immediately taken aback by the open hostility they showed towards the warders. One day, Tony was cutting a rock in the quarry when he noticed a guard walk past a young Sowetan and slap him round the back of the head to make him work faster. This was no more than routine to the warder, and Tony was staggered to see the prisoner twist around, a look of pure hatred in his eyes, and punch the warder smack in the face. Almost no one on the island had done that before, but soon acts of physical retaliation on the part of the younger prisoners became all too common.

The youngsters routinely defied orders, treated the guards with unrestrained contempt, and drew regular beatings for verbal abuse and arguing. Within weeks of the Soweto generation arriving on the island, the authorities were running out of isolation cells to use to punish them all.

The older men worked hard at trying to convince the newcomers that, unless they showed more restraint, the prison would descend into anarchy, but the youngsters showed the elders little respect. Worse, they suspected that the older prisoners had become the stooges of the white man. The very concept of co-operating with the prison system was alien to the mindset and experience of the Sowetan intake of prisoners. They felt they had every reason to distrust any tactics of conciliation. They hadn't worked on the mainland – why should they work on Robben Island?

The existing prisoners tried to convince them to find ways to make the best of their imprisonment and to use their time on the island to strengthen themselves for the struggle, but the younger men were instantly suspicious of their motives and questioned their dedication to fighting for freedom. For many of these new prisoners, the failure to strike back at the warders and the officers meant surrendering any role in the struggle and abandoning hope for change.

The arrival of the Sowetan wave caused a wholesale breakdown in social cohesion. Suddenly, there was a vast number of new men on the island who had little in common with those already there, and plenty of disagreements. The cell blocks were now, as they had been in the early days, completely overcrowded. Young and old were living cheek by jowl and the once calm unity of the compound was fragmenting into resentful groups and factions.

Existing political factions made aggressive efforts to recruit new members. The political orientation of the new prisoners was often unclear or immature, and both the long-term ANC and PAC prisoners began to solicit for support.

Political recruitment had not been a major issue in the early days, since the men who arrived on the island in the Sixties had already formed their deep political allegiances. Now, there was a large pool of potential recruits. This new atmosphere led to arguments and dissension. It became more difficult for the prisoners to talk about any number of subjects without the situation turning into a political battle. Tempers were short. The culture of the prison seemed to have been transformed overnight.

Once again, the first generation had to use all its negotiating skills to bring a sense of unity and co-operation back to the cell blocks. It was hard for long-term inmates to convince the new men that they had to be better than their oppressors and to take steps to fulfil their potential on the island against all the odds. It was even more difficult to make them understand that co-operation with the authorities was a tactical decision they had made in order to improve conditions in the jail and to survive the effects of imprisonment.

Solomon Mabuse had been sentenced in 1963 to fifteen years on Robben Island for crimes against the state. He was active in the administration of the Makana Football Association, and had long served on its disciplinary committee throughout his sentence. Solomon was convinced that the new prisoners were just assuming that the system had broken their older comrades. They could not understand that the older men were seasoned politicians who had learned how to use the system to their advantage.

He told friends such as Tony Suze and Sedick Isaacs that one of the responsibilities of the older generation was to educate the new arrivals in what he regarded as the maxim of the veterans: that the struggle is outside. It wasn't possible to fight for the struggle and win it while on the island; here, you could only survive and aim to come out much better equipped to continue the struggle.

His philosophy was representative of that ascribed to by his generation – it was going to take work and patience to convince the new arrivals of the political wisdom behind it. More than a decade earlier, men like Marcus Solomon had sought men like Harry Gwala, who had the benefit of age, and tried to learn from them. The new generation was more impatient and less respectful of seniority.

It took months for the young prisoners to understand exactly how much of a struggle it had been throughout the Sixties and early Seventies but, gradually, the young talked more to the older prisoners – and, once again, it was football that would help build an important bridge between the two generations.

At the beginning, the new prisoners were scornful of two aspects of prison life which meant a great deal to the older men – the construction of the prison and the existence of organized sports.

The newcomers could not believe that the men had built the prison or, indeed, that they took pride in it. When Tony Suze discovered this, he was hurt. The building of the prison exerted a particular emotional pull on him, as he had become a master stonemason while working on it. His colleagues thought that was special and could understand that it was a matter of pride to him.

What displeased Tony even more was the extent to which the new arrivals took being able to kick a football around for granted, with no acknowledgement of the sacrifices the older inmates had endured to make it happen. It seemed to Tony that these young men were enjoying the sports the first generation had established on the island while calling them sell-outs for having negotiated the right to play. The youngsters just assumed that the men must have humiliated themselves to obtain something as pleasurable as football.

It was, however, out on the football pitch that a new mutual respect began to develop between the younger and older men. There was no doubt that the arrival of the new prisoners rejuvenated the clubs in the MFA. Younger, fitter, and anxious to play, the newcomers swelled the ranks of the existing five sides and immediately raised the quality and standard of football on the island. Full of themselves, the best of the young players expected to run rings round the old-timers. It didn't happen.

Something curious happened out on the pitch. Proud men all, the older players took the new prisoners' arrival as a challenge to show that they could still compete. It was their league, and their teams, and they weren't about to hand over supremacy easily. Elite players such as Tony Suze trained harder, thought ever more deeply about tactics, and used their vast experience to control and dictate play out on the field.

The surprising ability of many of the older players made the new prisoners sit up and take more notice of them. Watching how they played, and seeing how they ran things, made more of the youngsters respect them. One of the younger prisoners summed up the feelings of many: 'The new generation brought energy, but gradually we discussed things with the older men. We especially admired those who could play so well at that age.' They were beginning to appreciate the wisdom and experience of their elders.

In exchange, the older men admired the footballing talents of some gifted young players. One such was 'Terror' Lekota. Hardly anyone referred to him as Patrick, his given name, and many older prisoners assumed that his nickname referred to his fighting abilities back on the mainland. That was not the case: he acquired his new name because he was a terror to goalkeepers. His exploits as a high-scoring football player soon gave him a special status among his comrades.

Terror soon began to see just how important football had been to the older generation, recognizing that the game had made the men 'feel free in an unfree place'. He became one of the first new players on the island to fully understand how vital it was to re-establish and then run and maintain organized football there. For him, one of the first indications that his fellow newcomers shared his views was that some of his young comrades began to take football so seriously they gave up smoking in order to be able to play better and run faster.

Now, in 2008, Terror Lekota is better known as the current South African Minister of Defence and former premier of the Free State province. Reflecting back on the role of football on the island, he claimed that 'without it, we would have been so depressed. It took your mind away.'

Tokyo Sexwale was another good player in the new generation. An ANC activist, he was a powerful midfielder and a leader. Later to become one of South Africa's foremost politicians and businessmen, he explained to team-mates on the island that playing football made you realize your weaknesses and respect other people. This extended to something that had never dawned on him before his time in prison – the need to appreciate the work of referees. As he said, 'After all, someone had to do it, and it took courage to take the whistle ... the secret was not to be perfect, but to do your best so we could have a game.'

As mutual respect began to grow, the older prisoners would sit in the quarry during lunchbreaks, gaze out towards Cape Town and the mainland, and quiz the new inmates about the progress of their favourite clubs. They particularly wanted to hear about the exploits of a new black 'super club' – the now world-famous Kaizer Chiefs. Inspired by legendary former Pirates striker, Kaizer Motaung, the club was run along high-powered sports-model lines – a tribute to Motaung's time spent playing for the Atlanta Chiefs in the North American Soccer League.

The older prisoners were surprised to discover just how much football culture had changed back in the townships since they were free men. The youngsters described how young and hip the Kaizer Chiefs' supporters were, embracing counter-cultural ideas in their dress and behaviour. Fans adopted the two-fingers peace sign and wore afro haircuts, fashionable bell-bottomed trousers, and strikingly bright wide-collared shirts. The Chiefs had also given the younger generation a new black hero – the attacking midfielder Ace Ntsoelengoe, who was idolized in the townships for his uncanny ball control and mesmerizing dribbling skills.

As more of a kindred spirit began to grow between the older and younger prisoners, a degree of social cohesion returned to the prison, and just in time. There was to be period of renewed repression on Robben Island, and unity among this much larger band of prisoners would be vital.

The apartheid regime had been shocked rigid by the revolts in Soweto and the townships. The government responded to the events with a combination of repression and brutality – and it expected prison officials to do the same.

The commanding officer on Robben Island had unique new problems to cope with: a rapid increase in the number of inmates and a new militancy on the part of many of the prisoners. The equilibrium that had existed on the island had been shaken, both within the prison community itself and in the relationship between the prisoners and the authorities. There were too many prisoners, and too many political factions.

He was particularly worried that sport would be a source of conflict, and that the larger crowds would lead to a level of disorder beyond the warders' control. Some officials might have welcomed the disorder in the prisoner community as an excuse to clamp down even further on what many regarded as undue privileges which made life too easy. Many warders would have relished the opportunity to give the cocky young prisoners a good beating. The commanding officer thought he was sitting on a ticking bomb. He seemed not to understand that relations between older and younger prisoners were improving week by week, and decided to act.

First of all, he placed limits on how many men were allowed out at any one time to play and restricted spectator numbers severely: a mere handful were let out of their cells to watch the games from the touchlines. The old guard still left within the MFA was not about to take this lying down. Sedick Isaacs began to work on the authorities for concessions and in so doing gave the younger prisoners a lesson in the importance of negotiation.

Sedick requested that the commanding officer allow spectators from each section, pointing out that the fans were very disciplined and wanted nothing more than to watch high-quality football. He also emphasized the fact that there had been so many new clubs formed, the men needed more time, not less, for recreation. Sedick described the current situation as a burning issue and hoped that the CO would extend recreation time at each weekend session to three hours. His subtext was clear – the CO might have more disciplinary problems on his hands if he didn't let the prisoners out for longer and allow more inmates to watch the matches.

On a slightly more mundane issue, he reminded the authorities that the prisoners had been promised months ago that they could purchase kit from the sports shops in Cape Town for the new players. It was a bad idea to wear their prison shoes out playing football, and the game would look more attractive if the new clubs were allowed their own football kit. This argument harked back to how much wearing something other than drab prison garb had meant to his comrades right from the beginnings of the Makana Football Association.

The younger prisoners were now learning from a man who had become expert at playing the authorities. The commanding officer responded to Sedick's overtures with a compromise. His solution was to re-organize sports so that clubs and leagues were based in different cell blocks or sections. Pitches would be laid and sporting facilities obtained so that each block would be self-contained.

The compromise was accepted: it was all a matter of 'give and take'. The prisoners agreed because it enabled them to continue playing sport and to have more spectators there enjoying the games. The community was divided into four houses for the purposes of playing sports. Numerous new clubs in everything from football and rugby to tennis and even board games were formed in each cell block as so many men wanted to take part and, thanks to the compromise, sport on the island was rejuvenated.

One activity that the younger men particularly enjoyed attracted crowds three deep in the cells. Everyone would shout advice and cheer on the participants. It was not football, rugby, or even athletics that brought such smiles to people's faces but long-running games of Monopoly, a board game modelled on rapaciously acquisitive capitalism, here, ironically, played by men who, generally, strongly believed in socialism. One former inmate remembered that 'no one could cheat as well at Monopoly as the political prisoners on Robben Island'.

Once the Soweto generation had realized how much of a struggle it had been for the older men to establish sports on the island, they vowed that there was no way they were going to lose what they had won. They came to understand that unity was everything. If the actions of any one prisoner threatened it, he would be brought into line. Sport – and football in particular – was still the one thing on the island that held everyone together.

The new arrivals had learned to respect their elders on the island but still knew that younger men were needed to take the reins from Steve Tshwete, Sedick Isaacs, and others. It would be this new crop of men who would carry on the sports administration and maintain a structure through which they could negotiate with the prison authorities.

They made use once again of the tried and trusted approach of prisoners for more than fifteen years: they set up committees in each of the cell blocks and sections to deal directly with problems, and with the authorities. The Protest and Disciplinary Committee was put to a novel use: its members were allowed to step out on to the pitch and physically call a halt to a match in order to decide on a controversial decision made about a goal by a referee. It wasn't exactly on a par with the high-tech solutions for controversial goals being discussed by FIFA and UEFA now, in 2008, but it was at least a recognition that referees sometimes make mistakes.

It was not just in football that new leaders were needed. Mluleki George had been president of the Border Rugby Union on the mainland for two years before being sentenced to Robben Island in 1978. When George arrived on the island, sporting codes other than football were not faring too well. After 1976, much less rugby was being played, perhaps largely because the latest intake of prisoners was overwhelmingly from areas where football was the sport of choice. George took it upon himself to re-popularize his sport.

His opening gambit was ingenious: in a variation of the 'camping' tactics their predecessors had used to ensure practice time for club mates, those prisoners interested in establishing and playing rugby found ways to manoeuvre people between cell blocks to ensure that there would be enough rugby players in each to form rival clubs.

Some of the new prisoners had a particular dislike for 'the Afrikaaner sport' and refused either to participate in or watch it. Others, however, seized on it as a challenge. One of Terror Lekota's comrades pointed out that he 'didn't know a damn about rugby, but he became a star'.

Another thing the Soweto generation inherited and which gave them particular pleasure was the annual Robben Island Olympics. One prisoner active in the sporting community in the Eighties described it as the most emotional day of the year. The younger generation really took the event to their hearts. Training began in September. Events were tailored to different abilities and so men of all ages worked hard to get fit and to participate, and each cell chose one or more of its inhabitants to act as journalists to write stories about the events and make sure everyone received the recognition they deserved. They also used the Summer Games to pressure the authorities into allowing all cell blocks to come together to play sport rather than have separate activities in each section, as was now the practice.

One of the new sports committees sent a letter to the commanding officer with an 'Urgent Application for All-Sectional Summer Games'. The committee phrased their approach to the issue in seasonal terms:

Xmas was merry-making ... people are drawn together to celebrate in many parts of the world ... It is a time of togetherness. ... in our small world of Robben Island there is a need for this togetherness ... in the spirit of Xmas plus considering that games on the island are the one thing that keeps us together ... and that Xmas is the season of goodwill ... we make an urgent appeal to have all inmates allowed to jointly participate in the forthcoming Summer Games.

The committee did, however, base its case on more than just sentiment. Though the prison authorities had promised more sporting equipment and pitches, some of the sections still did not have proper facilities, and this affected 'play and general enthusiasm'.

Not all the sections yet had a football field, and some had no tennis courts; sharing facilities would diminish the experience for everyone. There were also a number of sections that did not have enough participants to field a meaningful Olympic team. Some were inhabited by 'only a handful of inmates for reasons best known to the authorities'. Cleverly, the committee pointed out that letting the sections mix for sports would help relieve the then current staff shortage, freeing some of the warders to be deployed elsewhere or, better still, giving them more leisure hours during the festive season. The committee hastened to say that it was not in any way trying to question staff management, 'undoubtedly' the CO's area of particular expertise.

The committee concluded its appeal by assuring the commanding officer that granting its request would bring everyone together in a spirit of 'mini-Olympics atmosphere with Xmas as the goodwill background'. It reminded him that he had earlier granted limited sporting activity between two sections, and that had proceeded with 'no hitches in discipline'. Clearly, the Soweto generation's earlier militant stance of refusing to negotiate with their oppressors had been replaced by the skilful deployment of the negotiating skills championed by the first generation.

The CO said he could not reverse the decision. The sports committee continued to press the issue, drawing his attention to the fact that there were so many elderly people in section C that the restrictions rendered some of the sports codes useless. It made sense to amalgamate the prisoners in C with those in E and F for the purposes of sport, to average out the age differences. This appeal had no effect, however, and the prisoners were left to re-fashion sports within each section.

Despite their failure in this one effort the new guardians of football and sports in general continued to believe that progress was only to be made through negotiation. They also became increasingly skilled at organization. Learning from both the successes and the mistakes of the previous generation, they began to look at methods of streamlining the way sports were run on the island.

At the start of the 1980–81 football season, the various sporting codes on the island held a series of meetings to resolve differences and issues among themselves. The committees decided to do away with the structure whereby each sport had its own representative governing body, one of those rare instances when a governing body decided to abolish itself in order to create something more efficient. It was replaced by a much more flexible five-man committee, the General Recreation Committee (GRC), which was charged with the overall administration and planning of all sports on the island.

The main issue at its first AGM would not have been alien to the earlier generation; it concerned the responsibility and powers of every officer and committee and the need for periodic reports and meetings. It contained the kind of legalisms and detail that would have satisfied even Moseneke, Malepe, Gwala, or Naidoo and concluded with a statement of its role in the life of the community.

It shall be the task of the General Sports Committee Meetings to keep sound healthy relations with the authorities in the area of sports ... Most importantly, it is the duty of the GSCM to effectively articulate and firmly represent the Community in all matters of sports ... The GSCM has no interests separate from those of the Community.

Some of the same old issues persisted, and committee members found themselves having to face similar challenges to their predecessors. The committee had to insist upon a full accounting from the prison officials about expenditures for sports and leisure equipment and explanations as to why goods ordered had not been delivered. One difference, though, had occurred over time: the money now involved would have been unimaginable to men such as Indress Naidoo and Marcus Solomon.

When the Makana Football Association was fielding its maximum number of teams, it had a total expenditure of a few thousand rand. In 1981 the GRC spent close to R11,000 and still had a balance of R8,164 left in the bank. Some of the money had come from prisoners, but outside sources were crucial to the new order of things. The Red Cross had donated a grant of R15,000–20,000 for expenditure on sports and recreation equipment. The prison authorities were also now meant to contribute a sum of money from state funds, but the new committee constantly had to chase up this money. Its members were regularly told that the funds were 'somewhere in the bureaucracy'. In 1981 just R1,600 was handed over. The prisoners had been expecting R25,000.

The committee was concerned that it had not received this money, despite having sent a protest letter to Pretoria over a year earlier reminding them that the state had the responsibility of catering for the sporting and recreational needs of the inmates. The inattention of the state in this matter meant that the GRC was having to draw on the interest in its own account to cover ongoing costs.

A memo was distributed around the cell blocks: 'In view of the shocking news that the state is not prepared to pay for the purchase of the TVs and VCRs, the GRC resolved to make arrangements to pay for them.'

This memo made it clear how much had changed in the running of and approach to sports and recreation on the island. Which would have been more of a shock to Sedick Isaacs, Indress Naidoo, Marcus Solomon, Tony Suze, Steve Tshewete, Harry Gwala, and their comrades? The size of the account handled by the GRC, the anger the committee expressed at the failure to receive the budget it required, or the very fact that televisions and video players were now allowed on the island?

Changes in prison regulations and the introduction of new technologies were transforming life on Robben Island. For years, smuggled newspapers and news brought in verbally by people returning to the island from trips to the mainland had been the regular source of news about sports or anything else. In 1978, the authorities decided to let the prisoners listen to the news on the radio. Heavily censored newscasts were broadcast over the intercom system. Many of the prisoners felt that the authorities chose news items that would be particularly depressing to them but, after a short while, the target audience learned how to read between the lines and discern the news that had slipped past the censors' attention. Somehow, they came to know about sports boycotts and the increasing withdrawal and lack of renewed investment in the South African economy. All of this gave the inmates great hope and assured them that the fight against apartheid was on the right track. In 1980 category-A prisoners were even allowed to buy newspapers, which came on to the island uncensored. Although this privilege was restricted to that small group, the contents were soon circulated around the entire island community.

The committee that co-ordinated sports activities now had a number of other responsibilities. Films were shown regularly, and the committee had to attempt to obtain extra recreation time so that the time spent watching them would not cut into that allowed for team sports. The prisoners built up a large record collection, and the committee had overall charge of which records were played and when. Their decision of classical music in the morning and jazz at the weekends met with general approval, but there probably was no way to satisfy complaints such as that of one prisoner, who wrote to his cousin, 'I was listening to Nat Cole, only to have it spoiled by Sinatra.'

Eventually, the prison authorities made an announcement that would send shock waves around Robben Island, and give real hope that a change was going to come: radio news would no longer be censored above the usual stringent censorship practices the government applied in the rest of the country.

A prisoner released in 1974 returning to the island in 1980 would have seen so much that was familiar, and so much that had changed. The pitches may have been in different places, but the enthusiasm for sports was as high as it had ever been. The colours and names of the clubs had changed, the players were younger, and the clubs and spectators had been broken up into cell-based segments, but sports, and football in particular, still remained a unifying force.

Robben Island was still a maximum-security prison, the place of confinement for many of the most feared opponents of the regime in Pretoria, but so much else had changed on the island, and in ways that reflected the beginnings of profound political shifts on the mainland.

By the end of the Seventies, nearly all of the original political prisoners had left or were about to leave the island. (Lifers, such as Nelson Mandela, would remain in the isolation block for years to come.) The men issued with the longest sentences in 1963 and 1964 were the last to make their way home, Sedick Isaacs and Tony Suze among them, leaving in 1978. It was hardly a return to freedom because, like most of the former Robben Island prisoners, they would be placed under strict banning orders on their return to the mainland. They would not be able to attend gatherings, or speak to more than one person at a time. They would be barred from certain places, such as factories and schools, and restricted to living and moving in certain named districts. Tony and Sedick would have to report to the police at regular intervals for three years, and to stay in their homes for specified periods of time, usually nights and weekends. Sedick would soon discover that he even had to seek official permission to attend his own wedding, because the mosque was outside his named district.

One aspect of the banning orders came as a particular blow: the men were forbidden to communicate in any way with others under banning orders. Tony and Sedick, who had developed such a close and supportive friendship during all their years spent together on the island, were now forbidden to meet, phone, or even write letters to one another. As ingenious men, they knew they could and would find ways around this personal ban, but they both realized that it would be clandestine, illegal, and put them in danger of further arrest and imprisonment.

They left the island separately. They did not know what the future would hold, but there was room for optimism. Not only had they survived their time on Robben Island, Sedick and Tony returned to the mainland in a good physical and mental state, ready to fight for a better, post-apartheid South Africa and, though they would not realize it at the time, what they left behind them on the island would become testament to one of the most remarkable stories in modern sporting history. From nothing, and with the devoted, committed leadership and support of so many determined men, they had, against all the odds, created a vital sense of freedom among the men on Robben Island through football, and given thousands of prisoners hope, motivation, and a sense of purpose.

After the initial problems with the assimilation of the new prisoners back in 1976, they had worked tirelessly to pass on the baton to the next generation. The game had been left in good, safe hands. Organized football would continue to be successfully played on Robben Island until the closure of the prison in 1990 – the year when apartheid was finally dismantled, and a new, young, rainbow, multiracial democratic republic was finally born.

Many of the extraordinary footballers and officials within the prison would take the wisdom, skills, and self-confidence reaped from organizing and playing the sport to become major players in creating and running a new South Africa. On Robben Island, football had always been much more than just a game.

Epilogue

Life After the Island

'The maxim amongst us was that the struggle is outside. You have to come off of the island much better equipped for the future.' Solomon Mabuse, Prisoner 505/63

Tony Suze was released from Robben Island in June 1978, having earned a Bachelor of Arts degree and a postgraduate diploma in marketing and advertising, as well as a vocational diploma and a certificate in carpentry awarded by the prison authorities. Despite his many qualifications, Tony struggled to find work. Prospective employers were constantly warned not to hire him by BOSS operatives.

Thanks to Dikgang Moseneke's father, he finally got a job teaching at the Nkomo Secondary School in Atteredgeville. Dikgang's father was the principal and put his neck on the line by employing Tony as a private teacher of economics and English. The job lasted just six months. Mr Moseneke Snr was ordered by the Education Department to get rid of him. Someone had discovered that school-children were being exposed to an 'undesirable element'. There were protests and representations from various quarters, including the school's governing body itself, but to no avail. Tony had to leave. Throughout the Nineties, Tony managed to find more regular work in industry and, by the turn of 2000, had become a successful commercial property developer. He lives in Pretoria.

Marcus Solomon was released in 1974 and continued in what has been a lifetime's involvement in fostering social change. As a free man, however, he deals with a different constituency: children. The uprising of 1976 made him realize that traditional approaches to the role of children could not work in South Africa. He taught in a school for a while and then joined forces with other adult activists who were working in alternative forms of education. Marcus and his colleagues founded the Children's Resource Centre (CRC), aimed at helping to build and sustain a social movement for children.

Throughout the Eighties Marcus was active in the United Democratic Front, the broad-based political movement that pressured the government into finally negotiating the end of apartheid and the beginnings of a democratic South Africa. After the 1994 election, he felt free to put all of his energies into the CRC, which had become a nationwide organization. He secured some funding from European foundations and governments as well as from the South African government. Sport is an integral part of the programme of the CRC, and Marcus campaigns with the government and local authorities to ensure that sport for all becomes more than just a slogan.

Lizo Sitoto was given a taste of what the future would hold when he went looking for work on his return from the island in 1975. He managed to secure a job with Volkswagen, but it lasted only two weeks. The security police paid the company a visit and told his new employers that he was a political agitator who would cause trouble among his fellow workers. Lizo was 'let go'.

As soon as his banning order was lifted in 1980, Lizo was rearrested, for possession of an unlicensed firearm, and sentenced to eighteen months. Rather than return to prison, he left South Africa without a passport and became a refugee in Lesotho. He was joined by his girlfriend Margaret and, two years later, they received scholarships to study early childhood development in Sweden. Married, in 1990 they returned to South Africa and spent the next five years raising money to build a pre-primary school in the township Lizo had grown up in. To this day, they continue to run the school.

Sedick Isaacs was not able to return to teaching. He was harassed by the security forces and had a number of jobs before he was allowed to start postgraduate work at the University of Cape Town. While under a banning order, he wrote a doctoral thesis on medical information and worked as a researcher at the Groote Schur Hospital and University of Cape Town School of Medicine. When freedom finally came to South Africa, he rose to the rank of professor. His work is well known throughout the academic world of medical infomatics, and he serves as the regional president and international vice-president of the leading professional organization in his field. In 2010 he and Cape Town will host a major international conference on medical information – a visible sign that the international cultural boycott of South Africa is a thing of the past and that at least some of the victims of apartheid whom the boycott was supposed to help have been able to achieve the place they deserve in the intellectual world of South Africa.

Indress Naidoo left the island and went into exile to train fellow ANC fighters in Mozambique. He soon became a major assassination target for the secret police. Talking to him years later, a senior BOSS officer told him: 'You are under a lucky star.' He then went on to list at least four attempts that had been made on Naidoo's life, involving poison, snakes, and scorpions.

In 1982, Indress published *Island in Chains: Ten Years on Robben Island*, written in conjunction with Albie Sachs. The book was translated into a number of languages and dramatized on radio and stage. Needless to say, the book was banned in South Africa, but many copies were smuggled into the country.

One of Naidoo's comrades in Mozambique was the former captain of Rangers FC, Jacob Zuma. Released in 1973, he worked for two years re-establishing the ANC underground resistance in KwaZulu-Natal, and then spent over a decade in Swaziland and Mozambique training the young exiles who had left South Africa after the Soweto uprisings.

By 1977 he had been elected to the ANC's National Executive Committee and, following the lifting of the ban on the ANC in 1990, he was appointed its Deputy Secretary General. In 2007 Jacob Zuma was elected president of the African National Congress and was one of the leading advocates in South Africa's successful bid to host the 2010 FIFA World Cup.

Having been such an important figure in sport on the island, Steve Tshwete left in March 1978. He eventually became the Army Commissar of the ANC's military wing in Zambia. Over the next few years, Tshwete's efforts to bring together ANC leaders and prominent white South Africans laid the basis for the negotiations that resulted in the country's peaceful transition to democracy.

His vast experience of playing and helping to run sport on Robben Island was put to good use in South Africa's first truly democratic government. Steve Tshwete became the first Minister of Sport and

Recreation and then played a key role in starting the racial integration of South African sport. It was no easy matter. Decades of racial segregation had caused a lot of distrust and anger, and it took a major effort to create single bodies to control sports for the first time in South Africa's history.

The International Cricket Council was persuaded to readmit South Africa into world cricket, even though, at this early stage of its democracy, they were still fielding an all-white team. At the time, Steve Tshwete reasoned that South African cricket was an 'embryo that needs oxygen to grow. To suffocate it now would be terrible.'

In 1995 Tshwete played a major role in bringing the Rugby World Cup to South Africa. Thanks to his powers of persuasion, he became known as the 'voice of reason' by sports officials. When Sam Ramsay, one of the leaders of the international sports boycott of South Africa, became the President of South Africa's National Olympic Committee, he complimented Steve, dubbing him 'Mr Fixit', a nickname that soon stuck. Tshwete later took on an even more challenging responsibility when he became South Africa's Minister for Safety and Security.

After a short illness, Steve Tshwete died in Pretoria on 26 April 2002 – the eve of the anniversary of Freedom Day, South Africa's new beginning.

After his release in 1974, Harry Gwala returned to Pietermaritzburg. Banned from working as a teacher or for trade unions, he made ends meet by setting up his own laundry business. He immediately returned to active service within the ANC, helping to reorganize the Natal underground movement but, targeted by security police, he soon found himself back in the dock and on the boat to Robben Island.

After enduring two punishing spells in the prison, Harry Gwala discovered he had a new battle to fight: he was diagnosed with motor neurone disease. However, despite his arms being paralysed, he still had the dogged determination to become the ANC's Chief Whip in 1994. Just one year later, his long fight against illness came to an end. At his funeral, Nelson Mandela described him as one of 'the true makers of history'. Around the nation, the new South African flag flew at half mast for the 'old communist referee'.

Released back on to the mainland, Dikgang Moseneke began to carve out an astonishing dual career in law and business and has become one of South Africa's most respected leaders. A founder member of the Black Lawyers Association, he was called to the Bar in 1983 and then worked as an advocate in Johannesburg and Pretoria. In 1993 he was appointed a member of one of the committees that helped draft South Africa's very first democratic constitution, then he became Deputy Chairperson of the Independent Electoral Commission, which conducted the nation's first democratic elections. Eventually, he rose to become Deputy Chief Justice of the Constitutional Court of the Republic of South Africa.

Moseneke also became a leading member of South Africa's business community, variously serving as Chairperson of Telkom South Africa, the African Merchant Bank, Metropolitan Life Ltd, and African Bank Investments, plus becoming a director on the boards of a number of the country's major companies.

Tokyo Sexwale was one of the most active and enthusisastic footballers of the Soweto generation. He was released in 1990, immediately becoming a senior member of the ANC on the mainland. In 1994 he was elected premier of South Africa's largest province, Gauteng.

He left high-level politics in 1998 in order to further a career in business. He is now a major player in South Africa's oil and diamond-mining industries. In 2005, he hosted South Africa's version of the television reality game show *The Apprentice*. He is a member of the organizing committee for the 2010 FIFA World Cup in South Africa.

Sexwale was joined in the highest levels of the ANC by his fellow prisoner and footballer, 'Terror' Lekota, who became chairman in 1997. In 1999 Lekota was appointed Minister of Defence, which meant that the South African Cabinet contained representatives of two generations of Robben Island footballers, Steve Tshwete representing the earlier one.

Mark Shinners was released in 1973, the same day as his cousin Dikgang Moseneke. In June 1976 the Soweto uprising drew him back into an active role in the struggle. He and a colleague made repeated trips into the troubled areas to try to convince the students to pull back from open confrontation with the army and police since stones and courage were no match for automatic weapons and shoot to kill orders. As a result of these activities, in January 1977 he was arrested by the security forces and charged with involvement in terrorism. Once again, he went through severe torture during the detention before his trial. He joined Harry Gwala as one of the few men who were sentenced more than once to imprisonment on Robben Island.

After his second release from prison, Shinners again became involved in PAC activities. When the negotiations that led to the writing of the new constitution for a free and democratic South Africa started, Shinners became one of the PAC representatives.

In June 1997 Shinners assumed a very public role when he appeared before the Truth and Reconciliation Commission to present first-hand testimony about the physical and emotional torture that was inflicted upon the men who were involved in one of the most high-profile court cases of the post-Soweto period – the Bethel trial. Shinners recounted the supposed suicide of comrades and the cover-up that followed. He described the travesty of a trial held in camera and tried to impress on people what it felt like to know that your life was, literally, in the hands of men who thought you were both worthless and dangerous.

His opening statement to the TRC that the trial came about because 'the African people refused to accept that they had to live with oppression and injustice ... and would not live with the things that were intended to make them feel sub-human' echoes what he and his comrades were doing twenty-five years earlier in their struggle to win the right to play football on Robben Island.

The Story Behind
More Than Just a Game
by Professor Chuck Korr

'*Unless you sing your own song, the hymn sheet will be buried away, your history will disappear, no matter how noble it is.*'
Anthony Suze, Prisoner 501/63

'*Sports is a way of building character, of teaching proper values, of finding ways to persevere in the worst of conditions.*'

These might be the sentiments of a Victorian schoolmaster of the generation of men such as Thomas Arnold, who were convinced that hard play and team sports were the best way to turn wayward boys into the courageous men needed to build the Empire. The playing fields of Eton had nothing to do with the victory at Waterloo, but generations of British leaders felt there was a direct connection between manly virtues and the lessons learned by playing sports. Links such as these, between sport and courage, virtue and victory, became the standard vocabulary for coaches and sports administrators around the world, especially where British culture was influential.

'*Sport is for recreation, for entertaining the players and the spectators. It is for keeping our spirits high and for cultivating, encouraging, and maintaining the good and healthy relations among the residents of this place.*'

This could be the view of someone like the Victorian shipbuilder Arnold F. Hills, who started a football club for his workers at the Thames Ironworks. Hills was the paternalistic capitalist *par excellence*. His intention was that the new club would raise the morale of the workers, give them a sense of belonging to something more than the factory, and 'thus united, they would crown the labour of the Works on the field'. He thought also that the workers' interest in football would keep them away from distractions such as pubs and trade unions.

'Sports is a way of alleviating the distress and frustrating conditions which our community is always faced with.'

This statement is representative of the feelings of residents of innumerable poor communities around the world – from the *barrios* of Latin America to the ghettos of the United States, to any number of predominantly poor working-class industrial areas throughout Britain. It could just as easily have come from the leadership in POW camps throughout Europe in the First or Second World Wars, where the inmates welcomed the chance to play sports as much needed relief from the disappointment of having been captured and the hardship of imprisonment.

It will be no surprise to the reader of this book that all those quotes come from the writings of prisoners on Robben Island between 1964 and 1977. The value and joy of sport made it an antidote to much of what the island was supposed to inflict on the prisoners. The men seized on sport as something that they could exploit for themselves – but this could only have been the case if they had come to the island with notions of what made sport special.

This book has been fifteen years in the making. My involvement with this story started when I was teaching at the University of the Western Cape (UWC) in August 1993. It was an exciting time to be in South Africa. Freedom was coming, and the first democratic election would be held the following year. Negotiations were going on between the various political factions to write a constitution and ensure a peaceful path to majority rule. One afternoon, my friend and colleague at UWC, Professor André Odendaal took me into a room that housed the archives of the Mayibuye Centre.

Odendaal is the leading sports historian in South Africa. An Afrikaaner raised on a farm in the Eastern Cape, he had played cricket at a high level in South Africa, and at Cambridge University (where he earned a PhD in history). After returning home he chose to play multiracial cricket and accepted a teaching post in a university that was known throughout the country as part of the struggle against apartheid. By 1993 he was the Director of the Mayibuye Centre, an institution established to encourage research into the struggle and to preserve documents from across the world dealing with the fight to end apartheid. A few years later, when the Robben Island Museum was established, Odendaal would be its first director.

Odendaal directed my attention to a set of almost seventy cardboard archive boxes labelled simply 'Robben Island – Sports' and remarked: 'Those might interest you.' At that time I was totally unaware that there had been any sport on Robben Island. If anyone had mentioned the two words together, I would have said that it was an oxymoron. Robben Island was horror incarnate, not a place where prisoners would play games. It did not take very long for me to see just how wrong my assumptions had been.

I was invited to look at the archives less than a week before I was going back to my home in St Louis, Missouri. I started to look through some of the boxes and discovered that they were a historian's treasure trove. They contained a variety of documents handwritten on paper ranging from lined foolscap to bits and pieces torn from notebooks, to scraps that looked as if they had been torn from brown paper bags. Even before I had a chance to look closely at what was in the text of the documents, I knew that something very special had been happening on the island.

As I read through the letters in the first few boxes I began to wonder why men who were living in communal cells, breaking rocks in work groups, showering together, and spending almost all their time together would write letters to one another. Why not just ask someone a question or tell him what you thought about a terrible decision by the referee the previous week? Even more puzzling was the fact that almost every letter contained a formal interior address for both the sender and the recipient, and a formal mode of address, for example, from The Secretary, Gunners Football Club, Robben Island Prison, Local to The Secretary, Makana Football Association, Robben Island Prison, Local. This seemed a statement of the obvious. Wasn't it a waste of both time and paper? Time may have been plentiful on the island but paper was not. The other striking feature of the letters was the use of formal names. Everyone mentioned in them was Mr so and so, or addressed with their first and last name. Reference would therefore always be to, for example, Mr Isaacs or Sedick Isaacs, never to Sedick. Virtually every letter ended with the same phrase: 'Yours in sports'.

The prose was formal, often stilted. The level of detail was overwhelming. The prisoners left nothing to chance or open to misinterpretation. This was serious correspondence dealing with a variety of often detailed and technical issues about matches, rules, disciplinary matters, and relationships between the men. In some instances, it was easy to identify the author of the letters by their style, especially those written by a couple of men who demonstrated a remarkable flair for sarcasm, especially in letters addressed to the prison authorities.

Other boxes contained hundreds of pages of material dealing with the operations of leagues and clubs. There were match reports filed by club secretaries and referees, fixture lists and tables, and match summaries. Each club had filed a copy of its constitution and a detailed roster of its members and officials. The most surprising feature of the documents was the large number of pages devoted to detailed summaries of meetings of clubs, associations, and committees. Whoever kept the minutes took great care to attribute the remarks made at these meetings to the individuals who made them rather than just reporting their substance.

I have spent more than thirty years studying the role that sport has played in a number of societies. I am familiar with the development of team sports in Britain and the so-called Victorian ideals that it involved. Nowhere had I come across people who had such a strong belief that sport could create a sense of community, teach values, and build character than was expressed in those documents. It was also clear that, as much as the men wanted to play football for its own sake (there are countless times when they describe themselves and one another as 'football mad'), they regarded it as one activity in their ongoing struggle against the prison and the apartheid system that had sentenced them to Robben Island.

It took two research trips to go through most of the paper trail, then I began to seek out former prisoners to talk to them about their experiences. It was obvious from the papers which of them had played the most significant role in the organizational and adminis-trative side of sports. Luckily for me, many of them lived in Cape Town, where I was based when I returned to South Africa in 1997. The sequence of interviews that took place over the next nine years gave me special insights into both the experience of the prisoners and the changes that are the hallmark of post-apartheid South Africa. It also provided me with the chance to meet remarkable men and to form close friendships with many of them.

The settings of the interviews, the efforts that went into arranging them, and the tenor of the conversations give a sense of what is so extraordinary about the men who used sport to fight apartheid as prisoners.

The first men I interviewed were Indress Naidoo and Sedick Isaacs. They were authors of more documents than all their fellow prisoners combined.

My first meeting with Indress Naidoo took place in the visitors' gallery of the South African Parliament. He approached me with the words, 'Naidoo here. Are you Korr? We must speak soon.' We made plans to meet, and he left to go downstairs and take his seat in the Senate. The man who had arrived on Robben Island in chains and spent years in exile after his release was now a member of the first democratic parliament in South Africa. He was enthusiastic about talking to me about sports on the island, although somewhat bemused as to how an American professor knew anything about it and why I was so interested. So many people had talked to him about his experiences on the island and no one had ever mentioned sport.

Naidoo is an intense man, who came to politics from birth. Members of his family had been involved in political struggles in India and South Africa for generations. In my meetings with him he spoke with bursts of energy, and the intensity of his feelings was obvious from the first moments of our conversation. His role in sport on Robben Island was more as an administrator than a player and he recalled proudly the care with which he took down the minutes and kept things going at the meetings. Indeed, his summary of how football began was: 'We got permission, we got soccer balls, we blew them up, we formed our committees, and then we could start playing.'

The broad smile that so often comes across Naidoo's face was first visible when I asked him why the prisoners spent so much time organizing sports rather than just getting hold of some balls and having casual kickarounds to amuse themselves. He reminded me that the one thing the prisoners had the most of was time, and it was a lot better to spend it in meetings setting up sport than in idle thoughts about their life in prison and what they were missing at home.

Naidoo had another more important point to make. He knew that I was a historian of England and had lived there so he assumed that I would understand that a country such as South Africa, which had inherited much of its culture from the British Empire, was a place 'where we knew that sports is much too important to be just fun'.

In so many ways, Isaacs is the opposite of Naidoo. Isaacs had very little interest in formal political organizations. When sentenced to prison, he was part of a small political faction in Cape Town and, on the island, he tended to be identified more with PAC than the ANC.

He is a slight man whose demeanour disguises his incredible toughness. He served longer in solitary confinement than anyone on the island and was beaten repeatedly by the guards for his apparent insolence and willingness to bend the rules of the prison to breaking point.

Sedick's speech is punctuated with long pauses, the silence emphasizing what he has said. His pattern of conversation reflects his career choices. He has a number of academic degrees in the sciences, including a PhD in mathematics. We met in his office in the Groote Schur Hospital, just down the hall from where Dr Christian Barnard performed the first successful heart transplant. Isaacs was curious about why I should be so interested in sport on Robben Island, as no one else had enquired about it. He seemed almost surprised that I wanted to talk to him, since he was not a political leader and he had not spoken publicly or written very much about his time on the island. I showed him photocopies of some of the documents he had written and a small smile and look of recognition came across his face. The documents I handed to him were examples of the incredible thoroughness and attention to detail he exhibited. Some of them also illustrated his stunning talent for sarcasm.

It is almost impossible to overestimate the effect Isaacs had on the lives of so many other prisoners. He was the secretary of sports organization, the librarian, the organizer of the first-aid group, tutor in a number of classroom subjects, and the man who could be counted on to be a forceful advocate in disputes with the authorities. His efforts transcended any of the political differences that existed within the prison community.

Other interviews demonstrated how much South Africa has

changed since 1990. An interview with ex-Robben Island residents Cristo Brand and Vusumzi Mcongo took place in a busy coffee shop in the Waterfront shopping centre in Cape Town. The restaurant was a few yards from the Nelson Mandela Robben Island Museum Centre, from where boats leave for tours of the island. The two men were taking a break from their work in the Centre, where Brand manages the shop and Mcongo organizes the boat trips.

They have an easy, friendly relationship and asked to be interviewed together. Mcongo arrived on the island in 1977 and was there for more than thirteen years. Brand arrived a couple of years later and left in the late Eighties. They each talked about how much sport meant to the prisoners and how much it contributed to the good order within the community on the island. They reinforced one another's conclusions about how much more difficult life would have been for each of them if sport had not been a part of everyday life there. The significant difference between them is that Mcongo is black and was a political prisoner, and Brand is white and was a warder.

Marcus Solomon and I sat in his office at the Children's Resource Centre, a nationwide organization founded by Solomon in the Eighties, looking at photographs of children involved in its various programmes. As we talked about his role in sport on the island, he kept mentioning that sport was used in the centre's programmes in the same way it had been by the prisoners on the island. He talked about the need for South Africa to provide more fields and playgrounds for children, because play is a human need. Then he launched into a discussion about that, and remembered how he had argued with comrades in the Dynaspurs Football Club that they should have as many members play in matches as possible, even if that made winning less likely. I have never met anyone who believes more in the character-building potential of sports than does Solomon.

Lizo Sitoto sat in his home in the Kwanobuhle township of Uitenhage talking about how he grew up playing rugby and learned football on Robben Island. Through his front window, we could see children running around in the sun, playing games in the Khanyisa Cultural Ensemble, a pre-school that Lizo and his wife Margaret established in 1994. Lizo's understanding of the extent to which sport made his life bearable on the island has been translated into a recognition that sport should be an important part of children's lives.

An extended interview with Dikgang Moseneke was filmed in 2007 in his office. He wore a starched white shirt, with a tie, and was standing in front of shelves packed with law books – an appropriate setting for a man who had been sentenced to the island as a fifteen-year-old PAC activist in 1963 and in 2007 was appointed the Deputy Chief Justice of the Constitutional Court of South Africa.

My interview with Patrick Matanjana took place in the staff canteen of the Robben Island Museum. All the guides who take visitors through the restored prison are former political prisoners. In the midst of our conversation, a colleague of Matanjana's sat down with us and started to talk about his experiences on the island and how much football had contributed to breaking down barriers there, in creating a sense of community, and giving the men a sense of self-worth. These sentiments echoed what Matanjana had said earlier, but he interrupted his friend to say, 'Remember, man, we could only have so many political discussions and then had to have some fun.'

In the background throughout the interview the voices and laughter of a number of small children could be heard. It's easy to take those sounds for granted, but it was something that prisoners such as Mantanjana did not hear the whole time they were imprisoned on the island.

Later that day, I spoke with one of Matanjana's fellow guides, a man who had served a lengthy sentence on the island. A mutual friend had asked him to talk with me. Our conversation began haltingly, almost as if he was trying to decide whether he wanted to talk at all about his experiences but, once he began to tell his stories, the words flowed out of him. After close to two hours, we ended the interview. I thanked him for his willingness to talk; he thanked me for my inter- est, we shook hands and he started to leave. Midway across the room he returned and said there was something else I should know. He did not like talking about his personal experiences. He felt that most people were only interested in the ex-prisoners who had become famous and that the public treated men such as him almost as a kind of sideshow to the struggle. The reason he had decided to talk to me was that I was the first person who had wanted to talk to him about 'anything that happened on the island besides politics and misery'.

My investigation into sport on Robben Island had started with an almost chance encounter between myself and a huge cache of miscel- laneous documents stored in deteriorating cardboard boxes. The next step had been to talk to the men behind the papers, to hear them describe what had happened and to understand what they felt about it. The interviews in Cape Town had gone very well, but there was much more to do.

The idea of networking has become almost a cliché, but the term took on a whole new meaning for me when I tried to talk to the men whose letters and reports I had spent months reading. Ahmed Kathrada and Sedick Isaacs, both said they would help me in any way they could and then went ahead and did it. From the start, I was dependent on the goodwill of some former prisoners and their willingness to pass me along to friends with requests that they talk to me. Phone calls from them opened up possibilities that would never have existed otherwise, but it wasn't as easy as it might seem.

In 1999 my research ran into what could have been a roadblock bringing it to a standstill. Philemon Tefu and Isaac Mthimunye (Tefu and Ike to their friends) had a business office in downtown Pretoria. They were active in organizations made up of former political prisoners and devoted much of their time to the welfare of comrades whose lives had not recovered from what the apartheid system had done to them. After Sharpeville, these two men, comrades in PAC, had dedicated themselves to the armed struggle. They were arrested in 1963 and sentenced to life imprisonment.

If anyone could help direct me to the right people and encourage them to talk, it was them. I had come to them with the support of comrades they trusted, and I felt confident that that Friday afternoon was the start of the next important phase of the research – talking to the Gauteng-based former prisoners who were the backbone of football in the early years of the island.

They took turns asking me detailed questions about why I was there and what I expected from them. They alternated these questions with statements about the current poor status of many ex-prisoners. They couldn't quite figure out why they should help me with anything. There was never a hint of hostility in their remarks, but it became increasingly clear that my research in Pretoria might have come to an end before it had even started. My sense of confidence continued to diminish rapidly when, every few minutes, one of them would excuse himself to speak on the phone. These conversations were conducted in various African languages, all of which were unknown to me, but the substance was clear. They were talking about me, and the tone made me believe that my position was deteriorating with each phone call.

After almost two hours, Ike leaned back in his chair and told me that it had been very interesting to meet me. He suggested that I go to my friend's home in Pretoria and phone him later that night to see if it was worth my returning the next morning. Over the next few hours, he and his comrades would 'caucus' to decide what to do.

I was asked to return the following morning and was greeted by my hosts and three more men in the office. Each one of them repeated in different ways what had been asked of me the previous day: who I was and why they should want to talk to me? I recognized the names of two of the new guests: Tony Suze and Solomon Mabuse. The former had been a star player, often leading the league in goals, and had been one of the ringleaders in the Atlantic Raiders affair. The other had been heavily involved in administration and one of the stalwarts of the disciplinary committee – just the men I had hoped to meet and interview.

The conversation began to turn more towards what had happened on the island and less about what I was doing in that office. When I finally asked if I could record some of what they would say, Ike laughed and asked why I hadn't started the tape as soon as they had begun talking in English about life on Robben Island. Tony Suze and what I've come to think of as 'the Pretoria Connection' became the bedrock of much of the work that took place in the subsequent years that enabled me to put together the fullest possible picture of what happened on the island.

A Sunday-afternoon gathering in Pretoria in 2000 was a dramatic time in my effort to understand sports on the island and to explain it to others. Fourteen old friends had gathered at the home of Tony Suze in a tree-lined suburb of Pretoria. Collectively, they had served more than two hundred years in Robben Island Prison. If the apartheid government had not been replaced in a free election, at least two of them would have still been there, having been sentenced to life. There were two outsiders at the table – myself and a tape recorder. The men had come at the invitation of Tony Suze, to talk to his American friend about their lives on Robben Island and what sport had meant there. Almost everyone expressed curiosity about why anyone, let alone an American professor, had come so far to talk to them about this. After all, in the hundreds of articles they had read about men's experiences on the island, no one had ever said much about sport.

The conversation among the men was lively, punctuated by laughter, exclamations, and shaking of heads. They reminded one another of what had happened decades ago: the 'crimes' that had led to their imprisonment, the terrors during interrogation, the harshness of the prison regime, and the brutality of some of the guards – and the hopes and fears they had shared. Much of the talk was about the ways in which they had stood up to the authorities and what the prisoners had done to make life tolerable.

As they had been invited with the expectation that they would talk about sport, the conversation was filled with reminiscences about tension-filled matches, great goals, terrible refereeing, and everything else you would expect when friends got together to talk about years of watching and playing football together. Peripheral conversations broke out constantly as individuals reminded someone else of an event or asked if he remembered it in the same way. There were arguments about both the details and the meaning of what had happened almost forty years ago.

The former prisoners kept interjecting comments about the lessons they had learned from sport and how football had provided them with a diversion from prison life and enabled them to avoid the depression and sadness which the authorities hoped would be their lot. Phrases about the need to organize sports, to know the rules, and to acquire administrative abilities came easily to them. They were clearly enjoying this opportunity to meet and to talk to one another – and to me.

About ninety minutes into the discussion, everyone became silent and started looking at one another. Their discomfort was obvious. I had asked them whether anyone wanted to talk about the Atlantic Raiders. Suze broke the tension by saying to his friends, 'Let's talk about it, and don't try to fool around with him. Remember: he probably knows more about it than you can remember.' Three of the men sitting around the table had been Raiders. In the future, I would discover that every former prisoner who had been on the island in 1969–70 had strong memories and feelings about the Atlantic Raiders affair.

In 1970 the Atlantic Raiders affair had forced the prisoners to question just how much they were willing to live by their self-professed goal of sportsmanship. In 2000, the former Raiders talked about how the events provided a diversion and how they had simply been trying to get justice. But they confessed that they had taken a dangerous course, and one finally summed it up, saying, 'We were just being naughty.'

In a later interview, Marcus Solomon expressed a different attitude. As both a referee and a hard-working member of the disciplinary committee, he had been opposed to everything the Atlantic Raiders had done. In his eyes, they had shown scant respect for the association and for what the prisoners had built up, and no respect for the need to follow the rules. Almost forty years after the events, he is still upset at how his comrades and friends behaved.

A fellow prisoner, one of Tony Suze's closest friends from childhood, sat with him and me in his home and told me that, though he loved Tony like a brother, he still hadn't forgiven him for all the trouble he had caused with the Atlantic Raiders. That conversation took place in 2001 – almost thirty years after the event.

The world at large knows all about Nelson Mandela, the horrors of the island, and the stories of the leading political figures in the prison. None of the men at Suze's home fell into that category. The lives of ordinary prisoners figure little in the public understanding of what life on Robben Island was all about. The men knew Robben Island had become a symbol in the history of the struggle to end apartheid. They knew how important for the future of South Africa it was that people learned what men had done there. They were concerned that people had ignored something that meant so much to them. Towards the end of one day spent talking about life on the island, Suze turned to me and said, 'Unless you sing your own song, the hymn sheet will be buried away. Your history will disappear, no matter how noble it might be.'

There was no question about the passion in his voice or the intent behind what he said. The silence and nods around the table made it clear he was speaking for the others, and that they were counting on me to tell their story. They had been under no compulsion to be there that day. Clearly, they enjoyed the opportunity to get together as a group and talking about something of which they had fond memories. They were surprised how much I knew about what they had done on the island. It came as a shock to many of them that so much of their history had been maintained and was now in a university archive. They made a decision, both collectively and individually, to do whatever they could to help me tell their story as fully as possible.

I conducted numerous interviews in Cape Town, Johannesburg, Pretoria, Port Elizabeth, and other places over the next few years. Former prisoners suggested others whom I should interview and did everything possible to make the arrangements. The sites of these interviews included the office of the Minister of Defence, the office of a corporate executive, the newly paved streets of an informal settlement, a parliamentary office, and a banquet hall playing host to FIFA representatives when South Africa was bidding for the 2006 FIFA World Cup.

The most dramatic setting for any interview was a day walking around the island itself. In 2005 we took a camera crew over to Robben Island with Marcus Solomon, Lizo Sitoto, Sedick Isaacs, and Tony Suze. The four of them represented a range of political affiliations, ethnic backgrounds, and home towns. They had also played hugely different roles in sport on the island. Suze and Sitoto had played for the best team, Solomon at a lower level, and Isaacs could, in his own words, hardly kick a ball. Isaacs was involved in the organization of almost every activity on the island. Solomon was active in the Referees Union and on the disciplinary committee. Suze was the main instigator of the Atlantic Raiders demonstration. Isaacs had been the 'attorney' who had prolonged the case for months.

It wasn't until we were on the boat halfway to the island that Tony turned to me and said simply that this was the first time he had been back since his release in 1978. I was shocked, since I assumed that, like the others, he had been there for reunions and to see what had been done with the island. Hours later, when we were getting set to return to Cape Town, we had to rush to get the last tour boat back. If we missed it, however, we would not be stranded, since the staff boat would leave later, taking those who worked on the island back to Cape Town. The boat they used was the Dias, the same boat that had taken each of the four to the island to begin their terms of imprisonment. Suze made it clear to me that he would find somewhere to stay overnight on the island 'before they would ever get me again on that boat'. Luckily for all of us, we didn't have to test the strength of his resolve not to relive that part of his Robben Island experience.

When we arrived on the island, the four men created their own tour of the facility. They reinforced one another's memories and talked about what had happened at the places we stopped and how much everything had changed. They looked with pride at the detailed masonry work they had done when they built the prison. They wandered around the football pitch, and Sitoto took his place in front of the goal posts he had defended as Manong's keeper. They went into the cells where they had first played with rag balls, where they had been prodded through drills by Pro Malepe, and where they had spent hours in meetings that ensured that football was run 'properly'.

They walked on the pitch, talking and arguing again about what the Atlantic Raiders had done to the prison community. There was a sense of sadness that the old pitch had been moved to make way for more cells, but the place that clearly brought back the strongest memories was not the cells or the pitch but the quarry. The men looked for the remnants of the road they had walked down twice a day on their way to and from it. There is now an artificial lake in the midst of the quarry and scores of birds have turned it into a virtual nature reserve. Its peacefulness stood in stark contrast to their memories of a place that combined misery and comradeship.

The hardest thing for the men to accept was that the quarry was so remote from the rest of the prison that visitors to the island had no knowledge of its existence and no sense of how big a role it had played in the prisoners' lives. As we walked back to the prison, each of the men reflected on both their experiences on the island and how important it now was to them that people learn about something more than the horrors of life there.

The men had been imprisoned because they knew how vital freedom was. Apartheid was evil, and the system would end only when people stood up and challenged it. On the island men found themselves in extreme circumstances, beyond what they might have imagined. They found ways to work together to ensure that the place that was meant to break them instead became one where they could find new resolve to continue the struggle. They created ways to prepare themselves for the new South Africa they hoped would come during their lifetimes. That day in 2005 was the first time the four of them had been together there since Solomon was released in 1974 and the first time Suze had been back on the island since his release. After thirty years they were more convinced than ever that football on Robben Island had been much more than a game.

On that same route between the prison and the quarry, Marcus Solomon said softly but firmly that, in his decade on the island, 'sports gave people a chance to make a statement with their bodies and their minds. It was a chance to test our values.' Those sentiments might appear to be the wistful nostalgia of someone finally living in a free South Africa but, almost thirty-four years earlier, in the midst of angry disputes between the prisoners about sport, Solomon had spoken out about its values when he addressed his Dynaspurs team-mates in 1971.

> Sporting activities here on the Island are aimed at making our stay less unbearable and intolerable than it is ... Our sports have played no small role in bringing us closer together ... They are a form of social cement. Let it not become a point of conflict and misunderstanding.
>
> Some of us might say: Noble ideals and big talk which has no bearing on the real situation. My reply to those people is in the form of a question: If we had no noble ideals, would we have been here today?

It would be a decade until, with the co-operation of many people, I would be able to bring this story to the public in ways that I felt did justice to the lives of the men and would engage the broadest possible audience.

The first instinct of an academic historian is to think in terms of writing articles and/or a scholarly book. The story of sport on Robben Island demanded something different. I saw the potential for a film version and was fortunate enough to work with Dave Crowe, an award-winning documentary filmmaker in Britain, and Anant Singh, an Academy Award-nominated film producer in South Africa and his team at Videovision. The resulting collaboration was *More than Just a Game*, a docudrama that had its premiere in November 2007 in South Africa as part of the qualifying draw for the 2010 FIFA World Cup.

The decision to write a book was more difficult. I felt that if the book were to reach the audience it deserved, it needed the talents of a writer who could bring out the dramatic potential and human interest inherent in the events on the island. I had worked with Marvin Close on early drafts for the film documentary, and it was evident to me then that his approach and enthusiasm for the importance of the story was the same as mine. I shared my research findings and dozens of hours of interview material with Marvin. He set about doing more background research, and then we embarked upon putting together this book.

Why was it so important to tell this story? It was remarkable to listen to so many former prisoners talk about how much sport on the island meant to them. The general tenor of their remarks is summed up in comments such as 'It's impossible to think of the island without sports,' 'I know that so many of us would not have survived the depression without sports,' or 'Football was as much a part of our lives as politics.'

There's an understandable temptation to listen to these decades-old recollections and to think that the stories represent a kind of sanitized nostalgia. One might scoff at these re-created versions of life on the island, but such scepticism runs into two problems. If the men were going to exaggerate anything about the island, it would be in their interest to remind the world about just how badly they were treated: to stress the deprivation and the hardships. Also, and perhaps even more telling, we can compare what they now say with what they wrote at the time.

If freedom had not come to South Africa, Isaac 'Ike' Mthimunye would still be on Robben Island. A few years after his release, Ike looked back on how much the 'pain of the island was being deprived of things, ordinary things we took for granted'. There was lots of 'hustle and bustle', and that enabled the men to overlook, at times, the surroundings and the treatment. 'When I went to the island, I didn't have any appreciation of the stars and the moon,' he says. He has a special fondness for the small garden that Indress Naidoo created which 'changed people's lives and gave them such a sense of hope'.

Naidoo made an even more important contribution to making life on Robben Island more bearable for his fellow prisoners – the hours he spent doing administrative work for various sporting codes. The appreciation in Ike's voice when speaking about Naidoo is noteworthy, especially given the differences that existed between the two men in the Sixties and which have increased since then. When Ike was sentenced to prison, he was accused of being the chief lieutenant to PAC leader Potlako Leballo when the PAC broke away from the ANC.

If some football supporters are said to bleed the colours of their team, Naidoo would bleed the colours of the ANC banner. His has spent his whole life in the service of the struggle for freedom as part of the organization he thought could accomplish it. As mentioned earlier, he co-authored the first widely read memoir of a former Robben Island prisoner, *Island in Chains*, first published in 1983, while he was in exile. It is no coincidence that the foreword to the book was written by Francis Meli, the Director of External Publicity for the ANC.

Over the years (especially after its reissue in 2000), many PAC-affiliated prisoners have complained that the book downplays the importance of the PAC on the island. The fact that their strongest criticism of *Island in Chains* concerns the passages about the creation of sport shows just how important that part of their life on the island remained to them so many years after their release from captivity.

Mthimunye is adamant in his belief that it is impossible for someone who was never deprived of sports to understand why the prisoners just could not countenance losing their games once they had obtained them. Sport was important for its own sake, but there was a broader principle at stake. The warders were constantly telling the prisoners, in deed and words, that they were not real people and they had no rights. Gaining the right to participate in sport by means of an aggressive campaign gave the lie to those assumptions. Maintaining the structure within which sports operated was further evidence that the prisoners were smart and courageous enough to maintain the rights they declared to be theirs.

In their internal correspondence and the mass of official documents exchanged between the prisoners, the men made their attitude towards sports clear. They felt the need to have as much as possible down in writing, despite the fact that there had been no expectation that they were creating a historical record to be read by anyone but themselves. Some prisoners had the responsibility of collecting the documents and keeping them safe on the island. When many ex-prisoners refer to Mark Shinners as the 'archivist', they are not using the term in the normal sense of 'librarian' or 'historian'. The archivist helped create a memory for the various sporting organizations and gave them, and their successors, a record of what had happened. Sport had to be run properly; any other approach would have been a denial of its importance and a terrifying recognition that life on the island had succeeded in depriving the men of normal standards of running things.

Some ex-prisoners remember brilliant goals, fiery meetings, and quarry-based post-mortems of matches in great detail. Others have vivid recollections of different types of events. Some can reconstruct the ebb and flow of a football match played forty years ago. Others quote the instructions they learned as referees, and some take pleasure in reconstructing the banter that took place on the touchline between supporters of opposing teams. All of them remember that the fight to play real football reinvigorated them and gave them new hope for the future.

The warders had been able to disrupt the prisoners' games in the cells, but it was always possible to find ways to start them again. Playing real football was different. The young men had grown up in a culture where the chance to play football and other sports was taken for granted. They had all the energy of youth, so much that not even the back-breaking work at the quarry could destroy it. They couldn't play real football in the quietness of the cell in groups surrounded by other prisoners. Something like football needed open space and free time, and that meant that the only way to obtain it was for the prisoners to stage a frontal assault on the restrictions placed upon them by the authorities.

When the commanding officer first granted the right to play football, the prisoners held a series of meetings among themselves to decide how to accept the offer. The majority of the prisoners thought that sports would be enjoyable and 'could reduce the immense tension that was part of the atmosphere in prison'. Others thought that it was a propaganda stunt by the authorities, that 'the authorities didn't permit sports for us. They did it for themselves,' and that sport should therefore be rejected. It was up to the prisoners to make sure that they controlled sport and used it for their purposes.

The passion for football went far beyond the men who played it or even those who organized and ran it. To these young men, it was almost 'like school was out. It was time to have some fun.' But football on the island was serious fun.

By the time the prisoners had won the right to play football, the African prisoners, who were the majority, had finally been issued with shoes rather than sandals fashioned from old car tyres, but these prison-issue shoes were not very good for football. There was the danger of ruining the only pair of shoes a prisoner could expect to receive for a long time. Instead, many of these 'greenclad barefoot prisoners' were transformed on Saturday mornings into 'soccer magicians'. Saturday had always been special because it signified the end of the work week in the quarry but, before football, the day had also brought depression. The prisoners were confined to their cells, where the gloom and the cold reminded them how much their lives had changed. Saturday meant the absence of the quarry, but it also meant the absence of the noise of the work gangs, the songs that the men sang, the sense of movement, and the open sky above them. Four walls and a concrete roof replaced that on Saturdays.

Later, Saturday's football became the greatest escape from the routine of the prison. What struck so many of the prisoners was the 'sheer happiness' of being out, either playing or watching. Even the harshest football weather was remembered as the 'brightness of Saturday morning'. Playing or watching football felt so natural to the men that at times they had to remind themselves of the bizarre setting in which the matches were taking place. They could daydream. They could even imagine being somewhere else and remember the friends with whom they had played football under very different circumstances only a few years earlier. It was a way to 'counteract prison unlike any other'.

Football was definitely more than a one-day or, later, two-day a week event. The excitement started on Saturday night or Sunday morning when the fixture list was announced for the following week and, throughout the week, an informal schedule revolved around it, the men talking about past games and predicting events in future matches. If you could imagine a community of supporters of various football clubs living together, that was Robben Island.

Some supporters became well known for their humour, their passion, and even their excesses of partisanship. There was constant banter and teasing, punctuated by the occasional threat that your club would die the following week or that it shouldn't even bother to show up for the match, the same as there would be at any match. There were, however, a couple of aspects of being a football supporter in the outside world that didn't apply: there was never any question of travelling to a match, and there was never any physical confrontation between rival supporters. Compared with the need to police football outside, in supposedly civilized communities, the problems with fans on the island were non-existent.

So much of what happened on the island was part of an enforced routine. When the prisoners woke up, washed, ate, worked, and slept was laid down by the authorities. Work quotas were established for them. Even the time they spent studying was set by the prison, and the subjects they studied for degrees had to be approved. There was almost nothing in the lives of the prisoners that was not set in stone except for what happened on the pitch at the weekends. Competitive sport shares many of the attributes of theatre, but has one significant difference: the outcome is unknown, and the final act plays itself out among the various elements present – the players, the officials, and the spectators. The sheer unpredictability of sport provided an excitement for the prisoners unlike anything else.

What happened on the field was also the material from which memories and legends were created. Like sports events everywhere, the feats performed there became bigger and more spectacular as they were retold over time. The recounted memory of goals scored turned players into Robben Island versions of Pelé or George Best and, to hear about them, the saves might have been worthy of the greatest Soviet goalkeepers of the era of Lev Yashin or England's Gordon Banks, who made an impossible wonder save against Pelé during the 1970 World Cup.

So many of the prisoners cherished their accomplishments on the field, and their comrades revel in retelling the glories. Someone as studious as Justice Dikgang Moseneke shared those emotional ties to sports. When he talks about his experiences on the island, what comes into his mind immediately are conjugating Latin verbs to himself as part of his law studies while pushing a wheelbarrow around the quarry, and scoring an unlikely try as a novice rugby player. He's not sure how many tackles he evaded or how far he ran and is positive that it must have been a fluke. He does know that his comrades talked about it for months, making his exploits grow each time.

Prisoners shared the vocabulary of football and sports. Men who had found little to talk about with one another found that they could discuss something free of tension. The usual hostilities between supporters were trivial in comparison to splits over how to stage a successful revolution and how to govern the nation when freedom finally came. Until the advent of soccer, whenever the prisoners spoke about their community, they identified it in opposition to the authorities. Now, they had a positive definition. The community was the totality of the prisoners united to do everything that was necessary to enable them to play a game. It required co-operation, across competing political factions, to create the new soccer pitch, to roll it, to water it, and to make sure that the lines were freshly made before each week's matches.

In the most visible example of co-operation, the players from various clubs trained together. Every one of them benefited from the skills and badgering of Pro Malepe. His affiliation to PAC disappeared once he was caught up in football. His objective was to teach skills and condition his comrades regardless of party politics. Their common goal was to have the highest quality match possible to provide enjoyment and excitement to them and the hundreds of spectators.

Even the physicality of football played a role in breaking down barriers between prisoners. It was a hard activity with a rigid set of rules that was enforced by referees who tried to be as impartial as possible.

The sight of a PAC referee signalling for an ANC player to take a penalty after being fouled by a PAC leader did more to neutralize the hostility between political factions than weeks of debate and discussion could ever have done.

Playing a hard sport did a lot to lessen the overall level of tension in individual prisoners. They could fight out their battles on the field or on the touchline. Some of the prisoners even began to wonder whether, if they could work together to get a football moving in the same direction against entrenched opposition, maybe they could work together to get the country moving in the same direction.

Football also contributed to improved relationships between the prisoners and the warders. When the prisoners started agitating for sports, most of the warders thought it was nothing more than the prisoners making silly complaints to annoy the guards, who were simply trying to protect South Africa from communists and terrorists. Why should these hardened criminals expect to have such privileges when they were on the island to be punished? Many warders were troubled when those in charge made concessions to the prisoners. Warders might dismiss the matches as nothing more than a bunch of Africans and coloureds running around after a ball. After all, it wasn't as if they were playing rugby, a game for real men, which required intelligence and planning. After a while, though, except for the most hardened warders, it was difficult to ignore the fact that the prisoners were not just playing at football. They had created an organized league. They were playing scheduled matches and they seemed to know what they were doing.

Warders tried to make fun of the time that prisoners spent having meetings and talking with one another about things that, to them, didn't seem to matter much; it must mean that they had nothing better to do with their time than talk. What had happened to these men, supposedly a threat to the future of South Africa? However, all that 'useless' talk ended up producing a set of teams that played each weekend on a field that rivalled anything beyond the island.

The sit-down demonstration by the Atlantic Raiders presented a unique problem for the guards on duty that day. By this time, most of the warders had come to look forward to the weekly football matches as a welcome diversion from the harshness of their service on the island. They were as puzzled by what was happening as were the players and fans. When it became clear that the prisoners were going to let the demonstration run its course, one of the warders bent over the protesters and, in the most colourful language, made his opinion known, by questioning their sense, their morals, and their parentage. At that moment, he was acting far more as a disappointed football fan than as an agent of the state.

Any effort to understand the special quality of sport on the island has to start by recognizing the importance of two words that the men use constantly to describe what they did – 'organization' and 'structures'. The constant emphasis on the need to organize and the respect for procedure stemmed in part from their political background, but there was much more involved. Putting together an organization with a written constitution and a set of committees, rules, and by-laws was a way to show both themselves and the warders that these prisoners were not common criminals. However, as well as these idealistic motives for organization, there were also pragmatic considerations. If sport could be maintained on Robben Island, the

prisoners would have to overcome two opponents, the prison authorities and their own disunity. They needed a united front to negotiate
guidelines with the authorities. They needed structures to govern the
activities of various sports bodies to ensure that everyone had a
chance to participate.

The action by the Raiders took place in front of hundreds of spectators and denied the pleasures of a day of football to the men who
had fought so hard to win the right to have it. In the eyes of many
prisoners who watched the events unfold, the Raiders were acting like
buffoons or spoilt children and making the whole community look
silly in the eyes of the warders.

When the prisoners' addiction to legalism and Isaacs' desire to
provide a diversion came into play, the situation deteriorated into
something that everyone wanted to end but no one seemed to know
how to. Why then did the community respond so mildly, and why did
it take more than five months to resolve a situation the basic facts of
which were so clear to everyone involved?

When anyone other than the former prisoners learns about the
long-drawn-out process of ending the Atlantic Raiders affair, the
obvious question is why the Makana FA leadership and the prisoners
who valued football so much allowed it to continue. The answer is
that all of the men involved understood how an unfair system
purporting to represent justice operated. They were all on Robben
Island because they lived in a country where arbitrary penalties
masquerading under the guise of the need for security and resolution
of disputes was the rule. That was the system that had brutalized
them and sent them to Robben Island as punishment for their
crimes. The most obvious example of how deeply the prisoners

understood the need for due process, a fair trial, and punishment to fit the offence was the way in which they handled the Atlantic Raiders affair. They were extending to the Raiders and their supporters precisely the justice that the South African legal system had denied to all of them and was continuing to deny to the vast majority of the residents of the country. The Atlantic Raiders were as 'guilty as sin' and they were 'threatening what we had built', and that was all the more reason to ensure that not only were they given the chance to defend themselves, but that everyone would see that the process had been fair and transparent.

Above and beyond the struggle by the prisoners to obtain the basic necessities of life, their fundamental battle was to retain their self-respect and remain true to the reason they had chosen to become a part of the struggle against apartheid. They had to remind themselves, and one another, that they were political prisoners, men with an agenda based on their hope for a new South Africa. The goal of their struggle within the prison was to survive to continue the fight, and to survive with their dignity intact or even enhanced. That meant maintaining a spirit of defiance even in the worst of circumstances. It meant responding to a warder that, for example, 'I am not a number, I am Mark Shinners,' knowing that simple phrase meant being bundled off to the isolation cells and a loss of meals for a few days.

Nowhere was the prisoners' need to fight for their sense of dignity more apparent than in the way they created, organized, and maintained the Makana Football Association and the other sporting bodies that came into existence in its wake. The reasons why sport was so important varied hugely from one man to another, but all of them agreed that it mattered. It's almost impossible to find a former prisoner who does not share the opinion that life on the the island would have been unimaginable without sports and that it is important to make sure that the story of sport becomes as well known to the public as the stories of the politics and hardships of Robben Island.

Index

K

Puskás, Ferenc 94

R
Ramsay, Sam 253
Ramsey, Sir Alf 90
Rangers FC 63, 79, 80
  concerns over rugby 174
  matches played 86, 92, 97-9
  motto 77
  strip 81
Red Cross 53, 55-6, 57, 68, 70, 73,
  81, 91, 117, 243
referees 77-8, 163, 165
Referees Union (RU) 76-7, 162,
  163-4, 165, 166, 205, 274
Robben Island Prison x–xii,
  21-2, 24, 274-7
  arrival of Soweto prisoners
    and hostility towards
    authorities 228-9
  Asian and coloured prisoners
    27, 37-8
  Badenhorst's tyrannical
    reign 145-7
  beating up of Namibian
    inmates incident 147-8

  beatings and assault of
    prisoners by warders 26,
    32, 33, 34, 36, 39, 102
  breakdown of social cohesion
    with arrival of Soweto
    prisoners 230-1
  communication between
    isolation block prisoners
    and other inmates 40
  conditions 28, 29
  cultural activities 195-6, 218
  daily routine on 30-1
  description 25
  escape attempt by prisoners
    111-15
  establishing of other sports
    on 183-4, 192-4, 215
  food rations and diet 26-7,
    37-8, 70-1, 91, 92, 117
  and football *see* football
    (Robben Island)
  Fourie's regime 157-8
  friendships formed 198
  humiliation of prisoners by
    warders 37, 39
  hunger strikes 70-1, 147
  improvement in relationship

Acknowledgements
Chuck Korr

While this book was in final production, the authors were saddened to hear of the death of Sipho (Sam) Tshabalala.

'Robben Island should be seen as a triumph of the human spirit against the forces of evil ... a triumph of courage and determination over human frailty and weakness. A triumph of the new South Africa over the old.' Ahmed Kathrada, Prisoner 468/64

I owe a great debt to innumerable former Robben Island prisoners for allowing and encouraging me to become involved in this hitherto untold story of their experiences during their battle to end apartheid. So many men went out of their way to talk with me about their experiences, even when recalling those days was unpleasant and troubling. This includes: Indress Naidoo, Ike Mithimuye, Philemon Tefu, Moses ('Big Mo') Masemola, Benny Ntoele, Solomon Mabuse, Solomon Phetla, Lucas Mahlangu, Klaas Mashishi, Mike Mohohlo, Patrick Matanjana, John Nkosi, Joas Mogale, Nqothwa Lucas Mahlongu, Dikgang Moseneke, Steven Tshwete, Vusumzi Mcongo, Richard Chauke, Dan Moyo, Duxumbana, Terror Lekota, Lionel Davis, Sipho (Sam) Tshabalala.

Over the years, I developed special personal relationships with some of the men who were on Robben Island.

I want to thank Ahmed Kathrada for his generosity of spirit and his friendship This man who jokes about his non-existent sense of geographic direction did so much to set South Africa on the right course for freedom.

Most off all, there was what the director of the film. *More Than Just a Game* called the 'five Ss': Shinners, Sitoto, Solomon, Suze, and Sedick Isaacs. Their experiences on the island and in apartheid South Africa provided the framework for the film and they are a significant part of the book. They have become an important part of my life over the past decade. I think of them as friends who like to laugh and tell stories, men with families who have a great faith in the future of their country, and men who showed how exceptional supposedly 'ordinary people' can be.

Many of the former prisoners have asked me why and how I became so involved in what happened in South Africa. The answer goes back to 1955, when my father challenged me to learn about apartheid and to understand why it was so wrong

My initial visit to South Africa was as part of a faculty exchange between the University of Missouri–St Louis and the University of the Western Cape. Professors Ron Turner, Joel Glassman, and Jan Persens, and Peter Magrath, former President of the University of Missouri share the credit for the creation and continuation of this important program. I was invited to UWC by Professor Denver Hendricks. Neither of us could have predicted that my prospective one shot teaching stint in his department would turn into a life-changing experience.

The vast majority of my research was based in the archives of the

Mayibuye Centre where the assistance and friendship of Lea Phayane and Anthea Josias was so important. Everything in the book that is in quotation marks is taken directly from the documents at the Mayibuye Centre/Robben Island Museum archives or the recorded or filmed interviews I did with former prisoners.

The work involved in the book was possible only because I was fortunate enough to have so many people who made me look forward to each trip to South Africa. Amongst them were: Joan Rapp, Ken MacGregor, Vaughan Johnson, Archie Henderson, Melanie and Wilhelm Verwoerd, Andre and Bev Travill, Phillip Tobias, Floris van der Merwe, Jeff Duffel-Canham, Ralph and Lucy Rosen, Winston Kloppers, Linda Biehl, and the late Peter Biehl and Solomon Makasana.

Professor Andre Odendaal is the reason I started the research about Robben Island He has been a constant source of support and encouragement. He, along with Zohra, Rehana, Adam, and Nadia have transformed Cape Town into a place that will always be a second home.

It is ten years since I gave my first public lecture about football on Robben Island. Since that time, the enthusiasm and support of colleagues and friends reminded me of the importance of the story. Among those who did so much to help me were: Ted Rowlands, Richard Holt, James Panter, Norrie Baker, Allen Guttmann, Patricia Vertinsky, Irwin and Pat Levin, Pierre Lanfranchi, Vladimir Bercovic, Erik Brady, Tom O'Toole, Vahe Gregorian, Bill Baker, Hugh McIlvanney, Martin Tyler, Steve and Donna Gietschier, Joseph Losos, Bob Lipsyte, Peter Alegi, Michael Apted, and the late Anthony Sampson and Leonard Koppett.

Jerome Champagne took a great interest in the story and did so much to help with the film. Many of my FIFA MA students went out of their way to tell me how much Robben Island had come to mean to them.

Two academics deserve special mention. Rich Lapchick and Bruce Kidd are internationally renowned scholars whose sense of injustice and strength of conscience led them to assume leadership roles (often at personal cost) in the anti-apartheid movements in the United States and Canada.

Thanks to Anant Singh. Helena Spring, Junaid Ahmed, and Tom Eaton, whose combined efforts and insight, brought the story of *More Than Just a Game* to the screen.

Dave Crowe will always have my respect for the unique contributions he made to ensure that the film was produced and that I had the opportunity to write this book.

It's one thing to have an idea for a book, a very different matter to do it. It would have remained an interesting possibility had it not been for Borra Garson, our agent, Jenny Heller, our commissioning editor, and Lizzy Gray, our editor.

Anne has been involved in many ways in each of the books I have written, but this one was special to her. She has spent a great deal of time in South Africa and has become immersed in both its history and its present. She knows as well as anyone what made Robben Island special and she has developed close personal ties to many of the people involved in the story. Many times when I wasn't sure what I intended to do about this story, she reminded me how much it meant to people who meant so much to us and why the story is important to the new South Africa.

It is a simple statement of fact that this book would not have been written if I had not been lucky enough to have Marvin Close as a co-author. I met Marvin when he was the prospective scriptwriter for the

London-based T.V. documentary we intended to do about football on Robben Island. We were looking forward to working together on the script. When the project turned into a South African-based docudrama, there was no role for Marvin, something that troubled both of us.

A number of people had spoken to me about the need to write a book that could go into the detail that was impossible on film. As much as I could see they were right, I was convinced that I was never going to write another first draft of a book-length manuscript. Three were enough for me. The prospect of a retirement that combined lecturing in England, giving talks about Robben Island in various venues, and writing a few articles was a much more appealing thought than looking at a blank screen.

When I approached Marvin about working together, it took a matter of minutes for us to agree on how we would do it. His deep commitment to the subject was obvious from the first. The amount of research he did contributed so much to the structure of the book and his style as a writer is evident throughout it. Over the months of exchanging notes, comments, chapters, and revisions we developed a strong friendship and discovered there were so many things besides Robben Island where we had common interests. Even if we never work together again, we will be friends who will talk about politics, football, wine, music, South Africa, and so many things, as well as sharing our admiration for people who have made a difference ranging from Roy Orbison to Peter Norman to the men of Robben Island.

Marvin Close

I wholeheartedly echo all of Chuck's above thanks to each and every one of the remarkable people whose passionate support, unstinting help, and sheer generosity of spirit made this book possible. I would like to add a further few, who also personally helped me greatly in the making of this book.

Cyril Connolly once memorably claimed that the enemy of the writer is the 'pram in the hall'. Not so for me. My four children Holly, Jacob, Edward, and Tilly are, along with my wife Sheily, a constant inspiration, ever thoughtful, encouraging, and enthusiastic about my work. The story of this book and of the remarkable men who made it happen, has also taught my children big and important lessons about the indefatigability of human spirit.

Great friends and fellow writers Julie Rutterford, Jan McVerry, Paul Coates, Gretchen Woelfle, Chris Thompson, Dave Simpson, Diane Whitley, and John Hilton have given me much sound advice and help. My brothers Claude and Mark, close friends Neil Scott, Stephen Bucknall, Richard Crossland, Peter and Ruth Davey, Dr Emma Dawber, David Annandale, Alice and David Burston, Adam Henninger, and Aidan McKenna have all directly, or indirectly, given me a huge amount of support and inspiration throughout the writing of this book. Thank you, one and all.

A very special heartfelt thanks must go to Borra Garson – you've always been there for me.

Finally, I've made many new friends during the process of writing this book; and none greater than my co-author Chuck. Writing collaborations can sometimes become rather like the unraveling of an unhappy marriage: a wonderful honeymoon, the early joy of a shared new adventure. Then disagreements and rows occur, inexorably leading to a realization that the two partners simply don't share common ideals, goals, or a vision of how to achieve them. As a writer, I've been there a few times in the past.

From day one, it became clear that Chuck and I shared similar and passionate beliefs about most things. Principal amongst them, that in this strange, often cruel, but constantly surprising world, there are always reasons to believe in the possibilities for hope, change, and renewal.

Writing with Chuck was a sheer joy. As our working relationship progressed and we got to know one another better, we increasingly became of one mind about the direction that this book should take. In the process, I was privileged to enjoy the wisdom, warmth, and sheer infectious wit of a great man. As ever Chuck, yours in sport.